PATRICK KAVANAGH

The Complete Poems

PATRICK KAVANAGH
The Complete Poems

Collected, Arranged and Edited by Peter Kavanagh

THE PETER KAVANAGH HAND PRESS
250 East 30th Street · New York 10016 · U.S.A.
THE GOLDSMITH PRESS
Newbridge Co. Kildare Ireland

First published in U.S.A., 1972
Reprint published by The Goldsmith Press Ltd.,
Newbridge, Ireland, 1984, 1987, 1990
Printed in Great Britain by
The Guernsey Press Co. Ltd., Guernsey, Channel Islands.

Cover: from a portrait of
Patrick Kavanagh
painted from life, 1965
by
ALEX SADKOWSKY

PREFACE

Dear Patrick,

It is now more than four years since I last wrote to you and I find that the longer I delay the less I have to say. A year or two ago I might have discussed your funeral, trying to decide which group was the most offensive, those who came or those who stayed away. There were a few genuine friends in attendance, of course. Information on your departure came to me from the Gardaí in Carrickmacross, which will give you some idea of the prevailing mood. Your philosophy of "not-caring" must have saved the day for you. Just the same, I was very disappointed that I hadn't the opportunity of seeing you off, as you saw me off on many 's the occasion.

Much talk of you since you have gone—at least half of it bitter and the remainder begrudging. Still, I suppose one should not complain. Perhaps they mean well. It is hard to say.

All of your writing has been out of print for some time; nothing at all of yours in the Dublin bookstores. Recently *The Green Fool* was re-issued but since you stated many times that this book was part of your juvenilia it is hard to know what is the motive behind the present edition.

Fortunately I continue to have my health, and so I have been whacking away on my own, publishing your papers. I began, as arranged, with our correspondence, *Lapped Furrows*. Then last year, *November Haggard*, a selection from your un-collected prose and verse arranged by me in such a way that it was in essence an essay on your point of view.

Now *Complete Poems*, the biggest job of all! Not a penny contributed by anyone but myself to these enterprises—and this in a world of Cultural Committees, Art Councils, fellowships and the rest. When in 1952 you asked if I would help you start a newspaper I threw everything I owned into *Kavanagh's Weekly*, knowing I would never see it again. That is what I have been doing here but on an even larger scale—and as before, with no regrets. This is the third time, with the stakes rising with each occasion. There have been no offers of support. Even a release requested for this edition was not forthcoming.

You must not imagine that I have suddenly begun to suffer from delusions or from self pity. If anything, the reverse is more likely to be true. I am merely stating the position so that you may know the way things stand—not much different, I'd say, from when you were around.

I think I have collected all of your verse. There may still be a few stragglers overlooked but these will hardly be missed in so large a collection. A few also have been omitted because of doubtful provenance. I corrected those errors in *Collected Poems* that offended you—and many more besides. Much of your unpublished verse lacked titles and these I added. There was also much sorting and re-assembling. Everything is put together in chronological sequence or close to it. Your Author's Note to *Collected Poems* has been omitted because this is a new book with unique qualities and not a new edition. For the same reason your dedication of the book to me has been left out.

With *Complete Poems* I have finished the major part of my plan for your work, recalling that the first publication of my press was your *Recent Poems*, now widely acclaimed as you at your best but which no one but myself would publish at the time. Only a few pieces of yours still remain to be published and these I may allow to lie in manuscript.

And so, until we meet again in a few years,

As ever, Peter

CONTENTS

(Juvenilia excluded)

ix

INTRODUCTION

The *Complete Poems of Patrick Kavanagh* have now been in print for more than ten years. A new edition is in order.

Patrick lived during a period when Ireland, or at least the district in which we were born, was still largely mediaeval. In a very few years from about 1955 to 1970 Ireland jumped from the primitive ass-and-cart economy to that of the tractor-trailer. Many of the references, therefore, in Patrick's verse, though clear to me, are quite unfamiliar to younger people. To overcome this difficulty I have added a series of explanatory notes.

From a very early age I was Patrick's primary audience. Almost everything he wrote he read first to me and asked for my opinion. I therefore thought it would be useful if now and then I added my own personal recollection to help explain the genesis or environment of certain of his poems.

The arrangement is chronological, though not perfectly so. With Patrick the date of composition and the date of publication do not always correspond. I have tried to be exact without becoming excessively scholarly.

In making this collection I have consulted with the original manuscripts, most of which I have in my archives. Now and then I had to make a selection from two or more versions of the same poem. I also had to supply numerous titles.

I do not intend here to make a critical assessment of Patrick's poetry but in reading through the collection I observed that in all his verse, even the earliest, there is a consistent autobiographical note. So apparent is this characteristic that from a reading of the poems I could re-construct his life. His personality too is stamped on every piece. This unique feature bears out Patrick's own poetic philosophy:

What wisdom's ours, if such there be
Is a flavour of personality.

For as long as I can remember, Patrick practised the writing of verse every evening. For years a trunk upstairs in our house was crammed with his early writing. The contents alas disappeared, some destroyed by mice, some by members of the family in a cleaning operation and perhaps some by Patrick himself. When Patrick wrote he was not thinking of posterity—he wrote because he had to. For him poetry was the cure-all for any soul-sickness. After he had written a poem its survival was a matter of chance. I was able to save a number of important pieces—*Lough Derg*, for a sample, but there may have been many worthy pieces lost in spite of my vigilance.

In this edition I have included four or five pieces accidentally omitted from the first edition.

Peter Kavanagh,
New York 1984.

THE INTANGIBLE

Rapt to starriness—not quite
I go through fields and fens of night,
The nameless, the void
Where ghostly poplars whisper to
A silent countryside.

Not black or blue,
Grey or red or tan
The skies I travel under.
A strange unquiet wonder.
Indian
Vision and Thunder.

Splendours of Greek,
Egypt's cloud-woven glory
Speak no more, speak
Speak no more
A thread-worn story.

PLOUGHMAN

I turn the lea-green down
Gaily now,
And paint the meadow brown
With my plough.

I dream with silvery gull
And brazen crow.
A thing that is beautiful
I may know.

1

Tranquillity walks with me
And no care.
O, the quiet ecstasy
Like a prayer.

I find a star-lovely art
In a dark sod.
Joy that is timeless! O heart
That knows God!

TO A BLACKBIRD

O pagan poet you
And I are one
In this—we lose our god
At set of sun.

And we are kindred when
The hill wind shakes
Sweet song like blossoms on
The calm green lakes.

We dream while Earth's sad children
Go slowly by
Pleading for our conversion
With the Most High.

TO A LATE POPLAR

Not yet half-drest
O tardy bride!
And the priest
And the bridegroom and the guests
Have been waiting a full hour.

The meadow choir
Is playing the wedding march
Two fields away,
And squirrels are already leaping in ecstasy
Among leaf-full branches.

DREAMER

'A fool you are,' she said,
'Weaving dreams of blue
Deceiving sky. Evening folds them all
And what are you?
Squanderers of centuries and hours
Hold only faded flowers.'

'And why should I,' I answered,
'Walk among the dead?
And you are dead a million years,
The wolves are fed.
A fool who eats the leavings of the Wise,
Who tells me that he dies?'

GOLD WATCH

Engraved on the case
House and mountain
And a far mist
Rising from faery fountain.

On inner case
No. 2244
Elgin Nath. . . .
Sold by a guy in a New York store.

Dates of repairs
1914 M.Y., 1918 H.J.,
She has had her own cares.

Slender hands
Of blue steel,
And within the precious
Platinum balance wheel.

Delicate mechanism
Counting out in her counting-house
My pennies of time.

BEECH TREE

I planted in February
A bronze-leafed beech,
In the chill brown soil
I spread out its silken fibres.

Protected it from the goats
With wire netting
And fixed it firm against
The worrying wind.

Now it is safe, I said,
April must stir
My precious baby
To greenful loveliness.

It is August now, I have hoped
But I hope no more—
My beech tree will never hide sparrows
From hungry hawks.

THE GOAT OF SLIEVE DONARD

I saw an old white goat on the slope of Slieve Donard,
Nibbling daintily at the herb leaves that grow in the crevasses,
And I thought of James Stephens—
He wrote of an old white goat within my remembering,
Seven years ago I read—
Now it comes back
Full of the dreaming black beautiful crags.
I shall drink of the white goat's milk,
The old white goat of Slieve Donard,
Slieve Donard where the herbs of wisdom grow,
The herbs of the Secret of Life that the old white goat has
    nibbled,
And I shall live longer than Methuselah,
Brother to no man.

ASCETIC

That in the end
I may find
Something not sold for a penny
In the slums of Mind.

That I may break
With these hands
The bread of wisdom that grows
In the other lands.

For this, for this
Do I wear
The rags of hunger and climb
The unending stair.

SOFT EASE

The holes in my coat of want
Were the praise of good clothing.
Her chill indifference vaunt
Whom I loved was the proving
Of earnest young loving.

Now my chair of comfort is set
And the air in my room is warm,
Good things on my table, and yet
Beyond reach of my arm
The potion of charm.

The hand of Soft Ease is hard—
It was never raised in Heaven,
The eyes of Soft Ease are starred
In wastes where no driven
Truths have striven.

A STAR

Beauty was that
Far vanishing flame,
Call it a star
Wanting better name.

And gaze and gaze
Vaguely until
Nothing is left
Save a grey ghost-hill.

Here wait I
On the world's rim
Stretching out hands
To Seraphim.

TO A CHILD

Child do not go
Into the dark places of soul,
For there the grey wolves whine,
The lean grey wolves.

I have been down
Among the unholy ones who tear
Beauty's white robe and clothe her
In rags of prayer.

Child there is light somewhere
Under a star,
Sometime it will be for you
A window that looks
Inward to God.

MARY

Her name was poet's grief before
Mary, the saddest name
In all the litanies of love
And all the books of fame.

I think of poor John Clare's beloved
And know the blessed pain
When crusts of death are broken
And tears are blossomed rain.

And why should I lament the wind
Of chance that brought her here
To be an April offering
For sins my heart held dear.

7

And though her passing was for me
The death of something sweet,
Her name's in every prayer, her charm
In every face I meet.

I MAY REAP

I who have not sown,
I too
By God's grace may come to harvest
And proud,
As the bowed
Reapers
At the Assumption
Murmur thanksgiving.

A PRAYER FOR FAITH

O give me faith
That I may be
Alive when April's
Ecstasy
Dances in every
White-thorn tree.

O give me faith
That I may see
The angel of
The mountainy
Places of Dream's
Infinity.

TO A COLTSFOOT BLOSSOM

O coltfoot blossom
You're a hardy chap!
So early on Spring's
Shut door to rap.

You have the faith
Of a saint of God
If you can believe
In that frozen sod.

Now, you are not
A flower at all
For me, but a gap
In Winter's wall

That I may see
The fields that are
Bright with many
A daisy-star.

Coming so early
And gaysome yellow,
Oh coltsfoot blossom
You're a fine young fellow.

DARK IRELAND

We are a dark people,
Our eyes are ever turned
Inward
Watching the liar who twists
The hill-paths awry.

O false fondler with what
Was made lovely
In a garden!

TO THE MAN AFTER THE HARROW

Now leave the check-reins slack,
The seed is flying far to-day—
The seed like stars against the black
Eternity of April clay.

This seed is potent as the seed
Of knowledge in the Hebrew Book,
So drive your horses in the creed
Of God the Father as a stook.

Forget the men on Brady's hill.
Forget what Brady's boy may say.
For destiny will not fulfill
Unless you let the harrow play.

Forget the worm's opinion too
Of hooves and pointed harrow-pins,
For you are driving your horses through
The mist where Genesis begins.

FOR CELIA Christmas 1933

I shall not ruffle the fine grain of her soul
Or stain with my black finger-tips the flower.
I shall be silent long in the ancient meadows now
Till the Uncouth Monster perishes in holy fire.

I shall not bring her through the withering night
Whose wind rasps the love-chords of beauty's instrument,
Where every dream is caught in foils of clay
And cynic childhood is a brazen image.

GAY CITIES

In a city of many lamps
I stood,
In an alleyway among tramps
The Brotherhood—
Pitiless as pity
In a gay city.

In a high-lamped city they stood
Among
Beggars and beast. The rude
Unknowing throng
Crushed and shoved
One who loved.

TO M

I think to cure my love pain
By recalling the many poets who have been
Spliced on the ecstatic blade
Till from each divided body a man and a maid
Walked forth in the sufficiency never frustrated. . . .
Keats to his Fanny Braune of dream mated
And Dante a nobler Beatrice won
And Mangan calling to his Nameless One
And the pensive poets of the Gael
Embracing the stars of True Beauty. The flying flail
Missing the snowy-breasted swans. O I too
Am spliced and embrace a gay eternal you.

11

LONE FLAME

So far all men is love
A heady lie
So do all men meet love,
A passer-by.

A few steps past
But not beyond the ring
Of inner truth
And faery reasoning.

Mind is a poor scholar
O blind Mind
When is spun your chilly firmament
Souls nothing find.

One love lone flame
In a dark cell
Makes fuel of firmaments
And dims out Hell.

MY ROOM

10 by 12
And a low roof
If I stand by the side wall
My head feels the reproof.

Five holy pictures
Hang on the walls:
The Virgin and Child
St. Anthony of Padua
Leo the XIII
St Patrick and the Little Flower.

My bed in the centre
So many things to me—
A dining table
A writing desk
And a slumber palace.

My room in a dusty attic
But its little window
Lets in the stars.

SHANCODUFF

My black hills have never seen the sun rising,
Eternally they look north towards Armagh.
Lot's wife would not be salt if she had been
Incurious as my black hills that are happy
When dawn whitens Glassdrummond chapel.

My hills hoard the bright shillings of March
While the sun searches in every pocket.
They are my Alps and I have climbed the Matterhorn
With a sheaf of hay for three perishing calves
In the field under the Big Forth of Rocksavage.

The sleety winds fondle the rushy beards of Shancoduff
While the cattle-drovers sheltering in the Featherna Bush
Look up and say: 'Who owns them hungry hills
That the water-hen and snipe must have forsaken?
A poet? Then by heavens he must be poor'
I hear and is my heart not badly shaken?

FOUR BIRDS

Kestrel

In a sky ballroom
The kestrel
A stately dancer.
He is a true artist—
His art is not divorced
From life
And death.

Owl

Night-winged
As a ghost
Or a gangster,
Mystical as a black priest
Reading the Devil's Mass.

Lark

Morning star
Announcing the birth
Of a love-child.

Corn-crake

A cry in the wilderness
Of meadow.

BLIND DOG

I follow the blind dog
Over the twisted trail,
Bled by the wild-rose thorns
Where he lashes his comet tail.

I follow the blind dog,
Crying to my star: O star
Of a passionate pagan's desire,
Lead me to the truths that are.

TINKER'S WIFE

I saw her amid the dunghill debris
Looking for things
Such as an old pair of shoes or gaiters.
She was a young woman,
A tinker's wife.
Her face had streaks of care
Like wires across it,
But she was supple
As a young goat
On a windy hill.

She searched on the dunghill debris,
Tripping gingerly
Over tin canisters
And sharp-broken
Dinner plates.

TWISTED FURROWS

She walked with me yesterday
Guiding my plough
Straight from headland to headland. . . .
Lament with me now.

My furrow twists like falsehood
The field's length and breadth.
O straight is truth I cry out
But my cry is death—

15

She will not come again
My furrow to guide,
For I have sinned against Guidance
And my plough has lied.

She will not come again
Till my field is ploughed—
I have not gone humbly cheerful
With shoulders bowed.

WORSHIP

To your high altar I once came
Proudly, even brazenly, and I said:—
Open your tabernacles I too am flame
Ablaze on the hills of Being. Let the dead
Chant the low prayer beneath a candled shrine,
O cut for me life's bread, for me pour wine!

PHOENIX

Scrap iron—
A brown mountain at the Dublin docks:—
Twisted motor chassis
Engines that once possessed creative energy
Stoves, wheels,
Jumbled tumbled
A catalogue-maker's puzzle.

Minds sicken
In the sight of these served-their-purpose things. . . .
A dead culture.

Yet somewhere up the river
The Life One sings:—
A Leeds furnace
Is the phoenix
From whose death-wings on this scrap-heap
Will rise
Mechanic vigour.
We believe.
Now is the Faith-dawn.

THE LAKE POOL

The lake pool
Mirrors me nothing
Neither tree nor cloud
Nor my own image.

It is opaque
As frosted glass
Or a fool's eye
Or the door of death.

THE HOUR

Now is the clock hour
The triumphant stroke
Struck. This is the inexorable.
This rubber-band of life
Is stretched to violin sweetness.

Beware! If the gong clangs
On your passivity
Narrow despair is a grinning
Mandarin.

Now is desirable
Achieving ready sensuous to embrace
The hills marshal furrows
Soldierly. A marching tune is played

O children
Now have we borne the exultant
Hood on our shoulders.
Who will be the defeated after?

THE SOWER

I have scattered the grain over the brown clay
Visioning hunger triumphant in darkling day
Of a city builded in fields of terrible pain
Crying out want and sorrow and crying in vain.

I am the Giver's servant. Want and Sorrow
Lie with their long teeth shattered by my harrow.
Who sits at my table now and shares my crust
Shall rise amongst starry fields on winged dust.

INNISKEEN ROAD: JULY EVENING

The bicycles go by in twos and threes—
There's a dance in Billy Brennan's barn to-night,
And there's the half-talk code of mysteries
And the wink-and-elbow language of delight.
Half-past eight and there is not a spot
Upon a mile of road, no shadow thrown
That might turn out a man or woman, not
A footfall tapping secrecies of stone.

I have what every poet hates in spite
Of all the solemn talk of contemplation.
Oh, Alexander Selkirk knew the plight
Of being king and government and nation.
A road, a mile of kingdom. I am king
Of banks and stones and every blooming thing.

PIONEERS

They wandered through the dark places and they kept
The prideful passionate horse tight-reined that would have leapt
The fence dividing star from meaner dust.
To trample down the corn which yields all men a crust.

They hungered as they went the sharp-stoned road,
And only one small lamp above them glowed. . . .
I too have eaten of the holy bread,
A crust they spared for me who no name had.

THE CHASE

I followed Wisdom
A night and a night
And a day and a day
Clay-knowing to spite.

I went quickly
As gulls over fallow,
As goats among crags,
As winds through a hollow.

Yet never I
Caught up with slow-footed
Wisdom who took
The lanes deepest rutted.

She left me with
My gangster ambition
In remorse—and remorse
Is the Devil's contrition.

APRIL

Now is the hour we rake out the ashes
Of the spirit-fires winter-kindled.
This old temple must fall,
We dare not leave it
Dark, unlovely, deserted.
Level! O level it down!
Here we are building a bright new town.

The old cranky spinster is dead
Who fed us cold flesh.
And in the green meadows
The maiden of Spring is with child
By the Holy Ghost.

TO A CHILD

O child, will you now share with me
The laughter of wise innocence?
My seer is love's infirmity!
My seer is love's incompetence.

Child, remember this high dunce
Had laughter in his heart and eyes,
A million echoes distant thence,
Ere Dublin taught him to be wise.

Sour is he as spinster's mouth
At kissing-time or time of praise,
His well of gladness dry, the drouth
Of desert knowledge is his days.

O child of laughter, I will go
The meadow ways with you, and there
We'll find much brighter stars than know
Old Aldebaran or the Bear.

A WIND

There's a wind blowing
Cold through the corridors,
A ghost-wind,
The flapping of defeated wings.
A hell-fantasy
From meadows damned
To eternal April.

And listening, listening
To the wind
I hear
The throat-rattle of dying men,
From whose ears oozes
Foamy blood,
Throttled in a brothel.

I see brightly
In the wind vacancies
Saint Thomas Aquinas
And
Poetry blossoms
Excitingly
As the first flower of truth.

AT NOON

I will not burn these rags,
The cast-off clothing of my soul,
In the chill of dawn they covered
Its nude ugliness.

Now in the passionate noon
The no-good dames
Tattoo my flesh with the indelible
Ink of lust.

What are these dim rooms
And red ghost-lamps?
Tell me this city's name,
New York or Paris?

Heaven was somewhere about
A child ideal.
Ah! the disillusioned one cried,
You have come far.

MARCH

The trees were in suspense,
Listening with an intense
Anxiety for the Word
That in the Beginning stirred
The dark-branched Tree
Of Humanity.

Subjectively the dogs
Hunted the muted bogs,
The horses suppressed their neighing,

No donkey-kind was braying,
The hare and rabbit under—
Stood the cause of wonder.

The blackbird of the yew
Alone broke the two
Minutes' silence
With a new poem's violence.
A tomboy scare that drove
Faint thoughts of active love.

MORNING

Do not awake the academic scholars,
Tradition's hairy god last night departed.
This morn the huge iconoclastic rollers
Blot out the roads where long the Spirit carted
The prayerful dream, the scientific load,
The cobwebbed preacher-stuff of Portobello.
To-day will find a new straw-bodied god
Much brighter than the other morbid fellow.

And when they wake—the scholars—they will be
Toothless, unvoiced and maybe half-way gone,
With nothing but a clouded memory
To lead them to the hieroglyphic stone
On which old Scholarship had proudly scratched
A list of doors that Truth had left unlatched.

AFTER MAY

May came, and every shabby phoenix flapped
A coloured rag in lieu of shining wings;
In school bad manners spat and went unslapped—

Schoolmistress Fancy dreamt of other things.
The lilac blossomed for a day or two
Gaily, and then grew weary of her fame.
Plough-horses out on grass could now pursue
The pleasures of the very mute and tame.

A light that might be mystic or a fraud
Played on far hills beyond all common sight,
And some men said that it was Adam's God
As Adam saw before the Apple-bite.
Sweet May is gone, and now must poets croon
The praises of rather stupid June.

MY BIRTHDAY October 1935

My birthday comes as usual
As birthdays will;
You can't keep the eastern sun
On Cassidy's hill;
You can't stop the clock of Time
On Adam's mill;
You can't slip down your vest
Death's great pill;
You must grow old Paddy Kavanagh
So dream your fill.

At any rate, Felix Meegan
And crying Phil
Paddy Brennan and Jordan
Must run still
The same distance ahead of me. . . .
For good or ill,
You cannot, Paddy Kavanagh, liquidate
Life's little bill.

24

STRUCK DOWN

Three things through love I see
They are Sin and Death and Hell,
And the flame that she left in my mind
My mind remembers well.
And the pain of the love I gave
'Twere better I never had known
And the maiden, may God forgive you
This ruin that strikes me down!

NO CHARLATAN AM I

No charlatan am I
With poet's mouth and idiot's eye:
I may not be divine
But what is mine is mine
In naked honesty.

FEAR

Let me be beggar-wise
That no man may
Stoop to the secrecies
In my dark clay;
For I have learned to fear
All curious eyes that peer.

SANCTITY

To be a poet and not know the trade,
To be a lover and repel all women;
Twin ironies by which great saints are made,
The agonising pincer-jaws of Heaven.

PYGMALION

I saw her in a field, a stone-proud woman
Hugging the monster Passion's granite child,
Engirdled by the ditches of Roscommon,
Stone ditches round her waist like serpents coiled.
Her lips were frozen in the signature
Of Lust, her hair was set eternally,
No Grecian goddess, for her face was poor,
A twisted face, like Hardship's, to me.
And who she was I queried every man
From Ballahedreen to grassy Boyle
And all replied: a stone Pygmalion
Once lipped to grey terrific smile
I said: At dawn tomorrow she will be
Clay-sensuous. But they only smiled at me.

POPLAR MEMORY

I walked under the autumned poplars that my father planted
On a day in April when I was a child
Running beside the heap of suckers
For which he picked the straightest, most promising.

My father dreamt forests, he is dead—
And there are poplar forests in the waste-places
And on the banks of drains.

When I look up
I see my father
Peering through the branched sky.

STREET CORNER CHRIST

I saw Christ today
At a street corner stand,
In the rags of a beggar he stood
He held ballads in his hand.

He was crying out: "Two for a penny
Will anyone buy
The finest ballads ever made
From the stuff of joy?"

But the blind and deaf went past
Knowing only there
An uncouth ballad seller
With tail-matted hair.

And I whom men call fool
His ballads bought,
Found Him whom the pieties
Have vainly sought.

TWO WAYS

I know the misery of towns
The hunger and the drought,
Wise men on pavements built for clowns,
And poor forgotten Truth—

A turnip sculptor kneeling where
The heels of fashion fly—
A halfpenny for a poet's prayer
In the glare of the Savoy.

O for a country where the doors
Are hospitably wide,
Where clay is clean and parlour floors
Invite strong boots inside,

Where every arty fraud is jeered
Where shines no movie star—
The ancient fields where God is feared
And men are what they are.

FREE SOUL

Yesterday I saw the Earth beautiful
Through the frosted glass of November's tree
I peered into an April country
Where love was day-dream free.

And in the steam rising from the dung-heap
Another firmament was blown
Dotted over with fairy worlds
And lamped with silver stone.

Over the bleak grey-bearded bogs
I looked and beheld the last Atlantis
And surely it was not November
But a time the freed souls grant us.

DICTATOR'S GENEALOGY

My father strung for me
No genealogic Rosary
Beads of hypnotic power—
I am, as Napoleon said, my own ancestors.

My father licked the crumbs
Of existence and their thumbs
Profanely in the church
Which left them in the lurch—
I am, as Napoleon said, my own ancestors.

My father waved too wide
The flag of family pride,
When a sword cried
So fierce, so fierce
For hearts to pierce
And was denied—
I am, as Napoleon said, my own ancestors.

POET

Once the Golden Book was open to me
And I read
The answer to the Riddle
And I, an unschooled rustic
Was wise
As fool's laughter in an academy.

And my words flowed
With the waters of Life
Or with candle flame
Ascended dream spires.

And I carved images
In stone of Mind
That terrified
Children and pale priests of the Mass.

THE GIRL IN THE LENDING LIBRARY

You leaned your head
Against the shelf
And I saw your sided eyes
Like the sword at Orion's Belt
In the south passionate skies.
And I said:

Under Orion I was born
Vive la! for Nora Criona
And not under Capricorn
Or fettered Andromeda.

You leaned your head
And the dust covers
Came to life and the blurb
Told of starry lovers
Wonderful or superb.

Under Orion I was born
Vive la! for Nora Criona
Taurus trembles hoof and horn,
Thus to see you

PEASANT

I am the representative of those
Clay-faced sucklers of spade-handles,
Bleak peasants for whom Apollo blows
Aesthetic winds in nine-day laboured scandals.
I am the hoarse cry of creatures who
Have never scratched in any kind of hand
On any wall the signs by which they knew
The endurable stone in the phantasmic land.

Their history is a grain of wheat. A season
The cycle of a race that will persist
When all the scintillating tribes of reason
Are folded in a literary mist.
Fear-grey men of doom have kept for me
The foot-grip of an ancient surety.

THE HIRED BOY

Let me be no wiser than the dull
And leg-dragged boy who wrought
For John Maguire in Donaghmoyne
With never a vain thought
For fortune waiting round the next
Blind turning of Life's Lane;
In dreams he never married a lady
To be dreamed-divorced again.

He knew what he wanted to know
How the best potatoes are grown
And how to put flesh on a York pig's back
And clay on a hilly bone,
And how to be satisfied with the little
The destiny masters give
To the beasts of the tillage country—
To be damned and yet to live.

LISTEN

Listen!
There is surely something to be heard
That is told in this house warmly—
A new fire in the derelict walls of Poetry

O there is a flying word about us
For earth ears;
And a tune, yet not a marching tune,
For soldier-maddened feet,
But an air like peace and fullness in garnered wheat.
Let us listen!
Let us listen!

MONAGHAN HILLS

Monaghan Hills
You have made me the sort of man I am
A fellow who can never care a damn
For Everestic thrills.

The country of my mind
Has a hundred little heads
On none of which foot-room for genius.

Because of you I am a half-faithed ploughman
Shallow furrows at my heels,
Because of you I am a beggar of song
And a coward in thunder.

If I had been born among the Mournes
Even in Forkhill,
I might have had echo-corners in my soul
Repeating the dawn laughter.

I might have climbed to know the glory
Of toppling from the roof of seeing—
O Monaghan hills when is writ your story
A carbon copy will unfold my being.

APRIL DUSK

April dusk
It is tragic to be a poet now
And not a lover
Paradised under the mutest bough.

I look through my window and see
The ghost of life flitting bat-winged.
O I am as old as a sage can ever be,
O I am as lonely as the first fool kinged.

The horse in his stall turns away
From the hay-filled manger, dreaming of grass
Soft and cool in hollows. O does he neigh
Jealousy-words for John McGuigan's ass
That never was civilized in stall or trace.

An unmusical ploughboy whistles down the lane
Not worried at all about the fate of Europe
While I sit here feeling the subtle pain
That every silenced poet has endured.

AUDIENCE

God's blessing on all who listen to me,
To all who listen. But to
Closed ears be an Orange drum
A-beating and what falls due
To fools in the Kingdom Come.

THE BAT

I stand tonight
Leg deep in ripened white
Grasses that excite
Slow fires of mind.

33

And blind
Bat-winged I rise—
A bat—
Where little star-eyes
Round gables peer
For wondering at.

And I hear—
Eve-dropping—
The wiser-than-fool talking
Kitchen philosophy,
And the hum hum
Of a school-boy thinking out
A hard sum
Bat-winged my dream
Over the shadow meadows,
A bat.

DRIFTING LEAVES

We drift and we care not whither,
Why should we care?
For You are at the end of all journeys
By vision or prayer.

Blow us O Wind, O blow us
Whither you will.
Every leaf that November casts clay-ward
Shall its own place fill.

DROLL

His cursing lips are thin
And white as tin.

His eyes are old as age
He is the devil's sage.

His legs are bowed
Upon the world's road

And yet he can
Proclaim himself a man.

Proclaim himself a soul.
All so droll.

DRUNKARD

From your wine-cask I fill
My glass again
And I will drink to all
The happy men.

And I will drink to those
Dark passionate
Children who dance unto
Death's rusty gate.

And I will drink to every
Dog that goes
Bravely to that far country
No one knows.

EPILOGUE

And now close all books
Of piety and knowledge.
It is a little thing that one can learn
In Rhymer's College.

How deep love is
The terror of our knowing
Would silence all
Green winds in our dream blowing.

THE FALL

I do not know what you are
Angel or demon.
Wise men have invented names for you
Out of the happiness you bestowed
Where you stayed
Was life smooth as Death's peace
And gay as a child's praying.

I was very wise on a time
Telling to no man
Your secret hill
But in my own heart confiding. . .
Until, until
I broke with the iron hammer of vulgarity
The crystal bowl
And cupped my hands for common charity.

FIELD STONE

My father was a temple in the deep
Hill-secrecies where I today roll blindly,
The masonry of my generations
Has taken not kindly
To air, and sick of time
I roll upon the ridge of tribulations
And the bulls paw the wind
Where once was rhyme and chime.

FURROW

A furrow is a string by which
The Destinies draw up the coach of Fate.
O furrowed field! Who shall ditch
The boundaries and leave no shining gate.

A furrow is the depth of life, a furrow
In an old meadow, is the price of glory
A word in the Black Book of Durrow
Or anything of April-Gaelic story.

No man has walked the length of day
A furrow-road without being terrified.
No man can stand on headlands who can pray
The tinsel prayer of engines new-supplied.

O climbing at the last, the last furrow
Drawn in like an angler's line. Only the spools
Of Truth placed on the shelf of Morrow
Who'll have the laugh on Today's serious fools.

HELL

Once I imagined I
Myself sitting high
On the sacred seat
The whole base world at my feet.

I poet of light
Guiding the flight
Of the ecstatic child
Lest he be clay-defiled.

Upon a low death-stone
Beggar and unknown
Though One did love me
The whole base world is above me.

HOPE

The fire goes out
We sit with our palms over it
Like the priest at the Consecration,
We sit huddled, old forlorn folk
Remembering, striving to hold against the dark-to-come
Some of the ballad-liveliness
When minds were supple
And there were poems hidden under the black-oak couple.
We shall have long cold days before again
April will dance in our heart's ballroom
We shall suffer as modern savages must
Who have painted civilization brightness on the wheels of soul.
Ah, we shall survive
This is the hope will sustain
When the fire is black in the hearth of Ireland
And love is just a polished sophist on the last up-train.

IN ONE MOMENT

Dark, incomprehensible woman suddenly
Stepped down beside me out of a place of green leaves
Lovely as a remembered joy lighting up tragedy
Younger than the lark's dawn yet older than a million eves.

Once with long white fingers tapped my shoulder
I did not move. In a great moment out-stretching time
I stood. And somewhere far down in my dream stood an older
Seer weaving a frock for Truth from broken threads of rhyme.

IRONIC BEGGAR

I go empty
Who have begged all day
From beggars
The pennies of truth which they
Claimed was theirs
And theirs alone
And they were the heirs
Of every warm thought in a world of stone.

The dark is yours
The glory is ours
They said.
And I was a thing unnumbered.

THE JUDGMENT

I heard the children talking under breath
When I had turned my back a little way—
Winking quaintly, they asked: "What sort of fool
Is that old gabbler? His mind must be astray."

And that is what you think of my wise words!
O children to your verdict I bow here!
For children pronounce the judgment of Heaven
Harsh, harsh, resolute, touched by no tear.

JUNE EVENING

An old plough at rest,
Its work done.
The broad fields coming gay-dressed
To the Priests of the Sun.

A tired horse out on grass
Goats on a hill
A tinker driving an ass
By a corn mill,

A beggarwoman dim
As remembered love
Poised on the flaming rim
Of the World. A drove

Of steaming bullocks rush past
In cloudy terror.
A star-child stands aghast
Before a mirror.

TO KNOWLEDGE

You taught me far too many things
Filling my singing void
With signs and sounds until the kings
Creative could not bide.

Before you came I knew the speech
Of mountains, I could pray
With stone and water. O foul leech
That sucks truth's blood away!

The dark mysterious blind of Earth
You drew, and I could see
Only the walls of life, the girth
Of one ill-fruited tree.

You taught me how to steer by night
Unstarred and port no lie—
But my first dream had wings of light
And cherub witchery.

You said: This is the only way
Of truth. And the fool in me
Buried God's lantern in dark clay
That an angel might not see.

THE LAST LAP

This is the last lap
The bell rings
And the tape goes up.

Across the palings
Dumb-mouthed gape
Men at the taut
Terrific tape.

We the runners
All-out fling
Our bodies forward
Towards some vague thing.

We the athletes
Of Destiny strain
Towards a mean clay-god
For a crown all vain.

LATE AUTUMN

I saw her passing down the wet streets
Autumn in the bedraggled skirts of a beggarwoman
She walked as one who had been
Tricked out of something sometime.
The rainy-wind rat-tailed her thin hair
And blew whiteness into her face
Did I see her once before
When storms were rattling a broken door?

41

MIRRORS

Everything I look upon
I make
A mirror of
Wherein to see myself in all its seasons.

A tree, a woman, a flower,
Are nothing of themselves
Only when these
Throw back the image of my Egoist
I love them, call them pretty-pretty names.

NOVEMBER SONG

He is training his colt,
The Man in the Moon
I can see where the hooves have beaten down
A clear round ring.
Can it be this thing
Forbodes rainfall soon?

Now I must hurry away for the brown
Leaves fall from November's tragic trees
And love that once shouted goes whispering
Of fearful mysteries.

There shall be rain
Soon on the naked fields
Yet shall the Spartans fight again,
Here be their shields.

And Love shall come shouting in
The meadows once more.
But tomorrow—a mortal sin!
The rain will pour.

OLD MEN OF IRELAND

The Others dance while they on low stools sit,
Old men for whom Imagination lit
The Lamp of Dreaming once. Their eyes remember
Only the light of evenings September
That nickle-plates the stubble paths among
Straight wheaten stooks or rows of steaming dung.

The old men muse o'er bargains that were made
In horses and in women when the trade
Of Ireland was a gypsies' caravan
Merry from town to town with beast and man.

The old men sit on ancient log-made stools
In a dim place—four tragic-splendid fools.

MY PEOPLE

STRANGER:
    What kind your people are
    I would wish to know:
    Great shouldered men like rolling stock,
    Great in despair,
    Simple in prayer,
    And their hard hands tear
    The soil on the rock
    Where the plough cannot go?
POET:
    'Tis not so.
    Faint-hearted folk my people are,
    To Poverty's house they have never invited
    The giant Pride,
    But await the world where wrongs are righted.
    They till their fields and scrape among the stones

43

Because they cannot be schoolmasters—
They work because judge Want condemns the drones.
Dear stranger, duty is a joke
Among my peasant folk.

STRANGER:

Poet be fair,
You surely must have seen
Beneath these rags of care
Hearts that were not mean
And beggarly and faint.

POET:

O curious stranger, why
Should poet seek to prove
The spirit of a saint?
For one in love
Would never probe or pry
Into the mysteried cove
Where all that is God's
Is safe from the hurting clods.
I cannot tell you what you ask
But I will tell you other things—
I will fill the flask
Of your curiosity with bitterings.

STRANGER:

I will go
To my town back again
And never desire to know
The hearts of your women and men.

POET:

Our women are humble as dust,
They suck the hard crust,
They suckle our children, and we
Drink the milk of love's mystery.

44

STRANGER:

    I will go
    To my townland of vermin
    That sways to and fro
    Like fool heads at a sermon.
    I will pour out for them
    Your vitriol of hell.
    And may Christ condemn
    My name if I tell
    The dream of your folk
    That arose as you spoke.

LILACS IN THE CITY

There are lilacs in the city
I saw them looking over
Black walls like pretty
Nuns of an enclosed Order
Curious to know
How the earth-wheels go
I said to them: close down
Your eyelids on the town
And do not heed
The streeted ghosts of speed
And do not imagine that
God so excited at
The wonder machines
For Death will reap them all
But for you the Eternal queens
Blow kisses.
Do not look beyond your wall.

LOVE AND LAUGHTER

You have possessed me, distressed me in my nine mood muses
I walk around the jail parade-ring till your third degree bruises
Are a bloody net about my loins
The gravel under my bare feet is the shingle
Of the brimstone quoins.

Ting ting tingle
Goes your little bell of speech
And I grow daft and dafter. . . .
Free me, O God, put laughter
Within a lover's reach.

MIRRORS (2nd version)

Everything I look at I make
A mirror of
Wherein to see my soul in all its seasons.
A tree
A woman
A masterpiece of art
Are nothing of themselves.
Only when these
Throw back my image glorified
Saint-frenzied high
Only then
I love them
Call them inviolable truths.

OLD SOLDIER

I return to the fields
Of tillage and peace
Who have wandered and found
No Golden Fleece

But only a rag
On a lifting thorn
An ironic flag
Crow-pecked, forlorn.

Love's frosted buds
That could not shake
The nursing gods
Of green awake

Petty squabbling
My eyes did see
And Achilles wobbling
In jeopardy.

And men of thought
Being hustled on
Till there was not
Under the sun

An unflustered bird
Of evening mood
Or a poet's word
In the interlude.

Over the war-loud
Fields I went
Strumming the crowd—
False instrument.

One with the savages
And the insane
O War, that did ravage
My virgin Spain.

ORTHODOX

God keep you child
When you go down
The faithless streets
Of Pleasure's town.

High temples house
The meanest gods
And silken vested
Priests are clods.

And when you sell
Your beauty sweet
Beware! Love's coin
Is counterfeit.

And Night such glittering
Rainment wears
Day has but few
Admirers.

PLOUGH HORSES

Their glossy flanks and manes outshone
The flying splinters of the sun.

The tranquil rhythm of that team
Was as slow flowing meadow stream.

And I saw Phidias's chisel there—
An ocean stallion, mountain mare—

Seeing with eyes the Spirit unsealed
Plough-horses in a quiet field.

POPLARS

I walked under the tall poplars that my father planted
On a day in April when I was a boy
Running beside the heap of saplings
From which he picked the straightest spears of sky.

The sun was shining that day
As he shone for the Tuatha De Danann
And no one was old or sad
For life was just beginning

RAPE OF THE IDEAL

Open all windows
The savage begetting
Brute breaks the delicate glass
Ideal long in a sun unsetting.

REMEMBERED COUNTRY

No man lives the moment—the light
Is too crudely rudely staring. . . .
Oh I remember country in the flight
Of evening funerals after much child-bearing.

Not swallows septembered on waves of tile
Or the eagerings of apriltime is the full
Of my third eye—but the angel while
When God was unstirred mud in a shallow pool.

The Rages blow the dust out of the presses.
My two sense eyes are observant—I know
The fume and the fretful processes
Of world-thrown jail-birds and their face-brave show.

49

Thy Kingdom Come. They are gone
Flashed in the broken nimbus with a laugh
No man has worn the moment's perfect one,
Times torn tick delivers Now of chaff.

RENDEZVOUS

O once I talked with her
Whose voice all men
Cock ear for in every quiet,
Then move again.
I did not move, I knew
The prayer-gay rendezvous
Of love is anywhere.

THE RICH TRAMP

I am rich
Although I lie
On the shady side of a summer ditch.
I see the faery children pass by
To the wedding feast of the King's son,
In a ballroom under a big buck thistle.
The Queen has asked me to join the fun
And play gay reels on my tin whistle.
And won't I play the queerest tunes
Till they shout like mad
For the whistling lad
And rattle out time with old tea spoons.

What if the ballroom disappears
And the little dancers fade
Into the mists of long-shed tears!
I lie in the ditches' shade
Where the summer sun
At half-past-one
Scorches not one green blade.

THE RUSTIC

Simple love warm and kind
In the country I'll find
A daughter of nature young and sweet
Who has never learned city deceit.
A child of the unsullied muse
Who has never stood in cinema queues,
Who has never read the books that make
Women motherhood forsake.

I see her already so bashful, so
Awkward-tongued she cannot say
The pretty lyrical bunk or blow
Bubbles of laughter. Her name is May.
Her mother's an easy-going woman,
Very human,
And her father's a spade-man in the bog
Earning half-a-crown a day.

Simple and innocent love, by Johnie
What good is dirty money
Scattered over the floor of Hate
Like the pieces of a rage-smashed plate.
Heaven on Earth
The girth
Of a woman's waist.

THE SEEKER

All day I sought an easy peace
That would not wear away the flesh
Of my four bones.
In pleasure's chapel I heard the music of the zither
Blown in light like the down soft feather
Movements in zero zones.

And then you captivated me as the labour
Of black fields husbandmen for whom the sabre
Had giddily flashed too often
In balanced piety and hum drum quiet.
I prayed O Queen of Heaven after the riot
Where poet-soft fibres toughen.

THE SEED AND THE SOIL

Somebody is moving across the headlands
Talking to himself
A grey thinker.

The clay is whitening in the windy light
Where the sparrows are bathing.
Tomorrow surely
The seed will go under the harrow
Nothing must hinder
The wooing of grain and clay.

THE STONE OF THE TOURIST

Yankee tourist
He could sure
Talk to deafen a mill-race.

From his watch-chain
Platinum set
Hung
A chip of the Blarney stone.

I accept
He had been suspended
Head downwards
Two men holding his heels.
He had put his snout
To the stone mentioned
So favourably by Father Prout. .

TRAGIC AUTUMN

Autumn I'd welcome had I
Known love in Summer days
I would not weep for flowers that die
If once they'd bloom for praise.
I would not cry to any tree
Leaf lost, a word of misery
I would not make lament although
My harvest were a beggar's woe.

TRUTH

The light behind a written word
The silence of a singing bird,

The quiet at the root of trouble,
Not love, but love's ecstatic double,

A child asleep upon its prayer,
The glance of eyes that do not stare,

The beauty-spell of things uncouth—
These are the marks of living truth.

DREAM

When she in dream to you in manifest
Be quiet. Do not speak. She comes but once
And words do break her hold. Be silent lest
You mouth forever sorrow's impotence.
Do not cry "God", prostrating your body
Where all the dead lie prostrate, blind and blind
All in their seamy cloaks of pious shoddy.
There is no prayer can raise her once drawn.

TO ANNA QUINN

I'll make a song for you—
That should it be
That you return no more to me
In this song I may look and see
You smiling in at me—
You winking in at me.

And I can trace the line
Curving divine
From your neck to heel
And feel
Your sympathy of heart
Upon my tragic art.

O here I break
My heart in two
That you
May put your fingers in and take
All that to me is true
In love. . . .
Great God above
Must I forever see as in a glass
The loveliness of earth? the girls that pass.

CREATION

Vaguely unenterprizing floating in
A firmament whose stars do not change
Through frosty atmosphere or rain.

The gardens about us are faded
A little and over jaded
Eyes would be glad
To see the old gardener go mad
And shoulder his spade
And his rake
And let the weeds make
Their statement for falsehood or truth
O the agony of perpetual truth!

The leering god might be a plaster-cast
So fixed his putty smile.
His trade of creation has been suspended
And he waits for us at the end of the level mile.

His passive switch
Hangs like a cow's tail that beat
The flies of twenty summers which
Accounts for this decaying-grey conceit.
No one will be able hereafter
To boast a souvenir of once beauty
The firmament crashes rafter after rafter
Sin and sorrow and virtue sooty
And no one will be able to say
"I remember dawn's laughter
God was in the Beginning anyway."

BURIAL SERVICE

The old mare
Twenty-seven years old
Died; we buried her where
The brown turf-mould
Free from stones
Presses little
On her sapless bones—
Bones glass-brittle.

We marked the spot
With a smashed spade shaft
It was not
Evening. We laughed
At a cruel tale
A peasant told
Of a woman crushed and pale
And not old.

THE LADY OF THE POETS

O lady of the lonely and unloved
You are unmoved
By the lean anguish of a poet's cry
You have heard so many greater than I.

You I have long known
In tree and stone
And in all sealed tongues
Of sympathy. How many tongues
Of sympathy. How many songs
Of secret self have you heard—
Pitiful prayers that dared
Not turn to High
Heaven for mercy?

And have listened to the great
And yet you wait
To comfort me
In my lone house of poetry.

THE LAST VANITY

I will make you remember me:
O vain egoist:
Nothing remembers
But the part that is kissed
And mystic love
Is their lot where love missed
O none will remember you
Whom you haven't kissed.

I will make you remember me
O sensualist!
The seed that you throw
Flies back to your fist
For the earth-seeker's road
Has the silliest twist.

I will make you remember me
O simple priest
Love forgets her dark penance
In the dance-whirled mist
And your prayer has the power
A midge dares to resist.
To God's mill of slowness
You cannot bring grist
One grain more than Adam
Has put on man's list.

I will make you remember me
O Humanist
Hankering after
The dreams which consist
Of immortal sun-downs
In a poetic West
And forever longing
Creative incest.

PURSUIT OF AN IDEAL

November is come and I wait for you still
O nimble-footed nymph who slipped me when
I sighted you among some silly men
And charged you with the power of my will.
Headlong I charged to make a passionate kill,
Too easy, far too easy, I cried then,
You were not worth one drop from off my pen.
O flower of the common light, the thrill
Of common things raised up to angelhood
Leaped in your flirt-wild legs, I followed you
Through April May and June into September,
And still you kept your lead till passion's food
Went stale within my satchel. Now I woo
The footprints that you make across November.

IN THE SAME MOOD

You will not always be far away and pure
As a word conceived in a poet's silver womb
You will not always be a metaphysical signature
To all the poems I write. In my bleak room
This very year by God's will you may be

A woman innocent in her first sin
Having cast off the immortality
Of the never-to-be-born. The violin
Is not more real than the music played upon it
They told me that, the priests—but I am tired
Of loving through the medium of a sonnet
I want by Man, not God, to be inspired.
This year O maiden of the dream-vague face
You'll come to me, a thing of Time and Space.

THE IRONY OF IT

I have not the fine audacity of men
Who have mastered the pen
Or the purse
The complexes of many slaves are in my verse
When I straighten my shoulders to look at the world boldly
I see talent coldly
Damning me to stooped attrition.
Mine was a beggar's mission
To dreams of beauty I should have been born blind.

I should have been content to walk behind
Watching the reflection of God's delight:
A secondhand teller of the story
A secondhand glory.
It was not right
That my mind should have echoed life's overtones
That I should have seen a flower
Petalled in mighty power.

FOOL

Fool that has served
Do not go now
For I learn dignified ways
Too easily. I might crow
On the sun-caught tower
A vain praise-crowing
And forget my meanness
In the moment's power
Or on a weed bestowing
Love-fountained tears
Because of its greenness.

POET

Winter encloses me
I am fenced
The light, the laugh, the dance,
Against.

I am like a monk
In a grey cell
Copying out my soul's
Queer miracle.

What goes on out there
In the light
Is less than a blue-bottle's flirtation,
Yet spite!

I would be a blue-bottle
Or a house-fly
And let the monk, the task
In darkness lie.

PLOUGH

Plough, take your thin arms from around my middle
Leave me free to unscroll the wisdom of other flesh.
Ah, you are jealous plough, you drive the fingers
Of your lust-longing deep in my folds of manhood.

Release me, release me, my desires would run
In shallower furrows of passion. I am no Christ
Your breath is too strong. You hurry me towards
A monumental-immortal cowardice.

You have kissed me a thousand times,
You have twisted my shoulders and my will
O clinging, possessive mistress, O plough,
Though I break your hold your charms possess me still.

ANNA QUINN

O God above
Must I forever live in dreams of love?
Must I forever see as in a glass
The loveliness of life before me pass
Like Anna Quinn or sunlight on the grass?

SIREN

You scattered the house that I had built
From prayer and meditation
When I listened to your ingenuous lilt—
O empty--headed brazen!

You sang to me of pretty flowers
Young woman loud and merry;
Youth cannot live on ivory towers
Or granite hills of Kerry.

61

"Come down" you called "and play with us
Contemporary games,
Come down thou star-struck octopus
Not virgins we but dames.

While love on tandem bicycles
Pursues the sunny sprites
The poet's nose runs icicles
From spiritual heights.

Come down sad man and do not be
One of the lean begetters
Of the most tragic family
In the steel womb of letters.

Leave to the immutable gods
The House of Eternal Truth,
The light is on the impassioned clods
But the worm is sampling youth.

Do not heed the cry
Of the immortal birds—
Men are not made to fly,
Love speaks the plainest words."

And I came down and my house came down
Stone and slate and rafter
And unhoused I wandered in woman's town
Beggared by Woman's laughter.

SNAIL

I go from you, I recede
Not by steps violent
But as a snail backing
From the lewd finger of humanity.

I go from you as a snail
Into my twisted habitation.

And you
It does not matter how you
React. I know the shadow ways
Of Self
I know the last sharp bend
And the volleyed light.

You are lost
You can merely chase the silver I have let
Fall from my purse,
You follow silver
And not follow me.

THE PLOUGHMAN

In these small fields
I have known the delight
Of being reborn each morning
And dying each night.

And I can tell
That birth and death
Are nothing so fierce
As the Preacher saith.

But when a life's but a day
The womb and tomb
Press lips in fondness
Like bride and groom.

And when a man's a ploughman
As I am now
An age is a furrow
And Time a plough,

And Infinity a field
That cannot stretch
Over the drain
Or through the ditch.

ETHICAL

You who have not sown
Will eat the bitter bread
And beg the sweetness of a stone
Flung at Saint Stephen's head.

You who have not sung
Will hear the clang of brass
When fairies beat on April's gong
With stems of greening grass.

And you who have not prayed
The blackbird's evening prayer
Will kneel all night dismayed
Upon a frozen stair.

THE CALL

Did you call me
Or was it the wind
On my ill-carpentered window?
I am awake now
And all your prophecy
Is turned to dust.

DIFFERENT WISDOM

I know that I have heard spoken
A different wisdom as
The tree was shaken
Above the parlour grass.
That is not as it should be
I should have listened longer
Nor feared the tremulous tree
And that Stranger
With words that were not caught
Upon the difficult bough.
He was wise. And I fool taught
By Earth to know.
The laugh and the intense age
Awoke to look on
Reality diffused in the sigh
Of Sentiment's town.

OCTOBER WARRANT

Over the kind brown earth we bend
Knowing how warm a grave must be
In October. O Death send
In October-time your warrant for me.
And here as we lift the soil-baked bread,
The potatoes—we are not filled with dread
That hunger should touch Eternity.

We pick the potatoes and move aside
The withered flesh, and the gulls come down
Like a flock of angels. The countryside
Is emptied out. There is only town
And the place of souls beyond the night.
A star over Galway shines as bright
As a lamp in a cave or Mary's crown.

ONE WITH GOD

Over the kind brown earth we bend
And one with God are we.
It is October-time—the end
Of passions jittery.

The white bleached stalks
Are like the bones
Of long dead lovers
The lean-faced rocks
Unveiled in winds
Are Eternity's dictators.

IN DISTRESS

That song will not come
That child must be still-born
I shall lie dumb
A season fallow. O the sensuous corn
Green as innocent kisses cannot be.
I must be silent. Poet-God pray for me.
I cannot save myself and time runs on
A season of eternity. O the caress
Of a word.
O the laugh of the sun
O the light of a bird
The loveliness
Of the angelic absurd
In distress.

THE CIRCLE

The Circle is the Father
Diameter His Son
Spirit the mathematical centre
Thus truth is known
In all turning wheels
In all tumbling clowns
As in the firmament deep
Where the Prophet drowns.

Blessed are the followers
Of all wheel tracks,
Blessed the spoke-tortured
Christ. The axe
Traces a circle
And in that trace
Is the power the Word
And the tortured Face.

WEARY HORSE

The weary horse on which I ride
Is language vitiate
That cannot take in its stride
Bank, stream and gate.

Its eyes have the blank look
Of a memoried fool
Or a Victorian look
In a modern school.

NOT FOR THE ASKING

There is nothing to be said
When we are denied
The sense-bread.
Once a poet cried:
"I hunger"
And his song died.

I hunger! Christ!
Is it true
That Beauty has so high-priced
Her kisses? With you
O clay-wise men
I would eat
And laugh at the shame of it—

No music when
The dancers infinite
Called from a flower
Called my name
Through the Petalled flame
And I fell dumb
Fallen from power.
They come the dancers come!
Have I cried hunger.

SENSUALIST

Realize the touch kingdom
Do not stray
In the abstract temple of love.
There are no priests on the altars
Of Metaphysic

You have heard this truth before
Well, what matter!
Is the body not the temple of the Holy Ghost
And flesh eyes have glimpsed Truth.

SIMPLE FOLK

Around me everywhere
People are saying
The hard-edged words of reality
They are praying
To a solid god whose kick is no illusion
And whose house
Is not a poet's corner of confusion.

They arrive
By the stone stairway step a day,
While the winged children strive
Against hysteric winds to stay
Flapping vaguely in the tear-wet air
Calling on the spirit of Prophecy to witness their despair.

MEMORY OF MY FATHER

Every old man I see
Reminds me of my father
When he had fallen in love with death
One time when sheaves were gathered.

That man I saw in Gardiner Street
Stumble on the kerb was one,
He stared at me half-eyed,
I might have been his son.

And I remember the musician
Faltering over his fiddle
In Bayswater, London,
He too set me the riddle.

Every old man I see
In October-coloured weather
Seems to say to me:
'I was once your father.'

PRIMROSE

Upon a bank I sat, a child made seer
Of one small primrose flowering in my mind.
Better than wealth it is, said I, to find
One small page of Truth's manuscript made clear.
I looked at Christ transfigured without fear—
The light was very beautiful and kind,
And where the Holy Ghost in flame had signed
I read it through the lenses of a tear.
And then my sight grew dim, I could not see
The primrose that had lighted me to Heaven,
And there was but the shadow of a tree
Ghostly among the stars. The years that pass
Like tired soldiers nevermore have given
Moments to see wonders in the grass.

CHRISTMAS 1939

O Divine Baby in the cradle
All that is poet in me
Is the dream I dream of Your Childhood
And the dream You dreamed of me.

O Divine Baby in the cradle
All that is truth in me
Is my mind tuned to the cadence
Of a child's philosophy.

O Divine Baby in the cradle
All that is pride in me
Is my mind bowed in homage
Upon Your Mother's knee.
O Divine Baby in the cradle
All that is joy in me
Is that I have saved from the ruin
Of my soul your Infancy.

CHRISTMAS EVE REMEMBERED

I see them going to the chapel
To confess their sins, Christmas Eve
In a parish in Monaghan.
Poor parish! And yet memory does weave
For me about these folk
A romantic cloak.

No snow, but in their minds
The fields and roads are white.
They may be talking of the turkey markets
Or foreign politics, but tonight
Their plain, hard country words
Are Christ's singing birds.

Bicycles scoot by, old women
Cling to the grass margin,
Their thoughts are earthy but their minds move
In dreams of the Blessed Virgin
For one in Bethlehem
Has kept their dreams safe for them.

71

"Did you hear from Tom this Christmas?"
"These are the dark days"
"Maguire's shop did a great trade,
Turnover double—so Maguire says."
"I can't delay now Jem
Lest I be late for Bethlehem."

Like this my memory saw
Like this my childhood heard
These pilgrims of the North.
And memory, you have me spared
A light to follow them
Who go to Bethlehem.

SPRAYING THE POTATOES

The barrels of blue potato-spray
Stood on a headland of July
Beside an orchard wall where roses
Were young girls hanging from the sky.

The flocks of green potato-stalks
Were blossom spread for sudden flight,
The Kerr's Pinks in a frivelled blue,
The Arran Banners wearing white.

And over that potato-field
A lazy veil of woven sun.
Dandelions growing on headlands, showing
Their unloved hearts to everyone.

And I was there with the knapsack sprayer
On the barrel's edge poised. A wasp was floating
Dead on a sunken briar leaf
Over a copper-poisoned ocean.

The axle-roll of a rut-locked cart
Broke the burnt stick of noon in two.
An old man came through a cornfield
Remembering his youth and some Ruth he knew.

He turned my way. 'God further the work.'
He echoed an ancient farming prayer.
I thanked him. He eyed the potato-drills.
He said: 'You are bound to have good ones there.'

We talked and our talk was a theme of kings,
A theme for strings. He hunkered down
In the shade of the orchard wall. O roses
The old man dies in the young girl's frown.

And poet lost to potato-fields,
Remembering the lime and copper smell
Of the spraying barrels he is not lost
Or till blossomed stalks cannot weave a spell.

STONY GREY SOIL

O stony grey soil of Monaghan
The laugh from my love you thieved;
You took the gay child of my passion
And gave me your clod-conceived.

You clogged the feet of my boyhood
And I believed that my stumble
Had the poise and stride of Apollo
And his voice my thick-tongued mumble.

You told me the plough was immortal!
O green-life-conquering plough!
Your mandril strained, your coulter blunted
In the smooth lea-field of my brow.

You sang on steaming dunghills
A song of cowards' brood,
You perfumed my clothes with weasel itch,
You fed me on swinish food.

You flung a ditch on my vision
Of beauty, love and truth.
O stony grey soil of Monaghan
You burgled my bank of youth!

Lost the long hours of pleasure
All the women that love young men.
O can I still stroke the monster's back
Or write with unpoisoned pen

His name in these lonely verses
Or mention the dark fields where
The first gay flight of my lyric
Got caught in a peasant's prayer.

Mullahinsha, Drummeril, Black Shanco—
Wherever I turn I see
In the stony grey soil of Monaghan
Dead loves that were born for me

KEDNAMINSHA

You wore a heather jumper then,
A hat of cloud and on your feet
Shoes made by craft-gods out of peat.
No poet ever drew a pen
To bind with words wild goats and men
In such a glen. O, Time's deceit
Flirts here in Dublin's Grafton Street.

Yet I recall your quarrymen
Shouting among the granite gables,
Sitting on stone-stools sipping tea,
My eye that scans dull restaurant tables
In the glass of memory plain can see
Great iron men and the loves they seize
And young goats praying on broken knees.

THE 6.40 P.M. FROM AMIENS STREET

O, is it nineteen forty
Or a thousand years ago?
We are not going home by train
We're riding through the snow.

Riding our horses warily,
Among the ancient trees,
Strange beasts are howling fearfully
Somewhere deep in Meath.

We saw beside the Boyne
A kern keeping guard,
But we waved our green silk banners
As we galloped across the ford.

We saw upon a hill
A Christian church in flames:
Some said it was a candlelight
But it might have been the Danes.

"O listen to the chanting
Of the monks in Monasterboice"
An old man said, and pulled
His horse's bridle tight.

75

There's John de Courcy ahead of us—
What! It cannot be
Perhaps 'tis Collier the Robber
Heading for Dunleer

Though our lamps are cold blue ghosts
We ride in triumph north
Cheering, laughing. . . . What voice said to me
"Change at Dundalk!"

Some thought that we were in a train—
But my cloak was stiff with snow!
We were riding home to Christmas
A thousand years ago

AFTER MASS

"An acre a day
With the Kitty mare and the Grey."
Thus spoke Pat Dooley at the chapel gate after Mass
On a morning that was
Crisp as a biscuit at the fire of March.
"From eight till six without a bit of trouble
I'd belt an acre of stubble
Or lea
If the ground was free
Of rocks or running stones. . . ."
He puffed his pipe. Then David Martin said
While he winked at the crowd behind the graveyard beech,
"It's surely blowey weather
When God and Ploughman Dooley blow together."
We laughed and David said: "O Dooley diddler
You'd make a decent ploughman foal a fiddler."
Father Brennan came down the steps

And we saluted
"Good morning Father."
The Joker's hand was looted
And we were solemn as the graveyard tree. . . .
"I think I'll sow a bit of wheat tomorrow
If it keeps dry overhead:
Will you be using your spring-toothed harrow?"
Silence.
"McMahon, did you hear what I said?"
"You were talking, Dooley. . . . Oh yes, I agree
The war is no great benefit to you and me;
The ships are sinking a holy living dread
It will break the world."
Oh see! the grass is making a move—
But graveyard grass grows greenest—it is blest
And under is no hate but only love
The roots have fed on tears. Let us be gone
The dead have rest
But we must turn our wheels against the sun.

ART McCOOEY

I recover now the time I drove
Cart-loads of dung to an outlying farm—
My foreign possessions in Shancoduff—
With the enthusiasm of a man who sees life simply.

The steam rising from the load is still
Warm enough to thaw my frosty fingers.
In Donnybrook in Dublin ten years later
I see that empire now and the empire builder.

Sometimes meeting a neighbour
In country love-enchantment,
The old mare pulls over to the bank and leaves us
To fiddle folly where November dances.

We wove our disappointments and successes
To patterns of a town-bred logic:
'She might have been sick. . . . No, never before,
A mystery, Pat, and they all appear so modest.'

We exchanged our fool advices back and forth:
'It easily could be their cow was calving,
And sure the rain was desperate that night . . .'
Somewhere in the mists a light was laughing.

We played with the frilly edges of reality
While we puffed our cigarettes;
And sometimes Owney Martin's splitting yell
Would knife the dreamer that the land begets.

'I'll see you after Second Mass on Sunday.'
'Right-o, right-o.' The mare moves on again.
A wheel rides over a heap of gravel
And the mare goes skew-ways like a blinded hen.

Down the lane-way of the popular banshees
By Paddy Bradley's; mud to the ankles;
A hare is grazing in Mat Rooney's meadow;
Maggie Byrne is prowling for dead branches.

Ten loads before tea-time. Was that the laughter
Of the evening bursting school?
The sun sinks low and large behind the hills of Cavan,
A stormy-looking sunset. 'Brave and cool.'

Wash out the cart with a bucket of water and a wangel
Of wheaten straw. Jupiter looks down.
Unlearnedly and unreasonably poetry is shaped
Awkwardly but alive in the unmeasured womb.

CHRISTMAS CAROL 1941

I see the North Star
And the North Star sees me,
But who sees the Star of Peace
In the East, cloudy?

I see the donkey plod
Through the deep snow
But where can the Mother of God
In this storm go?

I see the Three Wise Kings,
They've lost their way,
Wandering around in rings
Day after day.

I see the Son of God
In the straw where he lies,
But I hear no angel sing
Peace in the skies.

I see countless stars
And the countless stars see me,
But no one sees the Star of Peace
In the East, cloudy.

THE GREAT HUNGER

I

Clay is the word and clay is the flesh
Where the potato-gatherers like mechanised scarecrows move
Along the side-fall of the hill—Maguire and his men.

If we watch them an hour is there anything we can prove
Of life as it is broken-backed over the Book
Of Death? Here crows gabble over worms and frogs
And the gulls like old newspapers are blown clear of the hedges,
   luckily.
Is there some light of imagination in these wet clods?
Or why do we stand here shivering?
                              Which of these men
Loved the light and the queen
Too long virgin? Yesterday was summer. Who was it promised
   marriage to himself
Before apples were hung from the ceilings for Hallowe'en?
We will wait and watch the tragedy to the last curtain,
Till the last soul passively like a bag of wet clay
Rolls down the side of the hill, diverted by the angles
Where the plough missed or a spade stands, straitening the way.

A dog lying on a torn jacket under a heeled-up cart,
A horse nosing along the posied headland, trailing
A rusty plough. Three heads hanging between wide-apart
Legs. October playing a symphony on a slack wire paling.
Maguire watches the drills flattened out
And the flints that lit a candle for him on a June altar
Flameless. The drills slipped by and the days slipped by
And he trembled his head away and ran free from the world's
   halter,
And thought himself wiser than any man in the townland
When he laughed over pints of porter
Of how he came free from every net spread
In the gaps of experience. He shook a knowing head
And pretended to his soul
That children are tedious in hurrying fields of April
Where men are spanging across wide furrows.
Lost in the passion that never needs a wife—
The pricks that pricked were the pointed pins of harrows.

Children scream so loud that the crows could bring
The seed of an acre away with crow-rude jeers.
Patrick Maguire, he called his dog and he flung a stone in the air
And hallooed the birds away that were the birds of the years.

Turn over the weedy clods and tease out the tangled skeins.
What is he looking for there?
He thinks it is a potato, but we know better
Than his mud-gloved fingers probe in this insensitive hair.

'Move forward the basket and balance it steady
In this hollow. Pull down the shafts of that cart, Joe,
And straddle the horse,' Maguire calls.
'The wind's over Brannagan's, now that means rain.
Graip up some withered stalks and see that no potato falls
Over the tail-board going down the ruckety pass—
And *that's* a job we'll have to do in December,
Gravel it and build a kerb on the bog-side. Is that Cassidy's ass
Out in my clover? Curse o' God—
Where is that dog?
Never where he's wanted.' Maguire grunts and spits
Through a clay-wattled moustache and stares about him from the
    height.
His dream changes like the cloud-swung wind
And he is not so sure now if his mother was right
When she praised the man who made a field his bride.

Watch him, watch him, that man on a hill whose spirit
Is a wet sack flapping about the knees of time.
He lives that his little fields may stay fertile when his own body
Is spread in the bottom of a ditch under two coulters crossed in
    Christ's Name.

He was suspicious in his youth as a rat near strange bread,
When girls laughed; when they screamed he knew that meant

The cry of fillies in season. He could not walk
The easy road to destiny. He dreamt
The innocence of young brambles to hooked treachery.
O the grip, O the grip of irregular fields! No man escapes.
It could not be that back of the hills love was free
And ditches straight.
No monster hand lifted up children and put down apes
As here.
                              'O God if I had been wiser!'
That was his sigh like the brown breeze in the thistles.
He looks towards his house and haggard. 'O God if I had been
    wiser!'
But now a crumpled leaf from the whitethorn bushes
Darts like a frightened robin, and the fence
Shows the green of after-grass through a little window,
And he knows that his own heart is calling his mother a liar
God's truth is life—even the grotesque shapes of his foulest fire.

The horse lifts its head and cranes
Through the whins and stones
To lip late passion in the crawling clover.
In the gap there's a bush weighted with boulders like morality,
The fools of life bleed if they climb over.

The wind leans from Brady's, and the coltsfoot leaves are holed
    with rust,
Rain fills the cart-tracks and the sole-plate grooves;
A yellow sun reflects in Donaghmoyne
The poignant light in puddles shaped by hooves.
Come with me, Imagination, into this iron house
And we will watch from the doorway the years run back,
And we will know what a peasant's left hand wrote on the page.
Be easy, October. No cackle hen, horse neigh, tree sough, duck
    quack.

II

Maguire was faithful to death:
He stayed with his mother till she died
At the age of ninety-one.
She stayed too long,
Wife and mother in one.
When she died
The knuckle-bones were cutting the skin of her son's backside
And he was sixty-five.

O he loved his mother
Above all others.
O he loved his ploughs
And he loved his cows
And his happiest dream
Was to clean his arse
With perennial grass
On the bank of some summer stream;
To smoke his pipe
In a sheltered gripe
In the middle of July—
His face in a mist
And two stones in his fist
And an impotent worm on his thigh.

But his passion became a plague
For he grew feeble bringing the vague
Women of his mind to lust nearness,
Once a week at least flesh must make an appearance.

So Maguire got tired
Of the no-target gun fired
And returned to his headland of carrots and cabbage
To the fields once again
Where eunuchs can be men
And life is more lousy than savage.

III

Poor Paddy Maguire, a fourteen-hour day
He worked for years. It was he that lit the fire
And boiled the kettle and gave the cows their hay.
His mother tall hard as a Protestant spire
Came down the stairs barefoot at the kettle-call
And talked to her son sharply: 'Did you let
The hens out, you?' She had a venomous drawl
And a wizened face like moth-eaten leatherette.
Two black cats peeped between the banisters
And gloated over the bacon-fizzling pan.
Outside the window showed tin canisters.
The snipe of Dawn fell like a whirring stone
And Patrick on a headland stood alone.

The pull is on the traces, it is March
And a cold black wind is blowing from Dundalk.
The twisting sod rolls over on her back—
The virgin screams before the irresistible sock.
No worry on Maguire's mind this day
Except that he forgot to bring his matches.
'Hop back there Polly, hoy back, woa, wae,
From every second hill a neighbor watches
With all the sharpened interest of rivalry.
Yet sometimes when the sun comes through a gap
These men know God the Father in a tree:
The Holy Spirit is the rising sap,
And Christ will be the green leaves that will come
At Easter from the sealed and guarded tomb.

Primroses and the unearthly start of ferns
Among the blackthorn shadows in the ditch,
A dead sparrow and an old waistcoat. Maguire learns
As the horses turn slowly round the which is which
Of love and fear and things half born to mind.

He stands between the plough-handles and he sees
At the end of a long furrow his name signed
Among the poets, prostitutes. With all miseries
He is one. Here with the unfortunate
Who for half-moments of paradise
Pay out good days and wait and wait
For sunlight-woven cloaks. O to be wise
As Respectability that knows the price of all things
And marks God's truth in pounds and pence and farthings.

IV

April, and no one able to calculate
How far is it to harvest. They put down
The seeds blindly with sensuous groping fingers,
And sensual sleep dreams subtly underground.
To-morrow is Wednesday—who cares?
'Remember Eileen Farrelly? I was thinking
A man might do a damned sight worse . . .' That voice is blown
Through a hole in a garden wall—
And who was Eileen now cannot be known.

The cattle are out on grass,
The corn is coming up evenly.
The farm folk are hurrying to catch Mass:
Christ will meet them at the end of the world, the slow and
    speedier.
But the fields say: only Time can bless.

Maguire knelt beside a pillar where he could spit
Without being seen. He turned an old prayer round:
'Jesus, Mary and Joseph pray for us
Now and at the Hour.' Heaven dazzled death.
'Wonder should I cross-plough that turnip-ground.'
The tension broke. The congregation lifted its head
As one man and coughed in unison.

Five hundred hearts were hungry for life—
Who lives in Christ shall never die the death.
And the candle-lit Altar and the flowers
And the pregnant Tabernacle lifted a moment to Prophecy
Out of the clayey hours
Maguire sprinkled his face with holy water
As the congregation stood up for the Last Gospel.
He rubbed the dust off his knees with his palm, and then
Coughed the prayer phlegm up from his throat and sighed:
    Amen.

Once one day in June when he was walking
Among his cattle in the Yellow Meadow
He met a girl carrying a basket—
And he was then a young and heated fellow.
Too earnest, too earnest! He rushed beyond the thing
To the unreal. And he saw Sin
Written in letters larger than John Bunyan dreamt of.
For the strangled impulse there is no redemption.
And that girl was gone and he was counting
The dangers in the fields where love ranted
He was helpless. He saw his cattle
And stroked their flanks in lieu of wife to handle.
He would have changed the circle if he could,
The circle that was the grass track where he ran.
Twenty times a day he ran round the field
And still there was no winning-post where the runner is cheered
    home.
Desperately he broke the tune,
But however he tried always the same melody lept up from the
    background,
The dragging step of a ploughman going home through the
    guttery
Headlands under an April-watery moon.
Religion, the fields and the fear of the Lord
And Ignorance giving him the coward's blow,

He dare not rise to pluck the fantasies
From the fruited Tree of Life. He bowed his head
And saw a wet weed twined about his toe.

V

Evening at the cross-roads—
Heavy heads nodding out words as wise
As the rumination of cows after milking.
From the ragged road surface a boy picks up
A piece of gravel and stares at it—and then
He flings it across the elm tree on to the railway.
He means nothing.
Not a damn thing
Somebody is coming over the metal railway bridge
And his hobnailed boots on the arches sound like a gong
Calling men awake. But the bridge is too narrow—
The men lift their heads a moment. That was only John,
So they dream on.

Night in the elms, night in the grass.
O we are too tired to go home yet. Two cyclists pass
Talking loudly of Kitty and Molly—
Horses or women? wisdom or folly?
A door closes on an evicted dog
Where prayers begin in Barney Meegan's kitchen;
Rosie curses the cat between her devotions;
The daughter prays that she may have three wishes—
Health and wealth and love—
From the fairy who is faith or hope or compounds of.

At the cross-roads the crowd had thinned out:
Last words are uttered. There is no to-morrow;
No future but only time stretched for the mowing of the hay
Or putting an axle in the turf-barrow.

Patrick Maguire went home and made cocoa
And broke a chunk off the loaf of wheaten bread;
His mother called down to him to look again
And make sure that the hen-house was locked. His sister grunted
   in bed.
The sound of a sow taking up a new position.
Pat opened his trousers wide over the ashes
And dreamt himself to lewd sleepiness.
The clock ticked on. Time passes.

VI

Health and wealth and love he too dreamed of in May
As he sat on the railway slope and watched the children of the
   place
Picking up a primrose here and a daisy there—
They were picking up life's truth singly. But he dreamt of the
   Absolute envased bouquet—
All or nothing. And it was nothing. For God is not all
In one place, complete
Till Hope comes in and takes it on his shoulder—
O Christ, that is what you have done for us:
In a crumb of bread the whole mystery is.

He read the symbol too sharply and turned
From the five simple doors of sense
To the door whose combination lock has puzzled
Philosopher and priest and common dunce.

Men build their heavens as they build their circles
Of friends. God is in the bits and pieces of Everyday—
A kiss here and a laugh again, and sometimes tears,
A pearl necklace round the neck of poverty.

He sat on the railway slope and watched the evening,
Too beautifully perfect to use,
And his three wishes were three stones too sharp to sit on,
Too hard to carve. Three frozen idols of a speechless muse.

VII

'Now go to Mass and pray and confess your sins
And you'll have all the luck,' his mother said.
He listened to the lie that is a woman's screen
Around a conscience when soft thighs are spread.
And all the while she was setting up the lie
She trusted in Nature that never deceives.
But her son took it as literal truth.
Religion's walls expand to the push of nature. Morality yields
To sense—but not in little tillage fields.

Life went on like that. One summer morning
Again through a hay-field on her way to the shop—
The grass was wet and over-leaned the path—
And Agnes held her skirts sensationally up,
And not because the grass was wet either.
A man was watching her, Patrick Maguire.
She was in love with passion and its weakness
And the wet grass could never cool the fire
That radiated from her unwanted womb
In that country, in that metaphysical land
Where flesh was a thought more spiritual than music
Among the stars—out of reach of the peasant's hand.

Ah, but the priest was one of the people too—
A farmer's son—and surely he knew
The needs of a brother and sister.
Religion could not be a counter-irritant like a blister,
But the certain standard measured and known
By which man might re-make his soul though all walls were
    down
And all earth's pedestalled gods thrown.

VIII

Sitting on a wooden gate,
Sitting on a wooden gate,
Sitting on a wooden gate
He didn't care a damn.
Said whatever came into his head,
Said whatever came into his head,
Said whatever came into his head
And inconsequently sang.
While his world withered away,
He had a cigarette to smoke and a pound to spend
On drink the next Saturday.
His cattle were fat
And his horses all that
Midsummer grass could make them.

The young women ran wild
And dreamed of a child
Joy dreams though the fathers might forsake them
But no one would take them;
No man could ever see
That their skirts had loosed buttons,
O the men were as blind as could be.
And Patrick Maguire
From his purgatory fire
Called the gods of the Christian to prove
That this twisted skein
Was the necessary pain
And not the rope that was strangling true love.

But sitting on a wooden gate
Sometime in July
When he was thirty-four or five
He gloried in the lie:
He made it read the way it should,

He made life read the evil good
While he cursed the ascetic brotherhood
Without knowing why.
Sitting on a wooden gate
All, all alone
He sang and laughed
Like a man quite daft,
Or like a man on a channel raft
He fantasied forth his groan.
Sitting on a wooden gate,
Sitting on a wooden gate,
Sitting on a wooden gate
He rode in day-dream cars.
He locked his body with his knees
When the gate swung too much in the breeze.
But while he caught high ecstasies
Life slipped between the bars.

IX

He gave himself another year,
Something was bound to happen before then—
The circle would break down
And he would curve the new one to his own will.
A new rhythm is a new life
And in it marriage is hung and money.
He would be a new man walking through unbroken meadows
Of dawn in the year of One.

The poor peasant talking to himself in a stable door—
An ignorant peasant deep in dung.
What can the passers-by think otherwise?
Where is his silver bowl of knowledge hung?
Why should men be asked to believe in a soul
That is only the mark of a hoof in guttery gaps?
A man is what is written on the label.

And the passing world stares but no one stops
To look closer. So back to the growing crops
And the ridges he never loved.
Nobody will ever know how much tortured poetry the pulled
    weeds on the ridge wrote
Before they withered in the July sun,
Nobody will ever read the wild, sprawling, scrawling mad
    woman's signature,
The hysteria and the boredom of the enclosed nun of his thought.
Like the afterbirth of a cow stretched on a branch in the wind
Life dried in the veins of these women and men:
The grey and grief and unlove,
The bones in the backs of their hands,
And the chapel pressing its low ceiling over them.

Sometimes they did laugh and see the sunlight,
A narrow slice of divine instruction.
Going along the river at the bend of Sunday
The trout played in the pools encouragement
To jump in love though death bait the hook.
And there would be girls sitting on the grass banks of lanes.
Stretch-legged and lingering staring—
A man might take one of them if he had the courage.
But 'No' was in every sentence of their story
Except when the public-house came in and shouted its piece.

The yellow buttercups and the bluebells among the whin bushes
On rocks in the middle of ploughing
Was a bright spoke in the wheel
Of the peasant's mill.
The goldfinches on the railway paling were worth looking at—
A man might imagine then
Himself in Brazil and these birds the birds of paradise
And the Amazon and the romance traced on the school map
    lived again.

Talk in evening corners and under trees
Was like an old book found in a king's tomb.
The children gathered round like students and listened
And some of the saga defied the draught in the open tomb
And was not blown.

X

Their intellectual life consisted in reading
Reynolds News or the *Sunday Dispatch*,
With sometimes an old almanac brought down from the ceiling
Or a school reader brown with the droppings of thatch.
The sporting results or the headlines of war
Was a humbug profound as the highbrow's Arcana.
Pat tried to be wise to the abstraction of all that
But its secret dribbled down his waistcoat like a drink from a
    strainer.
He wagered a bob each way on the Derby,
He got a straight tip from a man in a shop—
A double from the Guineas it was and thought himself
A master mathematician when one of them came up
And he could explain how much he'd have drawn
On the double if the second leg had followed the first.
He was betting on form and breeding, he claimed,
And the man that did that could never be burst.
After that they went on to the war, and the generals
On both sides were shown to be stupid as hell.
If he'd taken *that* road, they remarked of a Marshal,
He'd have ... O they know their geography well.
This was their university. Maguire was an undergraduate
Who dreamed from his lowly position of rising
To a professorship like Larry McKenna or Duffy
Or the pig-gelder Nallon whose knowledge was amazing.
'A treble, full multiple odds. . . . That's flat porter . . .
Another one. . . . No, you're wrong about that thing I was telling
    you. . . .

Did you part with your filly, Jack? I heard that you sold her. ... '
The students were all savants by the time of pub-close.

XI

A year passed and another hurried after it
And Patrick Maguire was still six months behind life—
His mother six months ahead of it;
His sister straddle-legged across it:—
One leg in hell and the other in heaven
And between the purgatory of middle-aged virginity—
She prayed for release to heaven or hell.
His mother's voice grew thinner like a rust-worn knife
But it cut venomously as it thinned,
It cut him up the middle till he became more woman than man,
And it cut through to his mind before the end.

Another field whitened in the April air
And the harrows rattled over the seed.
He gathered the loose stones off the ridges carefully
And grumbled to his men to hurry. He looked like a man who
    could give advice
To foolish young fellows. He was forty-seven,
And there was depth in his jaw and his voice was the voice of a
    great cattle-dealer,
A man with whom the fair-green gods break even.
'I think I ploughed that lea the proper depth,
She ought to give a crop if any land gives. . . .
Drive slower with the foal-mare, Joe.'
Joe, a young man of imagined wives,
Smiles to himself and answered like a slave:
'You needn't fear or fret.
I'm taking her as easy, as easy as . . .
Easy there Fanny, easy, pet.

94

They loaded the day-scoured implements on the cart
As the shadows of poplars crookened the furrows.
It was the evening, evening. Patrick was forgetting to be lonely
As he used to be in Aprils long ago.
It was the menopause, the misery-pause.

The schoolgirls passed his house laughing every morning
And sometimes they spoke to him familiarly—
He had an idea. Schoolgirls of thirteen
Would see no political intrigue in an old man's friendship.
Love
The heifer waiting to be nosed by the old bull.
That notion passed too—there was the danger of talk
And jails are narrower than the five-sod ridge
And colder than the black hills facing Armagh in February.
He sinned over the warm ashes again and his crime
The law's long arm could not serve with 'time'.

His face set like an old judge's pose:
Respectability and righteousness,
Stand for no nonsense.
The priest from the altar called Patrick Maguire's name
To hold the collecting-box in the chapel door
During all the Sundays of May.
His neighbors envied him his holy rise,
But he walked down from the church with affected indifference
And took the measure of heaven angle-wise.

He still could laugh and sing,
But not the wild laugh or the abandoned harmony now
That called the world to new silliness from the top of a wooden
    gate
When thirty-five could take the sparrow's bow.
Let us be kind, let us be kind and sympathetic:
Maybe life is not for joking or for finding happiness in—
This tiny light in Oriental Darkness
Looking out chance windows of poetry or prayer.

And the grief and defeat of men like these peasants
Is God's way—maybe—and we must not want too much
To see.
The twisted thread is stronger than the wind-swept fleece.
And in the end who shall rest in truth's high peace?
Or whose is the world now, even now?
O let us kneel where the blind ploughman kneels
And learn to live without despairing
In a mud-walled space—
Illiterate unknown and unknowing.
Let us kneel where he kneels
And feel what he feels.

One day he saw a daisy and he thought it
Reminded him of his childhood—
He stopped his cart to look at it.
Was there a fairy hiding behind it?
He helped a poor woman whose cow
Had died on her;
He dragged home a drunken man on a winter's night;
And one rare moment he heard the young people playing on the
    railway stile
And he wished them happiness and whatever they most desired
    from life.

He saw the sunlight and begrudged no man
His share of what the miserly soil and soul
Gives in a season to a ploughman.
And he cried for his own loss one late night on the pillow
And yet thanked the God who had arranged these things.

Was he then a saint?
A Matt Talbot of Monaghan?

His sister Mary Anne spat poison at the children
Who sometimes came to the door selling raffle tickets
For holy funds.
'Get out, you little tramps!' she would scream
As she shook to the hens an armful of crumbs,
But Patrick often put his hand deep down
In his trouser-pocket and fingered out a penny
Or maybe a tobacco-stained caramel.
'You're soft,' said the sister; 'with other people's money
It's not a bit funny.'

The cards are shuffled and the deck
Laid flat for cutting—Tom Malone
Cut for trump. I think we'll make
This game, the last, a tanner one
Hearts. Right. I see you're breaking
Your two-year-old. Play quick, Maguire,
The clock there says it's half-past ten—
Kate, throw another sod on that fire.
One of the card-players laughs and spits
Into the flame across a shoulder.
Outside, a noise like a rat
Among the hen-roosts. The cock crows over
The frosted townland of the night.
Eleven o'clock and still the game
Goes on and the players seem to be
Drunk in an Orient opium den.
Midnight, one o'clock, two.
Somebody's leg has fallen asleep.
What about home? Maguire, are you
Using your double-tree this week?
Why? do you want it? Play the ace.
There's it, and that's the last card for me.
A wonderful night, we had. Duffy's place
Is very convenient. Is that a ghost or a tree?

And so they go home with dragging feet
And their voices rumble like laden carts.
And they are happy as the dead or sleeping . . .
I should have led that ace of hearts.

XII

The fields were bleached white,
The wooden tubs full of water
Were white in the winds
That blew through Brannagan's Gap on their way from Siberia;
The cows on the grassless heights
Followed the hay that had wings—
The February fodder that hung itself on the black branches
Of the hill-top hedge.
A man stood beside a potato-pit
And clapped his arms
And pranced on the crisp roots
And shouted to warm himself.
Then he buck-leaped about the potatoes
And scooped them into a basket.
He looked like a bucking suck-calf
Whose spine was being tickled.
Sometimes he stared across the bogs
And sometimes he straightened his back and vaguely whistled
A tune that weakened his spirit
And saddened his terrier dog's.
A neighbour passed with a spade on his shoulder
And Patrick Maguire bent like a bridge
Whistled—good morning under his oxter,
And the man the other side of the hedge
Champed his spade on the road at his toes
And talked an old sentimentality
While the wind blew under his clothes.

The mother sickened and stayed in bed all day,
Her head hardly dented the pillow, so light and thin it had worn,
But she still enquired after the household affairs.
She held the strings of her children's Punch and Judy, and when
    a mouth opened
It was her truth that the dolls would have spoken
If they hadn't been made of wood and tin—
'Did you open the barn door, Pat, to let the young calves in?'
The priest called to see her every Saturday
And she told him her troubles and fears:
'If Mary Anne was settled I'd die in peace—
I'm getting on in years.'
'You were a good woman,' said the priest,
'And your children will miss you when you're gone.
The likes of you this parish never knew,
I'm sure they'll not forget the work you've done.'
She reached five bony crooks under the tick—
'Five pounds for Masses—won't you say them quick.'
She died one morning in the beginning of May
And a shower of sparrow-notes was the litany for her dying.
The holy water was sprinkled on the bed-clothes
And her children stood around the bed and cried because it was
    too late for crying.
A mother dead! The tired sentiment:
'Mother, Mother' was a shallow pool
Where sorrow hardly could wash its feet. . . .
Mary Anne came away from the deathbed and boiled the calves
    their gruel.
O what was I doing when the procession passed?
Where was I looking?
Young women and men
And I might have joined them.
Who bent the coin of my destiny
That it stuck in the slot?
I remember a night we walked
Through the moon of Donaghmoyne,

Four of us seeking adventure,
It was midsummer forty years ago.
Now I know
The moment that gave the turn to my life.
O Christ! I am locked in a stable with pigs and cows for ever.

XIII

The world looks on
And talks of the peasant:
The peasant has no worries;
In his little lyrical fields
He ploughs and sows;
He eats fresh food,
He loves fresh women,
He is his own master
As it was in the Beginning
The simpleness of peasant life.
The birds that sing for him are eternal choirs,
Everywhere he walks there are flowers.
His heart is pure,
His mind is clear,
He can talk to God as Moses and Isaiah talked—
The peasant who is only one remove from the beasts he drives.
The travellers stop their cars to gape over the green bank into
    his fields:—

There is the source from which all cultures rise,
And all religions,
There is the pool in which the poet dips
And the musician.
Without the peasant base civilisation must die,
Unless the clay is in the mouth the singer's singing is useless.
The travellers touch the roots of the grass and feel renewed
When they grasp the steering wheels again.

The peasant is the unspoiled child of Prophecy,
The peasant is all virtues—let us salute him without irony
The peasant ploughman who is half a vegetable—
Who can react to sun and rain and sometimes even
Regret that the Maker of Light had not touched him more in-
tensely.
Brought him up from the sub-soil to an existence
Of conscious joy. He was not born blind.
He is not always blind: sometimes the cataract yields
To sudden stone-falling or the desire to breed.

The girls pass along the roads
And he can remember what man is,
But there is nothing he can do.
Is there nothing he can do?
Is there no escape?
No escape, no escape.

The cows and horses breed,
And the potato-seed
Gives a bud and a root and rots
In the good mother's way with her sons;
The fledged bird is thrown
From the nest—on its own.
But the peasant in his little acres is tied
To a mother's womb by the wind-toughened navel-cord
Like a goat tethered to the stump of a tree—
He circles around and around wondering why it should be.
No crash,
No drama.
That was how his life happened.
No mad hooves galloping in the sky,
But the weak, washy way of true tragedy—
A sick horse nosing around the meadow for a clean place to die.

XIV

We may come out in the October reality, Imagination,
The sleety wind no longer slants to the black hill where Maguire
And his men are now collecting the scattered harness and baskets.
The dog sitting on a wisp of dry stalks
Watches them through the shadows.
'Back in, back in.' One talks to the horse as to a brother.
Maguire himself is patting a potato-pit against the weather—

An old man fondling a new-piled grave:
'Joe, I hope you didn't forget to hide the spade,
For there's rogues in the townland. Hide it flat in a furrow.
I think we ought to be finished by to-morrow.'
Their voices through the darkness sound like voices from a cave,
A dull thudding far away, futile, feeble, far away,
First cousins to the ghosts of the townland.

A light stands in a window. Mary Anne
Has the table set and the tea-pot waiting in the ashes.
She goes to the door and listens and then she calls
From the top of the haggard-wall:
'What's keeping you
And the cows to be milked and all the other work there's to do?'
'All right, all right,
We'll not stay here all night.'

Applause, applause,
The curtain falls.
Applause, applause
From the homing carts and the trees
And the bawling cows at the gates.
From the screeching water-hens
And the mill-race heavy with the Lammas floods curving over
    the weir.

A train at the station blowing off steam
And the hysterical laughter of the defeated everywhere.
Night, and the futile cards are shuffled again.
Maguire spreads his legs over the impotent cinders that wake
no manhood now
And he hardly looks to see which card is trump.
His sister tightens her legs and her lips and frizzles up
Like the wick of an oil-less lamp.
The curtain falls—
Applause, applause.

Maguire is not afraid of death, the Church will light him a candle
To see his way through the vaults and he'll understand the
Quality of the clay that dribbles over his coffin.
He'll know the names of the roots that climb down to tickle his
feet.
And he will feel no different than when he walked through
Donaghmoyne.

If he stretches out a hand—a wet clod,
If he opens his nostrils—a dungy smell;
If he opens his eyes once in a million years—
Through a crack in the crust of the earth he may see a face
nodding in
Or a woman's legs. Shut them again for that sight is sin.

He will hardly remember that life happened to him—
Something was brighter a moment. Somebody sang in the dis-
tance.
A procession passed down a mesmerized street.
He remembers names like Easter and Christmas
By the colour his fields were.
Maybe he will be born again, a bird of an angel's conceit
To sing the gospel of life
To a music as flightily tangent
As a tune on an oboe.

And the serious look of the fields will have changed to the leer
   of a hobo
Swaggering celestially home to his three wishes granted.
Will that be? will that be?
Or is the earth right that laughs haw-haw
And does not believe
In an unearthly law.
The earth that says:
Patrick Maguire, the old peasant, can neither be damned nor
   glorified:
The graveyard in which he will lie will be just a deep-drilled
   potato-field
Where the seed gets no chance to come through
To the fun of the sun.
The tongue in his mouth is the root of a yew.
Silence, silence. The story is done.

He stands in the doorway of his house
A ragged sculpture of the wind,
October creaks the rotted mattress,
The bedposts fall. No hope. No lust.
The hungry fiend
Screams the apocalypse of clay
In every corner of this land.

LOUGH DERG

From Cavan and from Leitrim and from Mayo,
From all the thin-faced parishes where hills
Are perished noses running peaty water,
They come to Lough Derg to fast and pray and beg
With all the bitterness of nonentities, and the envy
Of the inarticulate when dealing with the artist.
Their hands push closed the doors that God holds open;

Love-sunlit is an enchanter in June's hours
And flowers and light. These to shopkeepers and small lawyers
Are heresies up beauty's sleeve.
The naïve and simple go on pilgrimage too,
Lovers trying to take God's truth for granted. . . . Listen to the
    chanted
Evening devotions in the limestone church,
For this is Lough Derg, St. Patrick's Purgatory.
He came to this island-acre of limestone once
To be shut of the smug too-faithful. The story
Is different now.
Solicitors praying for cushy jobs
To be County Registrar or Coroner,
Shopkeepers threatened with sharper rivals
Than any hook-nosed foreigner.
Mothers whose daughters are Final Medicals,
Too heavy-hipped for thinking,
Wives whose husbands have angina pectoris,
Wives whose husbands have taken to drinking.

But there were the sincere as well
The innocent who feared the hell
Of sin. The girl who had won
A lover and the girl who had none
Were both in trouble
Trying to encave in the rubble
Of these rocks the Real,
The part that can feel.
And the half-pilgrims too,
They who are the true
Spirit of Ireland, who joke
Through the Death—mask and take
Virgins of heaven or flesh,
Were on Lough Derg Island
Wanting some half-wish.

Over the black waves of the lake trip the last echoes
Of the bell that has shooed through the chapel door
The last pilgrims, like hens to roost.
The sun through Fermanagh's furze fingers
Looks now on the deserted penance rings of stone
Where only John Flood on St. Kevin's Bed lingers
With the sexton's heaven-sure stance, the man who knows
The ins and outs of religion. . . .
"Hail glorious St. Patrick" a girl sings above
The old-man drone of the harmonium.
The rosary is said and Benediction.
The Sacramental sun turns round and "Holy, Holy, Holy"
The pilgrims cry, striking their breasts in Purgatory.
The same routine and ritual now
As serves for street processions or congresses
That take all shapes of souls as a living theme
In a novel refuses nothing. No truth oppresses.

Women and men in bare feet turn again
To the iron crosses and the rutted Beds,
Their feet are swollen and their bellies empty—
But something that is Ireland's secret leads
These petty mean people
For here's the day of a poor soul freed
To a marvelous beauty above its head.
The Castleblaney grocer trapped in the moment's need
Puts out a hand and writes what he cannot read,
A wisdom astonished at every turn
By some angel that writes in the oddest words.
When he will walk again in Muckno street
He'll hear from the kitchens of fair-day eating houses
In the after-bargain carouses
News from a country beyond the range of birds.

The lake waves caught the concrete stilts of the Basilica
That spread like a bulldog's hind paws. A Leitrim man
With a face as sad as a flooded hay-field,
Leaned in an angle of the walls with his rosary beads in his
    hands.
Beside St. Brigid's Cross—an ancient relic
A fragment of the Middle Ages set
Into the modern masonry of the conventional Basilica
Where everything is ordered and correct—
A queue of pilgrims waiting to renounce
The World, the Flesh, the Devil and all his house.

Like young police recruits being measured
Each pilgrim flattened backwards to the wall
And stretched his arms wide
As he cried:
"I renounce the World, the Flesh and the Devil";
Three times they cried out. A country curate
Stared with a curate leer—he was proud.
The booted
Prior passes by ignoring all the crowd.

"I renounce the World," a young woman cried
Her breasts stood high in the pagan sun.
"I renounce. . ." an old monk followed. Then a fat lawyer.
They rejected one by one
The music of Time's choir.
A half-pilgrim looked up at the Carrara marbles,
St. Patrick wearing an alb with no stitch dropped.
Once he held a shamrock in his hand
But the stem was flawed and it got lost.
St. Brigid and the Blessed Virgin flanked
Ireland's national apostle
On the south-west of the island on the gravel-path
Opposite the men's hostel.

Around the island like soldiers quartered round a barrack-yard
There were houses and a stall where Agnus Deis
And Catholic Truth pamphlets were sold.
And at the pier end, the grey chapel of St. Mary's.

The middle of the island looked like the memory
Of some village evicted by the Famine,
Some corner of a field beside a well
Old stumps of walls where a stunted boortree is growing.
These were the holy cells of saintly men—
O that was the place where Mickey Fehan lived
And the Reillys before they went to America in the Fifties.
No, this is Lough Derg in county Donegal—
So much alike is our historical
And spiritual pattern, a heap
Of stones anywhere is consecrated
By love's terrible need.

On Lough Derg, too, the silver strands
Of the individual sometimes show
Through the fabric of prison anonymity.
One man's private trouble transcending the divinity
Of the prayer-locked multitude.
A vein of humanity that can bleed
Through the thickest hide.
And such a plot unfolds a moment, so—

In a crevice between the houses and the lake
A tall red-headed man of thirty slouches
A half-pilgrim who hated prayer,
All truth for which St. Patrick's Purgatory vouches.
He was a small farmer who was fond of literature
In a country-schoolmaster way.
He skimmed the sentiment of every pool of experience
And talked heresy lightly from distances

Where nothing was terrifying Today
Where he felt he could be safe and say or sin—
But Christ sometimes bleeds in the museum.
It was the first day of his pilgrimage.
He came to Lough Derg to please the superstition
Which says: "at least the thing can do no harm"
Yet he alone went out with Jesus fishing.

An ex-monk from Dublin, a broad-faced man
With his Franciscan habit, staggering in a megrim
Between doubt and vanity's courtesan.
He had fallen once and secretly, no shame
Tainted the young girl's name,
A convent schoolgirl knowing
Nothing of earth sowing.
He took her three times
As in his day-dreams
These things happened.
Three times finds all
The notes of body's madrigal.
'Twas a failing otherwise
Lost him his priestly faculties.

Barefoot in the kitchen
Of John Flood's cottage
Where the girls of Donegal sat, laughing round on stools,
And iron cranes and crooks
Were loaded with black pots,
And holy-looking women kept going in and out of the rooms
As though some man was a-waking. . . .
The red-haired man came in
And saw among the loud cold women one who
Was not a Holy Biddy
With a rat-trap on her diddy,
But something from the unconverted kingdom

The beauty that has turned
Convention into forests
Where Adam wanders deranged with half a memory;
And red-haired Robert Fitzsimons
Saw Aggie Meegan, and quietly
An angel was turning over the pages of Mankind's history.
He must have her, she was waiting.

By the unprotected gable
Of ascetism's granite castle. The masonry's down
And the sun coming in its blood
The green of trees is lust
He saw from the unpeopled country into a town.

Let beauty bag or burst
The sharp points of truth may not be versed
Too smoothly, but the truth must go in as it occurred
A bulb of light in the shadows of Lough Derg.

The first evening they prayed till nine o'clock
Around the gravel rings, a hundred decades
Of rosaries until they hardly knew what words meant—
Their own names when they spoke them sounded mysterious.
They knelt and prayed and rose and prayed
And circled the crosses and kissed the stones
Never looking away from the brimstone bitterness
To the little islands of Pan held in the crooked elbow of the lake,
They closed their eyes to Donegal and the white houses
On the slope of the northern hills
And these pilgrims of a western reason
Were not pursuing French-hot miracles.
There were hundreds of them tripping one another
Upon the pilgrim way (O God of Truth
Keep him who tells this story straight,
Let no cheap insincerity shape his mouth).

These men and boys were not led there
By priests of Maynooth or stories of Italy or Spain
For this is the penance of the poor
Who knows what beauty hides in misery
As beggars, fools and eastern fakirs know.

Black tea, dry bread.
Yesterday's pilgrims went upstairs to bed
And as they slept
The vigil in St. Patrick's prison was kept
By the others. The Evening Star
Looked into Purgatory whimsically. Night dreams are
Simple and catching as music-hall tunes
Of the Nineties. We'll ramble through the brambles of starry-
strange Junes.

On a seat beside the women's hostel four men
Sat and talked spare minutes away;
It was like Sunday evening on a country road
Light and gay.
The talk was "There's a man
Who must be twenty stone weight—a horrid size. . . ."
"Larry O'Duff . . . yes, like a balloon
Or a new tick of chaff. . . . Lord, did anyone ever see clearer
skies?"
"No rain a while yet, Joe
And the turnips could be doing with a sup, you know."
And in the women's talk, too, was woven
Such earth to cool the burning brain of Heaven.
On the steps of the church the monks talked
To Robert of art, music, literature.
"Genius is not measured," he said
"In prudent feet and inches
Old Justice burns the work of Raphael—
Justice was God until he saw His Son

Falling in love with earth's fantastic one,
The woman in whose dunghill of emotion
Grows flowers of poetry, music, and the old
Kind in the mind, the fascination
Of sin troubled the mind of God
Until He thought of Charity. . . .
Have you known Charity? have I?"

Aggie Meegan passed by
To vigil. Robert was puzzled, Where
Grew the germ of this crooked prayer?
The girl was thrilling as joy's despair.

A schoolmaster from Roscommon led
The vigil prayer that night
"Hail Queen of Heaven" they sang at twelve.
Someone snored near the porch. A bright
Moon sailed in from the county Tyrone
By the water route that he might make
Queer faces in the stained-glassed windows. Why should sun
Have all the fun?
"Our vows of Baptism we again take. . . ."
Every Rosary brought the morning nearer
The scholmaster looked at his watch and said:
Out now for a mouthful of fresh air—
A ten-minute break to clear the head."
It was cold in the rocky draughts between the houses
Old women tried
To pull bare feet close to their bellies.
Three o'clock rang from the Prior's house clock.
In the hostel pilgrims slept away a three day fast.

On the cell wall beside the sycamore tree
The tree that never knew a bird
Aggie sat fiddling with her Rosary

And doubting the power of Lough Derg
To save the season's rose of life
With the ponderous fingers of prayer's philosophy.
Robert was a philosopher, a false one
Who ever takes a sledge to swat a fly.
He talked to the girls as a pedant professor
Talking in a university.

The delicate precise immediacy
That sees a flower half a foot away
He could not learn. He spoke to Aggie
Of powers, passions, with the naivete
Of a ploughman. She did understand—
She only knew that she could not hold his hand
If he stood closer. "Virtue is sublime"
He said, "and it is virtue is the frame
Of all love and learning. . . ."
"I want to tell you something," she whispered
"Because you are different and will know. . . ."
"You don't need to tell me anything, you could not,
For your innocence is pure glass that I see through."
"You'd be surprised," she smiled. O God, he gasped
To his soul, what could she mean by that?
They watched the lake waves clapping cold hands together
And saw the morning breaking as it breaks
Over a field where a man is watching a calving cow.
New life, new day.
A half-pilgrim saw it as a rabbiter
Poaching in wood sees
Primeval magic among the trees.

The rusty cross of St. Patrick had a dozen
Devotees clustered around it at four o'clock
Bare knees were going round Saint Brendan's Bed
A boy was standing like a ballet dancer poised on the rock

113

Under the belfry; he stared over at Donegal
Where the white houses on the side of the hills
Popped up like mushrooms in September.
The sun was smiling on a thousand hayfields
That hour, and he must have thought Lough Derg
More unreasonable than ordinary stone.
Perhaps it was an iceberg
That he had glanced at on his journey from Japan,
But the iceberg filled a glass of water
And poured it to the honour of the sun.

Lough Derg in the dawn poured rarer cups. Prayer
And fast that makes the sourest drink rare,
Was that St. Paul
Riding his ass down a lane in Donegal?
Christ was lately dead,
Men were afraid
With a new fear, the fear
Of love. There was a laugh freed
For ever and for ever. The Apostles Creed
Was a fireside poem, the talk of the town. . . .
They remember a man who has seen Christ in his thorny crown,

John Flood came out and climbed the rock to ring
His bell for six o'clock. He spoke to the pilgrims:
"Was the night fine?"
"Wonderful, wonderful," they answered, "not too cold—
Thank God we have the worst part over us."

The bell brought the sleepers from their cubicles.
Grey-faced boatmen were getting out a boat.
Mass was said. Another day began.
The penance wheel turned round again.
Pilgrims went out in boats, singing
"O Fare Thee Well, Lough Derg" as they waved
Affection to the persecuting stones.

114

The Prior went with them—suavely, goodily
Priestly, painfully directing the boats.
They who were left behind
Felt like the well-wishers who keep house when the funeral
Has left for the chapel.

Lough Derg overwhelmed the individual imagination
And the personal tragedy.
Only God thinks of the dying sparrow
In the middle of a war.
The ex-monk, farmer and the girl
Melted in the crowd
Where only God, the poet
Followed with interest till he found
Their secret, and constructed from
The chaos of its fire
A reasonable document.

A man's the centre of the world,
A man is not anonymous
Member of the general public.
The Communion of Saints
Is a Communion of Individuals.
God the Father is the Father
Of each one of us.

Then there was war, the slang, the contemporary touch
The ideologies of the daily papers
They must seem realer, Churchill, Stalin, Hitler,
Than ideas in the contemplative cloister.
The battles where ten thousand men die
Are more significant than a peasant's emotional problem.
But wars will be merely dry bones in histories
And these common people real living creatures in it
On the unwritten spaces between the lines.

A man throws himself prostrate
And God lies down beside him like a woman
Consoling the hysteria of her lover
That sighs his passion emptily:
"The next time, love, you shall faint in me."

"Don't ask for life," the monk said;
"If you meet her
Be easy with your affection
She's a traitor
To those who love too much
As I have done."
"What have you done?" said Robert
"That you've come
To St. Patrick's Purgatory?"
The monk told his story
Of how he thought that he
Could make reality
Of the romance of the books
That told of Popes
Men of genius who drew
Wild colours on the flat page. He knew
Now that madness is not knowing
That laws for the mown hay
Will not serve that which is growing.
Through Lough Derg's fast and meditation
He learned the wisdom of his generation.
He was satisfied now his heart
Was free from the coquetry of art.
Something was unknown
To Robert, not long
For Aggie told him all
That hour as they sat on the wall
Of Brendan's cell:
Birth, bastardy and murder—

He only heard rocks crashing distantly
When John Flood ran the mid-day bell.

Now the three of them got out of the story altogether
Almost. Now they were not three egotists
But part of the flood of humanity
Anonymous, never to write or be written.
They vanish among the forests and we see them
Appearing among the trees for seconds.
Lough Derg rolls its caravan before us
And as the pilgrims pass their thoughts are reckoned.
St. Patrick was there, that peasant-faced man.
Whose image was embroidered on political banners
In the days of the A.O.H. and John Redmond.
A kindly soft man this Patrick was, like a farmer
To whom no man might be afraid to tell a story
Of bawdy life as it goes in country places.
Was St. Patrick like that?
A shamrock in a politician's hat
Yesterday. Today
The sentimentality of an Urban Councillor
Moving an address of welcome to the cardinal.
All Ireland's Patricks were present on Lough Derg.
All Ireland that froze for want of Europe.

"And who are you?" said the poet speaking to
The old Leitrim man.
He said, "I can tell you
What I am.
Servant girls bred my servility:
When I stoop
It is my mother's mother mother's mother
Each one in turn being called in to spread—
"Wider with your legs" the master of the house said.
Domestic servants taken back and front.

117

That's why I'm servile. It is not the poverty
Of soil in Leitrim that makes me raise my hat
To fools with fifty pounds in a paper bank.
Domestic servants, no one has told
Their generations as it is, as I
Show the cowardice of the man whose mothers were whored
By five generations of capitalist and lord."

Time passed
Three boatloads of Dublin's unemployed came in
At three o'clock led by a priest from Thomas Street
To glutton over the peat-filtered water
And sit back drunk when jobs are found
In the Eternal factory where the boss
Himself must punch the clock.

And the day crawled lazily
Along the orbit of Purgatory.
A baker from Rathfriarland
A solicitor from Derry
A parish priest from Wicklow
A civil servant from Kerry
Sat on the patch of grass
Their stations for the day
Completed—all things arranged
Nothing in doubt, nothing gone astray.

O the boredom of Purgatory
Said the poet then,
This piety that hangs like a fool's unthought,
This certainty in men,   .
This three days too-goodness,
Too neighbourly cries
Temptation to murder
Mediocrities.

The confession boxes in St. Mary's chapel hum
And it is evening now. Prose prayers become
Odes and sonnets.
There is a shrine with money heaped upon it
Before Our Lady Immaculate Succor.

A woman said her Litany:
That my husband may get his health
  We beseech Thee to hear us
That my son Joseph may pass the Intermediate
  We beseech Thee to hear us
That my daughter Eileen may do well at her music
  We beseech Thee to hear us
That her aunt may remember us in her will
  We beseech Thee to hear us
That there may be good weather for the hay
  We beseech Thee to hear us
That my indigestion may be cured
  We beseech Thee to hear us
O Mother of Perpetual Succor in temptation
  Be you near us.
And some of the prayers were shaped like sonnets—

O good St. Anthony your poor client asks
That he may have one moment in his arms
The girl I am thinking of this minute—
I'd love her even if she had no farms
Or a four-footed beast in a stable;
Her father is old, doting down the lanes,
There isn't anyone as able
As I am for cocking hay or cleaning drains
All this that I am is an engine running
Light down the narrow-gauge railway of life.
St. Anthony, I ask for Mary Gunning
Of Rathdrumskean to be my wife.
My strength is a skull battering the wall
Where a remand-prisoner is losing his soul.

119

Saint Anne, I am a young girl from Castleblaney,
One of a farmer's six grown daughters.
Our little farm, when the season's rainy,
Is putty spread on stones. The surface waters
Soak all the fields of this north-looking townland.
Last year we lost our acre of potatoes
And my mother with unmarried daughters round her
Is soaked like our soil in savage natures.
She tries to be as kind as any mother
But what can a mother be in such a house
With arguments going on and such a bother
About the half-boiled pots and unmilked cows.
O Patron of the pure woman who lacks a man
Let me be free I beg you, St. Anne.

O Sacred Heart of Jesus I ask of you
A job so I can settle down and marry;
I want to live a decent life. And through
The flames of St. Patrick's Purgatory
I go offering every stone-bruise, all my hunger;
In the back-room of my penance I am weaving
An inside-shirt for charity. How longer
Must a fifty-shilling a week job be day-dreaming?
The dole and empty minds and empty pockets
Cup Finals seen from the branches of a tree,
Old films that break the eye-balls in their sockets,
A toss-pit. This is life for such as me.
And I know a girl and I know a room to be let
And a job in a builder's yard to be given yet.

I have sinned old; my lust's a running sore
That drains away my strength. Each morning shout:
"Last night will's a bone that will not knit.
I slip on the loose rubble of remorse
And grasp at tufts of cocksfoot grass that yield
My belly in a bankrupt's purse.

My mind is a thrice-failed cropping field
Where the missed ridges give out their ecstasy
To weeds that seed through gaps of indiscretion.
Nettles where barley or potatoes should be.
I set my will in Communion and Confession
But still the sore is dribbling—blood, and will
In spite of penance, prayer and canticle.

This was the banal
Beggary that God heard. Was he bored
As men are with the poor? Christ Lord
Hears in the voices of the meanly poor
Homeric utterances, poetry sweeping through.

More pilgrims came that evening
From the pier.
The old ones watched the boats come in
And smothered the ridiculous cheer
That breaks, like a hole in pants,
Where the heroic armies advance.

Somebody brought a newspaper
With news of war.
When they killed in Time they knew
What men killed each other for—
Was it something different in the spelling
Of a useless law?
A man from the campanile said:
"Kipper is fish—nice"
Somebody else talked of Dempsey:
"Greater than Tunney." Then a girl's voice
Called: "You'll get cigarettes inside."

It was six o'clock in the evening
Robert sat looking over the lake
Seeing the green islands that were his morning hope
And his evening despair.

121

The sharp knife of Jansen
Cuts all the green branches,
Not sunlight comes in
But the hot-iron sin
Branding the shame
Of a beast in the Name
Of Christ on the breast
Of a child of the West.
It was this he had read.
All day he was smitten
By this foul legend written
In the fields, in the skies
In the sanctuaries.
But now the green tree
Of humanity
Was leafing again
Forgiveness of sin.
A shading hand over
The brow of the lover.

And as the hours of Lough Derg's time
Stretch long enough to hold a generation
He sat beside her and promised that no word
Of what he knew should ever be heard.
The bell at nine o'clock closed the last station,
The pilgrims kissed good-by to stone and clay.
The Prior had declared the end of day.

Morning from the hostel windows was like the morning
In some village street after a dance carouse,
Debauchees of Venus and Bacchus
Half-alive stumbling wearily out of a bleary house.
So these pilgrims stumbled below in the sun
Out of God's publichouse.

The Mass was said
Pilgrims smiled at one another
How good God was
How much a loving Father!
How wonderful the punishing stones were!
Another hour and the boats will sail
Into the port of time.
Are you not glad you came?

John Flood stared at the sky
And shook his head knowingly.
No storm nor rain.
The boats are ready to sail.

The monk appears once more
Not trailing his robe as before
But different, his pride gone,
Green hope growing where the feet of Pan
Had hoofed the grass.

Lough Derg, St. Patrick's Purgatory in Donegal,
Christendom's purge. Heretical
Around the edges: the centre's hard
As the commonplace of a flamboyant bard.
The twentieth century blows across it now
But deeply it has kept an ancient vow.
It knows the secret of pain—
O moralist, your preaching is in vain
To tell men of the germ in the grain.

All happened on Lough Derg as it is written
In June nineteen-forty-two
When the Germans were fighting outside Rostov.
The poet wrote it down as best he knew
As integral and completed as the emotion

Of men and women cloaking a burning emotion
In the rags of the commonplace, will permit him.
He too was one of them. He too denied
The half of him that was his pride
Yet found it waiting, and the half untrue
Of this story is his pride's rhythm.
The turnips were a-sowing in the fields around Pettigo
As our train passed through.
A horse-cart stopped near the eye of the railway bridge.
By Monaghan, Cavan and Dundalk
By Bundoran and by Omagh the pilgrims went
And three sad people had found the key to the lock
Of God's delight in disillusionment.

ON READING JACK YEATS' NEW NOVEL

I tried to find in this book of yours, Jack Yeats
Some growthy patch sown with the enchanted seed
Of Grimm or Caroll or Lear—as is the need
Of children in a world of rents and rates,
I thought I'd find the linch-pin of the Fates!
Great wheel pulled out and souls a moment freed
To live in a poet's extravaganza creed,
And rare new dawns shine through the loosened slates.
Another Jack who had a beanstalk did it
And a Jack who killed a giant did it too
Hans Andersen had a tinder-box could bid it
Find jewels in a hollow-rotten tree.
But nothing happens here, Jack Yeats, where you
Have spun your web of childish fantasy.

ADVENT

We have tested and tasted too much, lover—
Through a chink too wide there comes in no wonder.

But here in the Advent-darkened room
Where the dry bread and the sugarless tea
Of penance will charm back the luxury
Of a child's soul, we'll return to Doom
The knowledge we stole but could not use.

And the newness that was in every stale thing
When we looked at it as children: the spirit-shocking
Wonder in a black slanting Ulster hill
Or the prophetic astonishment in the tedious talking
Of an old fool will awake for us and bring
You and me to the yard gate to watch the whins
And the bog-holes, cart-tracks, old stables where Time begins.

O after Christmas we'll have no need to go searching
For the difference that sets an old phrase burning—
We'll hear it in the whispered argument of a churning
Or in the streets where the village boys are lurching.
And we'll hear it among decent men too
Who barrow dung in gardens under trees,
Wherever life pours ordinary plenty.
Won't we be rich, my love and I, and please
God we shall not ask for reason's payment,
The why of heart-breaking strangeness in dreeping hedges
Nor analyse God's breath in common statement.
We have thrown into the dust-bin the clay-minted wages
Of pleasure, knowledge and the conscious hour—
And Christ comes with a January flower.

POSSESSING EDEN

The Fallen Angels left all there
And hid from God under the laurels
Till the trouble passed, the war over
Eden was their own forever
If they did not become bold
Coming into the open, to argue, to scold.

The outsiders are always waiting
For some kinsman of the house to unlock the door
Businessmen, politicians they know
That mystery works but is not in their taking.

The outsiders are always asking
Why this is and that is:
Birthplace of what had no father,
Name of sister, name of brother.
The schools to which an idea went,
How many hundred pounds were spent?
How many miles to Babylon?

The wheat is green on
The sidey hill—walk backways up it:
There's a primeval plain to the south,
There's a flashing river-mouth.
There's virgin soil—no flesh hand can crop it.

3

A woman is washing potatoes for the dinner
And the stick she churns the water with is white
And you must not require to understand
But be the virgin surrendering to the delight.

An old man opens a garden gate and looks
Among the stumps of winter cabbages.
Through the unwakened poplars he lifts his glance
To watch a train go by drawing marvellous carriages.

And he wonders if on his eyes it is
A cataract delusion. A tin-can rings
On the flag-stones of a well that's running low
And a townland drinks from love's unreasonable springs.

An eight-bull harrow is thrown from a cart
Onto a black ridge by a young man who whistles—
He stops to ponder over something mislaid
And question a self that is too alive to listen.

A girl is leaning over the handle-bars
Of her bicycle and talking through a hedge
To a woman who is searching in the nettles
With a long pot-stick for the turkey's secret eggs.

A donkey is trying to open Rooney's gate
To get his daily feed from the pit of mangels
But the chain is twisted once too many round
The post and all he gets is rusty jangles.

4

Chickens on a kitchen floor
White wyandots like powder-puffs
Meaning nothing meaning most—
"Come, come" their mother calls severely,
"A raw potato is good for you."
They gather round. Her commentary
Is a deep important bass.
The cat sneaks past screwing his nature
To a denial of all his race.
Why should sin
Be the pleasure in the bite
Of day-old chickens when a sparrow
Can be eaten in daylight?
To eat a mouse is virtue,
To eat
A chicken is to be
Kicked out into the infernal street.

5

Day passes by the front window round by the stables
Like a neighbour coming to borrow a graip or a spade
Or to see how the farrowing sow is getting on.

Today he is a little taller than he was yesterday
And a little brighter of the eye. Now he is gone
Round by the end of the boiler house, shining on the west gables.

6

Girls linked in threes like factory workers
Waltz on the long evening roads of Lent
Dreaming of after-Easter when the dance-hall
Will be the womb of their world—of blocked cement.
A coloured paper placenta sticky with sweat
Will fold close to the embryo of a generation.
    See, there's Pat the Gent
Letting his cow to a bull! The girls stand
Upon the grassy bank of a fence and one holds a briar
That cuts the vision in two aside with her hand.

7

A boy who has not smoked or sinned
For nearly forty nights and days
Walks to the village with his head in the air;
Christ and his angels are around
In primroses, in daisies, in the east wind.
    His boots are white
With dried clay. His feet
Are sore from tramping pointed arrises,
His shoulders are tired from carrying a sowing sheet
And galled under his roped gallowses.
But in the still clouds, in the motionless trees
In the football that that scholboy is pumping, holding it between
    his knees
Profound wisdom is spoken for easy consciences.
He does not speak to the girls, he does not see them;
He only sees what is unmortal. He does not care
If this moment outside time he has lived in
Should be in time hereafter time's despair.

PEACE

And sometimes I am sorry when the grass
Is growing over the stones in quiet hollows
And the cocksfoot leans across the rutted cart-pass
That I am not the voice of country fellows
Who now are standing by some headland talking
Of turnips and potatoes or young corn
Or turf banks stripped for victory.
Here Peace is still hawking
His coloured combs and scarves and beads of horn.

Upon a headland by a whiny hedge
A hare sits looking down a leaf-lapped furrow
There's an old plough upside-down on a weedy ridge
And someone is shouldering home a saddle-harrow.
Out of that childhood country what fools climb
To fight with tyrants Love and Life and Time?

SURPRISE

Two women in black to the ears; both wearing
Large tin-rimmed spectacles; both hard-of-hearing:
Both chill and bleak as the hills of Leitrim,
Sat drinking cocoa in a restaurant.
They
Seemed from the pages of Emily Bronte
Till they slanged of 'Shenko and Rommel and Monty.

A LOVER'S LENTEN DREAM

This time when the birds are singing
Maybe I'll be sad no more
One I've waited aeons for
May be waiting at my door.

When the Lenten roots are swinging
Lamps of light above the grass
What I've dreamt may come to pass
At a holy Easter Mass.

O the growing corn and hedges
That made me want to cry
For something lost when I
Was wandering in the sky.

My birds are all in cages
Maybe now the doors will rise
And the grief that looked so wise
Dissolve in laughing skies.

BEYOND THE HEADLINES

Then I saw the wild geese flying
In fair formation to their bases in Inchicore
And I knew that these wings would outwear the wings of war
And a man's simple thoughts outlive the day's loud lying.
Don't fear, don't fear, I said to my soul,
The Bedlam of Time is an empty bucket rattled,
'Tis you who will say in the end who best battles.
Only they who fly home to God have flown at all.

GRAFTON STREET ADMIRATION

And have you felt that way too
That someone was in love with you
And was afraid to speak? The air
Vibrated with your mutual prayer . . .
Without an introduction you
Are doomed to love and never woo.

GONE WITH THE WIND

Through Gone With The Wind I yawned my way
So I might know what magic lay
In this slow story that to its author
Three million sterling must have brought her.
And here's the secret I found in it—
Barnum was wrong—there's two a minute.

IMAGINARY TRANSLATION FROM VERSE IN GAELIC
By P. Beaslai

The big world today is full of darkness and badness
But the Gael is keeping lit bright candles of gladness,
Candles of light that ought to be holy
Since we brought them at duskish from North Inis Foley.

WISE CINDERELLA

Beauty at the Beauty Ball
Lose your silver slipper where
Some man passing may recall
A virtuous woman's prudent care.
Silver slipper, symbol of
Modesty who understands
That to run is part of love
The wiser part. Men in all lands
Are searching for a princess who
Spilled the last cocktail in her shoe.

131

A KNIGHT AT THE TOURNAMENT
(Cole V. Mulcahy)

It was not Virgil I thought of last Friday at the Rotunda
Or his verse which tells of huge muscled fighters
In the Roman arena as they exhibited their bodies to the first
   nighters
I was thinking of what I would say on Monday,
Something that all readers would understand—a
Hint of Tunney's lefts and Dempsey's righters
In the Soldiers Field . . . Cole swings, Mulcahy sidesteps
The fight is on and the audience roars like thunder
Blood flows. O Cole think back to Meath's great glory
The battle fury of ancestors may descend
Upon you. But Mulcahy's footwork's perfect. Holy!
If that swing had got home the fight would end.
In the ninth round Mulcahy's science won,
Cole counted out. And here's your sonnet, Sir John.

CHRISTMAS CAROL 1942

Sing of the Childhood
That renews in our eyes
Beauty grown tired.
Tonight is inspired,
Land, sea and skies
With a Childhood surprise.

Sing of the Childhood
That renews in the heart
Of the hopeless hope's cheer:
Year after year
Giving a fresh start
Where Sin's gaolers depart.

Sing of the Childhood
That renews for us all—
Banker or farmer
Or soldier in armour—
The laugh of the soul.
Sing the Child in the Stall.

NEW YEAR

The New Year's unwritten page we view
As a lea field to plough and sow
The memory of weeds from the last
Turned page comes through
But only matters what this year we grow.

THE IRISH PINE
   (Irish ship lost at sea)

She has harboured in the Unknown
That we all sail unto
And send no message back
No more than this ship's crew.
Vain hopes to be remembered—
We brought you wheat
And two months gone forgotten
In hall and field and street.

THE PRESIDENT'S BIRTHDAY

He found the secret love of Ireland hiding
Among the stones of Connaught's potato patches
And led her forth as eternally delighting
As ever love in Campion, Ford or Nashe is.

133

VALENTINE

Next Sunday is St. Valentine's Day
And it is my design
To bring you to a cheap cafe—
I'll be your Valentine
If you don't use sugar in your tay
And leave it all for mine.

JACK DOYLE

Some think he might have won the crown
That now to Brown Joe's head seems glued
But he got tangled in the gown
Of Venus waiting as she would
For the handsome boy who comes to town.

JUSTIFIABLE HOMICIDE

"I killed a verse speaker" said the Playboy
"Through my radio he attacked me with that cry
So banshee-like I followed him through Dublin
And split him in the middle with my loy."

MARCH IS A SILVERSMITH

"March is a silversmith" I thought on Friday
As I looked in a jeweller's window at the bright
Cups for Horse Show and football prizes—
What once was foggy metal. I was right,
For the streets and houses and the river
And the faces of the people and the sky
And my own thoughts were polished silver. . . .

And saw Michael Stanton beat with a sledge
Of buffalo horn the crude white metal
To the smoothness of a leaf in a laurel hedge.
Tomorrow we shall hear the song of this kettle.

The jeweller whom I met an hour before
Gave me a tip that I pass on to you:
"In buying a wristlet watch make sure
It has a circular face. The dust comes through
The rectangular one no matter how fairly
The glass is ground. And if it breaks there's trouble
In getting one to fit the casing squarely."
When you marry your wife you marry your daughter's double.

So out in the streets I went once more
Noting my street-friends and eyesight loves go by
At the same hour. One who used to smile smiles no more
And I know she's got a lover now who's real. Her eye
Looks through me with a blank indifference. I'm not sorry
For March is paying out at every office
White shillings that are bribes enough for worry
And we won't need to mind about the coppers.
I think of the artists of O'Connell Bridge
Who squeeze from us the treacle of compassion
With drawings and sad stories of the grudge
Of Fortune. Art is here a fickle fashion:
The loaf that's "easy drawn but hard to get"
Is eaten and in its place we see
Warnings in chalk along the whole parapet
From some old almanac's philosophy.

A townland down in Monaghan! Ah surely
This makes me glad. I know these names. I can see
The Garlands and the Rooneys and the Quigleys
Neighbours' children in the field next to me
Playing where a bewitched blackthorn 's growing

135

Beside a pile of fairy whinstone rocks
That no man dreams of quarrying—not knowing
What's hid beneath, who here at midnight walks.
I saw it all not far from Tivadina—
But when I came to myself in Abbey Street
I was looking at the program of a cinema—
California here we come—the Gaels of Greece
Sweden or Czechoslovakia. . . .
Yesterday evening
I went to the Botanic Gardens and there
With the flowers and plants of Ceylon and Chile,
China and New Zealand I caught the air
Of fabulous travellers. These gardens are hilly
Which makes them more interesting than Kew
Which are flat and large and monotonous.
I talked to John Besant, chief gardener, who—
Born in Perthshire—has been forty years a botanist.
I remember the almond trees in blossom
And the polyanthus that are just primroses,
Palms from the Himalays and ferns from South Africa
And the Costa Rican—"Columnea gloriosa."

PLAY TIME

Anthony tonight to Cleopatra runs
From Actium again—his will was flabby.
At the Gate laughs the king of all the dandy ones.
A plebian O'Cuddy marches to the Abbey.

F. J. McCORMICK'S SILVER JUBILEE

Not as Fluther Good or Joxer,
Or even as King Lear—
I think of you as the man who made
An honest woman out of the jade
Whose name is Stage Career.

136

RESTAURANT REVERIE

O half-potato on my plate
It is too soon to celebrate
The centenary of '48
Or even '47.
You're boasted to the centre, too,
And wet, in soapy soil you grew,
But I am thankful still to you
For hints of history given.

There's something lonely far-away
In what you symbolise today
For me—the half that went astray
Of life, the uncompleted.
But up brown drills new pink buds start
With truer truth than truth of art,
Ignoring last crop's broken heart
And a generation defeated.
   O here is life
   Without a wife
A half potato. Eat it.

MAY EVENING

Consider the grass growing
As it grew last year and the year before
Cool about the ankles like summer rivers
When we walked on a May evening through the meadows
To watch the mare that was going to foal.

SEED WHEAT 1916–1922

We then were fed
On stars not bread,
And when we stepped
From hill to hill
'Twas logic—
Not a miracle,
For we were fed
On stars, not bread.
And we have still
From hill to hill
Men striding with
The ancient tread.
And what was myth
And high-star fed
Is the germ of a people's
Daily bread.

LOVE SONG

She looked as though she didn't care
He looked as though he didn't care;
Yet I heard by telepathy
The story of a love as rare
As ever trembled in the air.
They must not speak, they were afraid
Of what might happen: she might say
"Excuse me sir" and turn her head
Should he comment upon the day—
"Nice weather" in a lover's way.

She could smile as women can
With safety—but he might freeze.
So here the poet sought the plan
Of Dante, Petrarch—and for these
Mute lovers sang love's mysteries.

THE TWELFTH OF JULY

The Twelfth of July, the voice of Ulster speaking,
Tart as week-old buttermilk from a churn,
Surprising the tired palates of the south.
I said to myself: From them we have much to learn—
Hard business-talk, no mediaeval babble,
But the sudden knife of reality running to the heart
With experience. The pageantry of Scarva
Recalled the Greek idea of dramatic art.
The horse-dealers from the Moy or Banbridge,
The Biblical farmers from Richhill or Coleraine.
All that was sharp, precise and pungent flavoured—
Ah! an Ulster imagined! For here from the train
At Amiens street come gin-and-bitter blondes,
The slot machines that give us all the "answers,"
And young men out of Ulster who will dare
To drive a wedge in Dublin's Lounge Bar panzers.

A TOAST TO A MAN OF LETTERS—G.B.S. 87

O. G.B.S.
I a XX
R 2
2 U !
4 I B
O T T

BUDDA

A little man with a little heart
And a little talent for the poet's art
And a little idea cramped in his mind
Where the jealousy-hatred snakes are twined,
With their tetanus-toxins that strangle the song.
Squat and smug in his corner of musty lore
He sits and the littler he grows the more
Is his poison potent. O genius child
Do not pity for through pity have the poor been defiled.

JEROME CONNOR

He sits in a corner of my memory
With his short pipe, holding it by the bowl,
And his sharp eye and his knotty fingers,
And his laughing soul
Shining through the gaps of his crusty wall.

CANDIDA

Candida is one to-day,
What is there that *one* can say?
One is where the race begins
Or the sum that counts our sins;
But the mark time makes to-morrow
Shapes the cross of joy or sorrow.

Candida is one to-day,
What is there for me to say?
On the day that she was one
There were apples in the sun
And the fields long wet with rain
Crumply in dry winds again.

Candida is one and I
Wish her lots and lots of joy.
She the nursling of September
Like a war she won't remember.
Candida is one to-day
And there's nothing more to say.

TARRY FLYNN

On an apple-ripe September morning
Through the mist-chill fields I went
With a pitch-fork on my shoulder
Less for use than for devilment.

The threshing mill was set-up, I knew,
In Cassidy's haggard last night,
And we owed them a day at the threshing
Since last year. O it was delight

To be paying bills of laughter
And chaffy gossip in kind
With work thrown in to ballast
The fantasy-soaring mind.

As I crossed the wooden bridge I wondered
As I looked into the drain
If ever a summer morning should find me
Shovelling up eels again.

And I thought of the wasps' nest in the bank
And how I got chased one day
Leaving the drag and the scraw-knife behind,
How I covered my face with hay.

The wet leaves of the cocksfoot
Polished my boots as I
Went round by the glistening bog-holes
Lost in unthinking joy.

I'll be carrying bags to-day, I mused,
The best job at the mill
With plenty of time to talk of our loves
As we wait for the bags to fill.

Maybe Mary might call round . . .
And then I came to the haggard gate,
And I knew as I entered that I had come
Through fields that were part of no earthly estate.

CAMOGIE MATCH

Bright shone the sunlight on Peggy and Doreen
Wild swung the ash sticks. Be careful astooreen;
Josie is getting right into her stride now,
Kathleen is hurling with all her Cork pride now.
A shout from the side-line: "Mark your man, Kathleen Cody."
Kathleen pucks it. I tell you that puck was a dotie.
The game is exciting, it is indeed really,
Maureen Cashman is tackling bold Ide O'Kiely. . . .

IF WINTER COMES

It's cold enough to snow today,
Ah, year, there's no delaying
"It's only seven weeks till Christmas"
The children playing
At Mount Street Bridge were saying.

SANTA CLAUS

To end in verse without much cause;
Shop windows show old Santa Claus
Down from Artic's midnight sun.
Ghosts glimmer on planes and tanks and guns.

WEE BEAUTY

Gulliver he went to Lilliput
Swift, he was not silly, but
His man came back by the hilly rut
Riding on a pony.

WHITE BREAD

White bread, you give us hope; you break
The grey monotony of the story.
It is not how you look or taste,
But in the imagination that blossoms in the waste
When we look on the loaf that is not hoary.
White bread, you are a mirroring back
Reflecting mid-night lighted streets
Cigarettes, tea, sugar, gas always on,
Busses coming home at a quarter to one—
All that's evoked by the name of peace.

A CHRISTMAS CHILDHOOD

I

One side of the potato-pits was white with frost—
How wonderful that was, how wonderful!
And when we put our ears to the paling-post
The music that came out was magical.

The light between the ricks of hay and straw
Was a hole in Heaven's gable. An apple tree
With its December-glinting fruit we saw—
O you, Eve, were the world that tempted me

To eat the knowledge that grew in clay
And death the germ within it! Now and then
I can remember something of the gay
Garden that was childhood's. Again

The tracks of cattle to a drinking-place,
A green stone lying sideways in a ditch
Or any common sight the transfigured face
Of a beauty that the world did not touch.

II

My father played the melodeon
Outside at our gate;
There were stars in the morning east
And they danced to his music.

Across the wild bogs his melodeon called
To Lennons and Callans.
As I pulled on my trousers in a hurry
I knew some strange thing had happened.

Outside in the cow-house my mother
Made the music of milking;
The light of her stable-lamp was a star
And the frost of Bethlehem made it twinkle.

A water-hen screeched in the bog,
Mass-going feet
Crunched the wafer-ice on the pot-holes,
Somebody wistfully twisted the bellows wheel.

My child poet picked out the letters
On the grey stone,
In silver the wonder of a Christmas townland,
The winking glitter of a frosty dawn.

Cassiopeia was over
Cassidy's hanging hill,
I looked and three whin bushes rode across
The horizon—the Three Wise Kings.

An old man passing said:
'Can't he make it talk'—
The melodeon. I hid in the doorway
And tightened the belt of my box-pleated coat.

I nicked six nicks on the door-post
With my penknife's big blade—
There was a little one for cutting tobacco.
And I was six Christmases of age.

My father played the melodeon,
My mother milked the cows,
And I had a prayer like a white rose pinned
On the Virgin Mary's blouse.

LEGEND

They'll make him king of Connaught now
And generations will hear how—
Like Hercules or Finn McCoul—
A child at Spiddal National School
His tiny fist knocking giants down. . . .
Martin, you're heir to legend's crown.

CURTAIN

(In memory of Joseph Holloway)

Joe, I cannot let you pass on without saying
The way you were known to me and I to you.
The residue
Memory picks from many a meeting—delaying
The spirit in the stalls though the play is over
And in Darleys next Sunday evening in the big armchair
You will be there
Telling of McCormick as Fluther and Cusack as Covey,
And Darleys little dog will be looking up in your face
And you nibble at the cake to the tune of theatrical glory;
The dog knows the story
Of the Terrys, Mrs. Campbell and all the stage-stricken race,
Eleven o'clock! Don't go yet, Joe, that clock is fast,
Till you hear a Mozart quartette or a Swan-Hennessy tune—
It is too soon.
Come, children, a song for Joe—Just one last.

WAR AND PEACE

Do you hear that noise, Mother,
That comes over the sea?
Is that God the Father raging
In His Eternity?
That is only war, darling,
Drunk men returning
From the pubs of their pleasure,
They'll be sober by morning.
Do you hear that whisper, Mother,
That follows the sigh
From the house of Injustice?
What was that going by?

That was God raging, child,
Something to fright
More than the shouting
Of a whole drunken night.

FOR EMINENT PHYSICISTS

God must be glad to see them play
Like kittens in the sun
Delighted with the wisps of hay
Blown from His haggard on a breezy day. . . .
Time's kittens, have your fun.

OCTOBER 1943

And the rain coming down, and the rain coming down!
How lovely it falls on the rick well headed,
On potato pits thatched, on the turf clamps home,
On the roofs of the byre where the cows are bedded!

And the sun shining down, and the sun shining down!
How bright on the turnip leaves, on the stubble—
Where turkeys tip-toe across the ridges—
In this corner of peace in a world of trouble.

MEMORY OF BROTHER MICHAEL

It would never be morning, always evening,
Golden sunset, golden age—
When Shakespeare, Marlowe and Jonson were writing
The future of England page by page
A nettle-wild grave was Ireland's stage.

147

It would never be spring, always autumn
After a harvest always lost,
When Drake was winning seas for England
We sailed in puddles of the past
Chasing the ghost of Brendan's mast.

The seeds among the dust were less than dust,
Dust we sought, decay,
The young sprout rising smothered in it,
Cursed for being in the way—
And the same is true to-day.

Culture is always something that was,
Something pedants can measure,
Skull of bard, thigh of chief,
Depth of dried-up river.
Shall we be thus for ever?
Shall we be thus for ever?

A WREATH FOR TOM MOORE'S STATUE

The cowardice of Ireland is in his statue,
No poet's honoured when they wreathe this stone,
An old shopkeeper who has dealt in the marrow-bone
Of his neighbours looks at you.
Dim-eyed, degenerate, he is admiring his god,
The bank-manager who pays his monthly confession,
The tedious narrative of a mediocrity's passion,
The shallow, safe sins that never become a flood
To sweep themselves away. From under
His coat-lapels the vermin creep as Joyce
Noted in passing on his exile's way.
In the wreathing of this stone now I wonder
If there is not somehow the worship of the lice
That crawl upon the seven-deadened clay.

They put a wreath upon the dead
For the dead will wear the cap of any racket,
The corpse will not put his elbows through his jacket
Or contradict the words some liar has said.
The corpse can be fitted out to deceive—
Fake thoughts, fake love, fake ideal,
And rogues can sell its guaranteed appeal,
Guaranteed to work and never come alive.
The poet would not stay poetical
And his humility was far from being pliable,
Voluptuary to-morrow, to-day ascetical,
His morning gentleness was the evening's rage.
But here we give you death, the old reliable
Whose white blood cannot blot the respectable page.
Some clay the lice have stirred
Falls now for ever into hell's lousy hollows.
The terrible peace is that follows
The annihilation of the flesh-rotted word.
But hope! the poet comes again to build
A new city high above lust and logic,
The trucks of language overflow and magic
At every turn of the living road is spilled.

The sense is over-sense. No need more
To analyse, to controvert or turn
The laugh against the cynic's leer of power.
In his own city now he lives before
The clay earth was made, an Adam never born,
His light imprisoned in a dinner-hour.

PEGASUS

My soul was an old horse
Offered for sale in twenty fairs.

149

I offered him to the Church—the buyers
Were little men who feared his unusual airs.
One said: 'Let him remain unbid
In the wind and rain and hunger
Of sin and we will get him—
With the winkers thrown in—for nothing.'

Then the men of State looked at
What I'd brought for sale.
One minister, wondering if
Another horse-body would fit the tail
That he'd kept for sentiment—
The relic of his own soul—
Said, 'I will graze him in lieu of his labour.'
I lent him for a week or more
And he came back a hurdle of bones,
Starved, overworked, in despair.
I nursed him on the roadside grass
To shape him for another fair.

I lowered my price. I stood him where
The broken-winded, spavined stand
And crooked shopkeepers said that he
Might do a season on the land—
But not for high-paid work in towns.
He'd do a tinker, possibly.
I begged, 'O make some offer now,
A soul is a poor man's tragedy.
He'll draw your dungiest cart,' I said,
'Show you short cuts to Mass,
Teach weather lore, at night collect
Bad debts from poor men's grass.'
                            And they would not.
        Where the
Tinkers quarrel I went down
With my horse, my soul.

150

I cried, 'Who will bid me half a crown?'
From their rowdy bargaining
Not one turned. 'Soul,' I prayed,
'I have hawked you through the world
Of Church and State and meanest trade.
But this evening, halter off,
Never again will it go on.
On the south side of ditches
There is grazing of the sun.
No more haggling with the world. . . .'
As I said these words he grew
Wings upon his back. Now I may ride him
Every land my imagination knew.

BARDIC DUST

CHARACTERS:
    Austin Clarke
    The Editors of *The Irish Times*
    The Public (in the form of a chorus)
    Myself as Commentator
    Anyone else who thinks he has something to say.
CHORUS (Ad nauseum):
  We hate verse plays, we hate verse plays
  We do not think there are worse plays.
MYSELF (soliloquising)
  If I agree with the Public, they
  Will take me into their confidence;
  They'll say
  Eventually, there's nothing like the Royal—
  Even the ones who seem to be most loyal
  To symphony music and Jack Yeates' art
  Are only waiting for the chance to start
  An anti-intellectual campaign—
  I shall not give their poison-piety rein,

And yet, I cannot praise
Honestly, these ghostly lyric plays.
Enter Austin Clarke in the dusty robes of a mediaeval abbot.
COMMENTATOR:
He looks like a gargoyle,
Much weather-worn,
Can stone breed stone?
Is this poet manufactured or born?
This Clarke is always three removes from life—
EDITOR (*entering*)
Be easy critic with the butcher's knife
For I'll allow no man to say
That Clarke is not a good poet anyway.
MYSELF:
Then we'll let him speak for himself.
CLARKE (*reading from "The Viscount of Blarney"*)
Woman: Who's there?
Cauth: It's me, ma'am.
Woman: Who?
Cauth: Cauth Morrissey
             An orphan going out on service.
             I'm lost
             Entirely.
Woman: Lift the latch and walk right in
Cauth: O thank you ma'am.
COMMENTATOR:
This has some merit I agree
A Celtic Twilight world. Poetry
Is not in scansion, form, rhymes,
But in the intense gospel of our times.
Poetry is not something sweetly nice.
The Poet is a man twice
As much alive as any other man,
His time wounds him more deeply than

152

It wounds the common
Man or woman.
But—
The same knife, Life, makes that monstrous cut . . .
And take his unique names—Cauth, Fostermother,
Pookha, Old Monk, Young
Monk—Are these I wonder,
Universal symbols that imply
Queer counsels in the soul, the tragedy
Of living that is ever the same?
Or are they only a child's dusty game,
A problem that is private to the writer?
Scruple scratches that like a flea-bite, or
The tickle of the long-worn habit
Of the old Abbot,
Draw no blood worth speaking of
The catacombs, Newgrange and Dowth—
His priests have never been inside Maynooth,
His monasteries are as empty as O'Connor's,
Echoing the pathetic remorse of private dishonours.
EDITOR:
You are
Going too far
Clarke's student straying
Blazes with the terror of your moment's praying
And as you read
You'll see his cattle-raiders sweat and bleed
And all that's Catholic Ireland in
The poet's preoccupation with sin.
COMMENTATOR (*aside*)
John Knox has been here
I fear.
Enter half-a-dozen of Clarke's consistent praisers
All together:
Clarke is the doyen of all

Poets, we'll allow no critical
Remarks, but only praise, praise.
Hah! Yourself and Life are nuisances. A phrase,
Spondee, trochee, literary guff
In pubs, on radio, is quite enough
For us.
Go with na gCopaleen on his bus
To digs in slums,
We are Austin's imitative chums.

MYSELF:

Give Clarke a break
Your stupid praise of him will make
The Public here get sick, more
Indifferent than they were before,
See, he wants to say
Something interesting about the play.

CLARKE:

Alone I've come
To win the poet back his rightful home—
The theatre. Alone I've stayed
Unafraid
To carry on the fight.
And this small play that you will see tonight
With all its dusty years upon it
Yeates' preciousness and Synge's Calvinistic Connaught—
Is worthy of a hearing for the sake
Of those who may come after me—awake
To life, to public problems, to the terror
Of poetry revealing moral error.
I know my limitations, I have died;
To come alive again how hard I've tried.

MYSELF:

And not failed either, a warm breath
Is blowing in a room where once was death.

TARRY FLYNN

If one could say
On such a day
This man did what
The fates could not
Its following judgment set aside.
If one could show
How such a throw
Of a stone or a leaf
Had been the ever undenied
If one could keep the main
Road and not many a lane
That leads to full-stopped gaps.
Out to this field to wander again
The inevitable is the pointless journey, perhaps.

TARRY FLYNN

The scent of cut grass
Hung on a briar—
He sniffed through gaps till his mind
Was packed with twenty summers memories.
He held the stem of the briar and wondered
Something he had lost in grief piecemeal to find
And now the lane turned round
Keeping surprises up its green-sleeved arms.
He was walking through a quarry of iron stones
That was really the tomb of a king
The greatest of all kings,
A storybook king.
Dark boulders roll over the magical lanes.
At the boortree that has a curse but also a blessing.
The grass and ferns have powers
If a man only knew
Greater than the witches of Hans Andersen.
A castle might spring up here. . . .

TEMPTATION IN HARVEST

A poplar leaf was spiked upon a thorn
Above the hedge like a flag of surrender
That the year hung out. I was afraid to wonder
At capitulation in a field of corn.
The yellow posies in the headland grass
Paraded up and down in loud apparel;
If I could search their hearts I'd find a moral
For men and women—but I'd let them pass.
Hope guarantees the poor that they will be
Masters at haw-time when the robins are
Courageous as a crow or water-hen. O see
There someone on an ash tree's limb
Sawing a stick for a post or a drilling-bar!
I wish that I this moment were with him!

I should not have wished, should not have seen how white
The wings of thistle seeds are, and how gay
Amoral Autumn gives her soul away
And every maidenhead without a fight.
I turned to the stubble of the oats,
Knowing that clay could still seduce my heart
After five years of pavements raised to art.
O the devilry of the fields! petals that goats
Have plucked from rose bushes of vanity!
But here! a small blue flower creeping over
On a trailing stem across an inch-wide chasm.
Even here wild gods have set a net for sanity.
Where can I look and not become a lover
Terrified at each recurring spasm?

This time of the year mind worried
About the threshing of the corn and whether
The yellow streaks in the sunset were for fine weather.

The sides of the ricks were letting in; too hurried
We built them to beat the showers that were flying
All day. 'It's raining in Drummeril now,'
We'd speculate, half happy to think how
Flat on the ground a neighbour's stooks were lying.
Each evening combing the ricks like a lover's hair,
Gently combing the butt-ends to run the rain,
Then running to the gate to see if there
Was anybody travelling on the train.
The Man in the Moon has water on the brain
I love one! but my ricks are more my care.

An old woman whispered from a bush: 'Stand in
The shadow of the ricks until she passes;
You cannot eat what grows upon Parnassus—
And she is going there as sure as sin.'
I saw her turn her head as she went down
The blackberry lane-way, and I knew
In my heart that only what we love is true—
And not what loves us, we should make our own.
I stayed in indecision by the gate,
As Christ in Gethsemane to guess
Into the morrow and the day after,
And tried to keep from thinking on the fate
Of those whom beauty tickles into laughter
And leaves them on their backs in muddiness.

The air was drugged with Egypt. Could I go
Over the field to the City of the Kings
Where art, music, letters are the real things?
The stones of the street, the sheds, hedges cried, No.
Earth, earth! I dragged my feet off the ground.
Labourers, animals armed with farm tools,
Ringed me. The one open gap had larch poles
Across it now by memory secured and bound,
The flaggers in the swamp were the reserves

Waiting to lift their dim nostalgic arms
The moment I would move. The noise of carts
Softening into haggards wove new charms.
The simplest memory plays upon the nerves
Symphonies that break down what the will asserts.
O Life, forgive me for my sins! I can hear
In the elm by the potato-pits a thrush;

Rain is falling on the Burning Bush
Where God appeared. Why now do I fear
That clear in the sky where the Evening Star is born?
Why does the inconsequential gabble
Of an old man among the hills so trouble
My thoughts this September evening? Now I turn
Away from the ricks, the sheds, the cabbage garden,
The stones of the street, the thrush song in the tree,
The potato-pits, the flaggers in the swamp;
From the country heart that hardly learned to harden,
From the spotlight of an old-fashioned kitchen lamp
I go to follow her who winked at me.

ROOSEVELT

He did not wear the cruel mask of will
That little men put on to terrify
Poor human children climbing someone's hill;
These were not trespassers fearful of the eye
Of a policeman or the Lord God of Law.
He had the innocence of heart that's found
Not in the mighty husk, but in the awe
Of a spirit conscious of the Original Wound—
Original Sin, the gap through which Love passes
And Pity and Humility; that gap that lead
Through the wilderness to the summit of Parnassus
Was open wide to all misfortune's needs.
He was a man and not a mask of power,
Upon whose grave I lay this simple flower.

BLUEBELLS FOR LOVE

There will be bluebells growing under the big trees
And you will be there and I will be there in May;
For some other reason we both will have to delay
The evening in Dunshaughlin—to please
Some imagined relation,
So both of us came to walk through that plantation.

We will be interested in the grass,
In an old bucket-hoop, in the ivy that weaves
Green incongruity among dead leaves,
We will put on surprise at carts that pass—
Only sometimes looking sideways at the bluebells in the planta-
tion
And never frighten them with too wild an exclamation.

We will be wise, we will not let them guess
That we are watching them or they will pose
A mere façade like boys
Caught out in virtue's naturalness.
We will not impose on the bluebells in that plantation
Too much of our desire's adulation.

We will have other loves—or so they'll think;
The primroses or the ferns or the briars,
Or even the rusty paling wires,
Or the violets on the sunless sorrel bank.
Only as an aside the bluebells in the plantation
Will mean a thing to our dark contemplation.

We'll know love little by little, glance by glance.
Ah, the clay under these roots is so brown!
We'll steal from Heaven while God is in the town—
I caught an angel smiling in a chance
Look through the tree-trunks of the plantation
As you and I walked slowly to the station.

IN MEMORY OF MY MOTHER

I do not think of you lying in the wet clay
Of a Monaghan graveyard; I see
You walking down a lane among the poplars
On your way to the station, or happily

Going to second Mass on a summer Sunday—
You meet me and you say:
'Don't forget to see about the cattle—'
Among your earliest words the angels stray.

And I think of you walking along a headland
Of green oats in June,
So full of repose, so rich with life—
And I see us meeting at the end of a town

On a fair day by accident, after
The bargains are all made and we can walk
Together through the shops and stalls and markets
Free in the oriental streets of thought.

O you are not lying in the wet clay,
For it is a harvest evening now and we
Are piling up the ricks against the moonlight
And you smile up at us—eternally.

IN MEMORY OF MY MOTHER

Died November 10th, 1945

You will have the road gate open, the front door ajar
The kettle boiling and a table set
By the window looking out at the sycamores—
And your loving heart lying in wait

For me coming up among the poplar trees.
You'll know my breathing and my walk
And it will be a summer evening on those roads
Lonely with leaves of thought.

We will be choked with the grief of things growing,
The silence of dark-green air
Life too rich—the nettles, docks and thistles
All answering the prodigal's prayer.

You will know I am coming though I send no word
For you were lover who could tell
A man's thoughts—my thoughts—though I hid them—
Through you I knew Woman and did not fear her spell.

FROM FAILURE UP

Can a man grow from the dead clod of failure
Some consoling flower
Something humble as a dandelion or a daisy,
Something to wear as a buttonhole in Heaven?
Under the flat, flat grief of defeat maybe
Hope is a seed.
Maybe this's what he was born for, this hour
Of hopelessness.
Maybe it is here he must search
In this hell of unfaith
Where no one has a purpose
Where the web of Meaning is broken threads
And one man looks at another in fear.
O God can a man find You when he lies with his face downwards
And his nose in the rubble that was his achievement?
Is the music playing behind the door of despair?
O God give us purpose.

POOR CAT

In the woods there lived a cat,
White as snow and very fat.
He live on robins, larks. No mouse
Was ever eaten in his house.
Since he came to the woods he made
Fun of all the mousing trade.

Once he was a decent cat
In a farmer's house. He sat
On a rug beside a nice
Fire thinking about mice
In the evenings he said: Meow
It is time to milk the cow.
Then one day a little chick
That was very small and sick
Lay beside Tom's big claws
And he liked it better than
Any mouse that ever ran;
Next day he killed another
Chick and took it from its mother.
Bad cat, bad cat the woman cried
I will kill your dirty hide
I will have you left to die
On the loft.

THE GIFT

One day I asked God to give
Me perfection so I'd live
Smooth and courteous, calmly wise
All the world's virtuous prize.

So I should not always be
Getting into jeopardy,
Being savage, wild and proud
Fighting, arguing with the crowd;

Being poor, sick depressed,
Everywhere an awful pest;
Being too right, being too wrong.
Being too weak, being too strong,

Being every hour fated
To say the things that make me hated;
Being a failure in the end—
God, perfection on me spend.

And God spoke out of Heaven
The only gift in My giving
Is yours—Life. Seek in hell
Death, perfect, wise, comfortable.

LOVE IS BUT A SEASON

The bluebells are withered now under the beech trees
And I am there—the ghost of myself—alone
Trying to remember a truth I once had known
Poking among the weeds on bare knees
Praying, praying poetic incantation
To call back life to that once-green plantation.

A score of grey ungrowthy stumps stand up
Like an old graveyard in my mind: Dingle, Cooleen,
A shadowed corner of St. Stephen's Green,
A noisy corner of the Country Shop,
All chilly thoughts that bring no exaltation
No green leaf love to the beautiful plantation.

I dreamt it in my heart, it was not real,
I should have known that love is but a season
Like spring. The flowers fade. Reason
Knows it cannot find its old ideal
And yet her breath still blows some undulation
Of leaf and flower to charm my dream plantation.

HILDA

Unless you come
I shall die in a ditch.
There will be no bluebells there,
Only the vetch
Smelling of death.
Weeds round me,
The mud of hooves
That prance there
Falling over my eyes.

Rags of beggars that passed
Will clothe my soul.
The winter will come through the bushes,
Rain will fall
Making puddles in my face;
The snow will come
And cover me up
Like the Babes in the Wood:
Then no one will stop
To examine the heap,
No one will know where a poet's asleep.

I shall die in a ditch
Like a dog or a bum,
Poet dead in a ditch
Unless you come.

HILDA

Hilda, I have day-dreamed walking the streets
For years, and walking the fields I have filled the
Hours with happy imaginings. I have stood treats
To gods of fame who as I will they
Gave me whatever I asked. But no dream, Hilda,
Of mine was ever wild enough with dream's conceits
To shape you as you are beautiful. I'd say
If ever such a dream had been born
Out of my dream: it was not fair of them
Who handed out the opiate so to lay
Grief upon my heart. In fields of corn
By lanes where no one knew me I have gone
Flaunting upon my lonely, flowerless stem
Blossoms of love. But Hilda, she was the sun.

HILDA

By Raglan Road and Hollis street I shall walk blind
Remembering that through her eyes I first looked there
At walls and windows that became more rare
Than Eden flowering in a poet's mind
And down to Dunsany all that road will be
No road at all but only a dark streak of despair
I must avoid lest I go down to hell,
And I cannot see Kerry ever, for the spell
Of Hilda created it for me as sweet as prayer.
Round by Cooleen where the land broke into the sea
And men were gathering seaweed, and there were old gates
That let us through to heaven. Over Dingle Bay
I shall never be able to look till God sets free
His children from the earth. O Hilda waits
Somewhere in my imagination all the day.
She shall not leave me again: I shall. . . .

HOMEWARD

Now the crows fly home, fly home, fly high
To Caffrey's plantation through a mackerel sky,
The young ones gabbling of great eagles reported
From the west of the world by a wise crow of Clones.
It is night—

The bat takes over from the crow and snipe
The sentry post of the low sky.
A cobbler takes his apron off and lays by
His spectacles beside a ball of hemp.
The frogs are grunting in the swamp
And seem to shake the bog-road under
The unsteady feet of the half-tight servant-boy;
A ghost fear gives his red hair a creepy caress
For he remembers that a man who died in March
Was funeraled this long way round. The hearse
Shook the road as it is shaking now—

Home, home.
A long travel

SNAIL

Little snail, run, run
Into those weeds or under that stone
For the blackbird has stopped,
Has stopped,
Has stopped,
His singing and hopped
Down the stairs of the trees
And one eye has popped
Like a doll's glass eye—
Is it a snail or a pebble he sees?
Hurry snail if you do not want to die.

166

Little snail run, run
Into those weeds or under that stone
For the sun has come out,
Come out,
Come out
With a bang and a shout
And the hens are running into the garden
Through the haggard gate.

RIDING PEGASUS

Ride him. Are these boys and girls
Swine worthy of your pearls?
I wondered and I pondered long,
Made for these poor folks a song
Rhymed the racing page of papers
Copied all the jazzy capers
Degraded my soul. They laughed.
One said to the other, "Who's the daft
Man over there?" A small boy flung
A stone through the heart of my best song.
Still Peadar O'Donnell thinks Pegasus
Should be ridden by the masses.

WHY SORROW?

A Fragment

It was the month of May. Father Mat walked among
His cows that evening dreaming of a song
That Christ had closed the window on.

Now the priest's pride
Was a Roman poet hearing of the Crucified.
Apollo's unbaptised pagan who can show
To simple eyes what Christians never know—
Was it the unspeakable beauty of Hell?
The priest looked once—twice—and fell.

167

The bleeding body of sorrow, no pattern
Woven, the excitement of a child
That remembers the ditches where dead leaves have rotted
A suddenness of green and light.
And the balls of mud that were spun to spheres
Within the orbit of the road-roller's wheels.
All that was true before the piteous death of the Cross.
No earth-love was transfigured on that Hill
All flattened out most prostrate, muddy-mouthed.

The priest moved on. He swung
His blackthorn at a pebble of the sun.
He saw the daisies now and the white
Confirmation dresses of the alder trees,
And he heard the people passing, laughing—
                    "I might
Have eaten like these
Life's leavened bread that has mysteries
Marvellous as the wafer consecrate
Each morning with words that are blots in the book of my fate."

But his people needed him,
His people needed him,
His people needed him.

He was the sledge that smashed the dark resistance
Of time for those who never could fly
He was the people's need where the little fields
Of Cavan gagged the mouth of prophecy.

His pride lay between the hammer and the thing
That he was striking at. Every blow
Squashed flat something that knew of beauty
Drove joy into a wet weedy onion-row.

But his people needed him,
Needed him
Needed him.
His cows were heavy with calf. He liked to talk
Of things growing and growthy till the people thought
Him the old-time priest who took life as it came,
Looked into the hearts of his people, covered their shame
With the white cloak of Grace. Attended the sick
Gave Christ and then talked with Paddy and Mick
Of the work of the seasons: "Your potatoes are doing
Better than my own. . . ."

                         " 'Tis the farmyard manuring."

He was part of the place, as natural as
The stones in grazing fields that are not seen
By those who walk the ridges. Yet he was all
That the servant of the Lord needed to be
A mud-walled house that was Truth's citadel.

The children of Dromore looked up at him
Trustingly, hero-worshippingly. His humilities
Were of a high angel that stooped and carressed
The sinful heads of poor children. That man was blessed
Above all other priests that they had known
A soul with no sharp edges—a simple one.
His farmer's face, soft eyes, white hair
His slow flat tread, his thick tongue for bargaining fair,
Or for prayer.

His father was a farmer in Corofin
He had six fields with soil like soap
Where rushes grew and grasses like steel wires
Blue in the sunshine. Down the shivering slope
Water ran in sheets of winter.
And out of this sour soil he squeezed
The answer to his wife's wishes:
In steely grass and green rushes
Was woven the vestments of a priest.

169

The eldest daughter rose to be
A teacher in a school;
Mat was the youngest. Father took
His rosary and at a stool
Knelt and prayed for something special
Something that was never mentioned
And the fire went out behind their heels.
And Mat grew up like July in the fields.

And as he grew they prayed that he was growing
A priest. He was soft and easy-going.
No wild singing in the evening lanes
Or at the night cross-roads. But through the dusk window-panes
Looking out where ducks were coming gabbling in
From the frog-croaking bogs of Corofin.
A calf sucking the edge of a tub
The Evening Star musing in the East,
Behind the house the giggle of girls.
                   He was a priest
Already—he only had to grow
The flower was in the seed.
Twin flowers, perhaps—he sometimes saw
The magic worlds of another law.

It was the Garden of the Golden Apples,
A long garden between a railway and a road,
In the sow's rooting where the hen scratches
He dipped his fingers in the pockets of a rich god.

In the thistly hedge old boots were flying sandals
By which he travelled through the childhood skies,
Old buckets rusty-holed with half-hung handles
Were drums to beat when old men married wives.

170

The pole that lifted the clothes-line in the middle
Was the flag-pole on a prince's palace when
He looked at it through fingers crossed to riddle
In evening sunlight miracles for men.

It was the Garden of the Golden Apples
And when the Carrick train went by he knew
That he could never die till something happened
Like wishing for a fruit that never grew,

Or wanting to be up on Candle-Fort
Above the village with its shops and mill.
The racing cyclists' gasp-gapped reports
Hinted of pubs where love can drink his fill.

And when the sun went down into Drumcatton
And the new moon by her little finger swung
From the telegraph wires he knew how life had happened
And what the blackbird in the whitethorn sang.

It was the Garden of the Golden Apples
The half-way house where he had stopped a day
Before he took the west road to Drumcatton
Where the sun was always setting on the play.

And when years brought loving on
He was deep in love with one—
Mary Queen of Heaven.
She was every girl he knew,
Nimble-footed, daring too.

She was laughter on the stiles
In the evenings of July
When the lads were playing skittles
On the dusty road. Her cry

"Good man, Mat!" She could run
The hundred yards with any one.
And she could sling a stone above
McCabe's tall poplar. Love, ah, love!
All that was flesh of womankind
Was the Virgin Mary in his mind.
And lonely as a lover then
Separate in a world of men
He walked and wondered why
He could not reach the gaiety.
The gap was bushed and Christ was always
Like an old farmer guarding it
From neighbouring trespass.
He was a grey stooped old man of Cavan
Christ herding a ragged cow in a patch of dry grass.

Every penny that the school-teacher earned
Save fifteen shillings weekly for her keep
She posted home. And Mat went to college
And all things turned out as they had prayed.
This done
At thirty-eight herself became a nun.

Through the cool meadows that lay along the river
And through the flaggered swamp the priest went on
On the back of his neck there burned a disc of sun.
                                    Was this the river Styx?
And that man in shirtsleeves with a shovel, Charon,
Or only Michael McCabe? He who rowed sorrow over
To bluebell beauty on the wild hills of Seola.
Those hills that were always swinging their beauty in—
Original Sin—

Oh the screaming children on the greening ridges
The trees that were before the Cross was sawn
Were worthy to be worshipped. Come draw your wages
In evening silver, in pure gold at dawn.

Father Mat looked down at a coltsfoot blossom
And loved it more than ever he loved the Sacrament—
For here was the symbol of an old joy.
Success—the earth cheers Christ human not divine.

          In the dim chapel was the grey
Mumble of prayer
To the Queen of May
The Virgin Mary with her schoolgirl air.
The priest was seeing her, a girl
Of fifteen. She sits and listens to
The wandering poet who has come (indeed!)
To talk with her mother of times they both knew.
He sits one side of the fire dandling the tongues
The mother the other side, Mary by the dresser.
The tea is made and as they drink the mother
Marvels at the scholar
His indifference to girls and dancing and the world's bother.
The mother goes out to milk the cows. Says he:
"How many miles to Babylon? with me
Beside you it is just to dream. . . ."
The childhood of the priest cried out: "Beware
Of the evil spell in all poetry."
              And he was saying a prayer
In the dim chapel all the while.
But the Gospel was printed over an older writing
And its damnation was crawling under the Host.

O despair! O despair! O despair!
My people want and I must be
For them
Their final surety.
I doubt
But must not let them see
That I am signing with a lie
Their checks of holy constancy.

O Truth, I
This evening ask
How I may
Sieve my salvation
In the riddle of clay.
And from morning's temptation
To dally with day
Keep me I pray.
                    In a meadow

Beside the chapel three boys were playing football
At the forge door an old man was leaning
Viewing a hunter-hoe. A man could hear
If he listened to the breeze the fall of wings—
How wistfully the sin-birds come home!

It was Confession Saturday, the first
Saturday in May: the May Devotions
Were spread like leaves to quieten
The excited armies of conscience.
The knife of penance fell so like a blade
Of grass that no one was afraid.

Father Mat came slowly walking, stopping to
Stare through gaps at ancient Ireland sweeping
In again with all its unbaptised beauty:
The calm evening
The whitethorn blossoms,
The smell from ditches that were not Christian.
The dancer that dances in the heart of men cried:
Look! I have shown this to you before—
The rags of living surprised
The joy in things you cannot forget.

The Holy Ghost descends
At random like the muse

On wise man and fool
And why should poet in the twilight choose?
Within the dim chapel was the grey
Mumble of prayer
To the Queen of May—
The Virgin Mary with the schoolgirl air.

Two guttering candles on a brass shrine
Raised upon the wall
Monsters of despair
To terrify deep into the soul.

Through the open door the hum of rosaries
Came out and blended with the homing bees.
                    The trees
Heard nothing stranger than the rain or the wind
Or the birds—
But deep in their roots they knew a seed had sinned.

In the graveyard a goat was nibbling at a yew,
The cobbler's chickens with anxious looks
Were straggling home through nettles, over graves.
A young girl down a hill was driving cows
To a corner at the gable-end of a roofless house.

Cows were milked earlier
The supper hurried,
Hens shut in,
Horses unyoked,
And three men shaving before the same mirror.

The trip of iron tips on tile
Hesitated up the middle aisle,
Heads that were bowed glanced up to see
Who could this last arrival be.

Murmur of women's voices from the porch,
Memories of relations in the graveyard.
On the stem
Of memory imaginations blossom.

In the dim
Corners in the side seats faces gather
Lit up now and then by a guttering candle
And the ghost of day at the window.
A secret lover is saying
Three Hail Marys that she who knows
The ways of women will bring
Cathleen O'Hara (he names her) home to him.
Ironic fate! Cathleen herself is saying
Three hail Mary's to her who knows
The ways of men to bring
Somebody else home to her—
'O may he love me'.
What is the Virgin Mary now to do?

From a confessional
The voice of Father Mat's absolving
Rises and falls like a briar in the breeze
As the sins pour in the old priest is thinking
His fields of fresh grass, his horses, his cows,
His earth into the fires of Purgatory.
It cools his mind.
"They confess to the fields" he mused,
"They confess to the fields and the air and the sky,"
And forgiveness was the soft grass of his meadow by the river.
His thoughts were walking through it now.

"I vexed my father until he swore
And beat my mother till she screamed" (for more).

Father Mat listened with bowed head
As the earth came in to be burned, every stalk
That grew green in the heart to be uprooted,
Every memory that surprised with an unChristly pleasure
The clod growing a daisy, the oily black stones in the river
Put away forever.
                    All that was
His heart when he was happy must not be;
The way of Christ's sorrow is shaded by no trees.

His human lips talked on:
"My son,
Only the poor in spirit shall wear the crown;
Those down
Can creep in the low door
On to Heaven's floor."

All poetry in nature or in book
Must be outcast this night. We must not look
Behind us at the pitiful beauty of those
That lost the war, but kept their magic power,
O the wild fearful happiness of the poet
Is almost too great a load for Christ's shoulders.

A little girl came, and whisperingly
Said: "Father, I'm a Child of Mary";
She told him how she once had loved the pianist
Who taught the convent girls. One day
He came to her father's house to hear her play
He said her fingers on the keys were the hopping feet of hungry
    birds.
He told her of a strange world. And then?
He gave her loneliness forever.
She knew nothing about the ways of men
Until that day. "O Father heed my sorrow."

177

The Confessor sighed and thought: Who seizes a star
Breaks the balance of justice. Mercies are
A cone of loose rubble piled upon the Moon—
"My daughter, you are the mystery in the piano's tune".

As Father Mat walked home
Venus was in the western sky
And through her broken maidenhead
He saw the womb of poetry

And children dancing in the dusk
Cried with voices of surprise
That were never twice repeated:—
God the Gay is not the Wise.

Take your choice, take your choice
Called the breeze through the bridge's eye:
The domestic Virgin and her Child,
Or Venus with her ecstasy.

To the lives of the Saints he turned,
To Saint John of the Cross and Teresa of Avila
And all the chapters shouted, "Jesus, Jesus
The Defeated One is He whom we must follow".

Through his parlour window down the old yew path
A vista opened and a rhododendron
Swung sideways like a dancing girl and winked
Temptation to his heart, the dim temptation
Of middle-age.

A death-bed call today, yet even death
Up that long lane in a pocket of the hills
Was not the Cross of Christ; the old romantic
Waved death as merrily as a wedding feast.

Within the house he knew every rag and stick,
The mean unmade bed behind the kitchen
The sights they hurried to hide when he came in.
His soft eyes pierced
Into the secret rooms of their homes and hearts
Where everything was topsy-turvey: an unwashed shirt
Kicked under the bed, and the chamber-pot
That the women forgot to empty,
A stolen pitch-fork standing in a corner.
And the old man in bed, his beads in his fingers
Counting old sins.
Death was as easy as harvest in Seola.

His hand upon the dash-board of a cart,
Father Mat was standing
Talking to Michael Duky about fairs:
The price of pigs and store cattle—
Like a dealer in the Shercock fair bawling in the doorways of
  shops.

His heavy hat was square upon his head
Like a Christian Brother's.
His eyes were watery like an old man's eyes
And out of his flat nose grew spikey hairs—
Michael Duffy wondered as he saw him thus—
So like mere earth and yet not one of us.

It was the gap
Between the seasons, and the days moved slowly
With labouring men sleeping on headlands among the nettles
And long arms hooked over gates that brightened
The gravel patches on the June road.
The priest spoke wistfully, rurally, heavily
And no one could know that he was seeing
Down the shaft of the gate's light, horses growing wings,
The midges caught in the searchlight
Were beautiful unChristian things.

His curate cycled by—to the Village hall
He had the haughty intellectual look
Of the man who never reads in brook or book,
The man who has not climbed and cannot fall.

                                    Father Ned was fair
And freckled just the slightest bit. He was sharp
A diligent priest who never slurred a word
Of Mass or litany; a man who was never late
For train or chapel. He had the sins
Of men card-indexed—fixed in permanent values
He could tell the mortal ones at a mile's distance in all their
    several grins.
Each day he smoked five cigarettes
And never six. He could speak to Christ
As to his brother the publican of Coothill.

The old priest saw him pass
And, seeing, saw
Himself a mediaeval ghost.
Ahead of him went Power
One who was not afraid when the sun opened a flower,
Who was never astonished
At a stick carried down a stream
Or at the undying difference in the corner of a field.

                    The parish priest was afraid
There was a man
Who'd write and tell the Bishop tales of scandal
Or of how he, Father Mat, talked to himself
And worshipped more the flowers in the garden
Than God. But Ned was scarce of understanding
Everything that Maynooth had put a mark on.

Ned was the works that kept the parish going
The dance-hall, the new decorations in the chapel.
But the people were shy of him, from him they ran
To Father Mat who was both priest and man.

Again the unholy beauty struck his eyes
And Christ the coward of Gethsemanie
Cried out: Father, Father. . . .
                    The dancer that danced
In the hearts of men:

Look! I have shown it to you before,
The bogs, the grey hills, the dirty rags
Of living excited
That no man has seen and died.
                    I broke away
And rule all the dominions that are rare;
I took with me all the answers to every prayer
That young men and girls pray: Love, happiness, riches
Christ cannot give. His is the bitter-tasted, wrong-turned.
You will get
From Christ if you pray for love a laugh too late
And riches Christly-come will be desire
Without escape from it.

The sun crept round
And June was a hum over dusty ground,
Confirmation Day
The bishop of the diocese came that way.

He christened the children and slapped their humble cheeks
In token of the descending Paraclete.
  Be wife, be wife, be spread
  The Holy Spirit consumates.

He spoke, the bishop spoke, of Father Mat,
In him the people of that parish had
A priest who went the good old ways and asked
No questions. Doing his job in simpleness.
"You plough, you sow, you reap, you buy and sell
And sing and eat and sleep. All this is well
Done
In the Name of the Holy One".

Father Mat laughed with the mothers of the children
Who smiled acknowledging their approval of
The bishop's words—they seconded the motion.
And as the bishop passed down the centre aisle
Blessing to right and left, 'twas Father Mat
Their eyes were fixed on. A proud people
Proud of a parish priest whose words begat
Old music in the silences.

                              Of his own Confirmation Day
Father Mat was thinking—when he first found in clay
The secret of a different Deity written. . . .
Before the sun went down into Drumcatton.

O Fear
When consciousness blows through the debris
We are unhomed. Truth's insanity
Is a spell that men must hold to; when they wake
Not even dust is left for all their striving.

So one dull day he knelt and struck his breast
And denied the sun and the earth. And Jesus Christ
Turned him round in his path.

Everywhere he went no grief was come or arriving.
In Casey's house where merriment had been
Longer than scandalous gossip could recall,
Where they had drunk long and loved long
When the factory men love-seeking left their towns,

Lilacs grew before that door and roses
More prosperous than roses anywhere,
Forget-me-nots in rings—not marriage rings—
A cherry tree that swung a welcoming gate.

And you could hear.
On summer evening coming from the village,
Loud laughter from the kitchen of the silly
Girls that were bastardy's delight—
Their screams were larks by day and nightingales by night.

The Mothers—there were four—had never learned
To look outside the door when footsteps passed
They did not heed what talkers talking much
Said about them as they went to Sunday Mass.

Away back Octobers lamp-lit that house of pleasure
And memory many-windowed each one showed
A new crop of lovers gathered in the kitchen,
And an old crop blowing down the sleety road.

All within that house had learned of the earth
How to be quick like a season to grow and blossom
How to be without remorse when the windy weather
Takes down the leaves. Old lovers dream with Autumn.

The old priest crossed that threshold with the pity
Of Christ and what life taught to take and spend
Was forgotten, and four generations wept in a squalid corner
For tomorrows that would tell the shame of them.

Why should this be?
O easy, O rest
There are wool-packs in the west.
Rain fills the evening. At the sharp end of the Seola road
The whitethorns are drenched
The dripping branches on the carts going home
Is a holy-water blessing this hour.
But this that was once a miracle is now
To Father Mat the abominable symbol of
The golden Calf.

The rattle of buckets, rolling of barrels under
Down-spouts, the leading-in of foals
Were happenings dipped deep in pagan wonder
Springs of life.
                        He cast his soul's
Pride in the ditch and he was wearing
The charity-stained dress of grief.
The rain-lighted lanes of Seola were graveyards feeding
But in sorrow was the mystery of being.

One day he said: "I shall not rove
Out of the miserable groove".
Contrition. He confessed his sins
To his own curate, Father Ned.
And though 'twas degradation that
He saw when he had bowed his head,
He held to the belittlement
—Through the floor my soul. The Lord's
Tabernacle is underneath the flooring-boards.

Now he was with his people, one of them.
What they saw he saw too
And nothing more: what they looked at
And what to them was true was true
For him. He was in the crowd
A nobody who had been proud.
From the level of the people he could see
No hills beyond new-green: no raw flesh bleeding
No light astonishing as a knife drawn
In Shercock cattle-fair at dawn
The crowd is mud, mud to the knees
And Pride you were a star-high stand
Yet maybe I'll find in Charity's
Illiterate book of pieties
Apollo's writing in a Christian hand.

He went to Lough Derg, Saint Patrick's Purgatory,
Father Mat went to the Island of the poor
Where every leaf that is green is changed to fire
And everything that makes art and literature
Is a thing to be abhorred—impure desire.

On bare knees they prayed around the rings
Of stones that once were holy walls that bound
The floor of human desire
Into a turbine that sun Time's mill-wheels round.
They were monks then with wants—like women
Or flowers in winter—stretched on their backs
To ease their too strong loving. . . .

                               But today here were lacks,
Anaemic hearts that said to life: "Stay out"
Life that was not coming in—shopkeepers strolled about:
Then a young man painted his shadow on
Saint Brigid's ring of penitential stone.
His back was to the sun though he was praying
For what the sun has thrown to fools all time.
He was a clerk from Dublin, unemployed.
Twenty-seven years old. He was in love
With a waitress in the city.
"O God give me a job and I will prove
My faith and come each year. She is pretty.
Once when my passion broke
The thin banks of youth she held my wrists
And smiled away my shame as a joke.
There's a job in Thomas Street: I'm on their lists;
But the lists are long as roads that Hope is walking.
That shape at the rise, I know, is no house of rest
But the mist
Risen from tears that were wept at many a mocking. . . ."

Father Mat was tempted: Is the way of living
That you are praying for in this God's giving?
Ah lad, upon the road of life
'Tis best to dance with chance's wife
And let the road-menders that follow
Sweep remorse into a hollow.
A girl went round the holy stones,
About thirty-five she was with a long nose.
Was she too praying for what she
Herself was saying: keep from me?
Father Mat has seen her before—
The extra woman on the kitchen floor.
She had one chance.

"But no one ever came again
To ask why I was born a woman.
No one was ever man, but only men
Only crowds and never the companion.
I had to search, I had to be brave—
And bravery is piteous in a maid.
I danced, I danced
With dancing clowns
I smiled and planned—
I went to towns
And walked main streets and fair green
And saw no man but only men
Shouting the price of pigs and cows
Or quarrelling in a publichouse.
O the search that we know is vain!"

Day, night, vigil, dawn—
The Pilgrimage went on
The sun came up over Donegal
And jeered at what was pitiful.

Over cups of black tea they laughed
Shortening the day that was a measureless day
Of Purgatory. Women, their bare legs asplay
Lay on their backs upon the rise where grew green grass—
They were emptied out waiting for love that never was
A wink of the sun.
It was like a day by the sea.
New pilgrims came and yesterday's paper
Passed across panting bellies, fluttering
Hands reached to catch the stale news of war
What earth toy were earth's men fighting for?

Far beyond the water
The miles that are not miles
But ideas of death.

An old man pointed a finger to his face
Where was a cancerous hole
"Was God not good to me?" he said
As he moved back the pad of cotton wool.
"That happened coming from Mass
An accident, a fall upon stone it was.
But it will kill me painlessly, for I
Have asked this at Saint Patrick's Purgatory".
"O God is good", the listener said.
The Cynic whispered to Father Mat. . . .

ON RAGLAN ROAD
   (Air: *The Dawning of The Day*)

On Raglan Road on an autumn day I met her first and knew
That her dark hair would weave a snare that I might one day
      rue;
I saw the danger, yet I walked along the enchanted way,
And I said, let grief be a fallen leaf at the dawning of the day.

On Grafton Street in November we tripped lightly along the
   ledge
Of the deep ravine where can be seen the worth of passion's
   pledge,
The Queen of Hearts still making tarts and I not making hay—
O I loved too much and by such by such is happiness thrown
   away.

I gave her gifts of the mind I gave her the secret sign that's
   known
To the artists who have known the true gods of sound and stone
And word and tint. I did not stint for I gave her poems to say.
With her own name there and her own dark hair like clouds
   over fields of May

On a quiet street where old ghosts meet I see her walking now
Away from me so hurriedly my reason must allow
That I had wooed not as I should a creature made of clay—
When the angel woos the clay he'd lose his wings at the dawn
   of day.

ELEGY FOR JIM LARKIN
   Died February 1947

Not with public words can his greatness
Be told to children, for he was more
Than labour agitator, mob orator
The flashing fiery sword merely was witness
To the sun rising. Cried Larkin: Look!
The fields are producing for you and the trees;
And beyond are not the serf stockland, but seas
Rolling excitement in God's Poetry Book.
When the full moon's in the river the ghost of bread
Must not be in all your weary trudgings home.
The masts of once black galleys will become
Fir forests under the North's glittering Plough,
And the rusty gantries, the heroic ahead
With man the magician whom the gods endow.

It was thus I heard Jim Larkin shout above
The crowd who would have him turn aside
From the day's shocking reality. Their morphine pride
Hid in the fogs of unhope and would not move—
The smoke and the drug of the newspaper story;
And with mouths open they were glad to stare
Not at a blackbird, but a millionaire
Whose two-year olds ran off with all their worry—
Though battoned by policemen into Dublin's garbage.
Jim Larkin opened a window wide
And wings flew out and offered to slow rising things
A lift onto high altars with proud carriage.
And they swayed above the city in young knowledge
And they ate the loaf that nourishes great kings.

THINGS NOBODY DIES FOR

A bomb can kill twenty men at a time
It is bombs and cannons that count.
This is surely the end of the world
But it was a war between good and evil
And victory looked like being with the devil.

SECOND MAN:
      King Billy fought a mighty fight
      James was an amateur soldier.
      Who are these two down there
      In the corner where the fat cattle stand
      Knee-deep in the grass of Meath
      Who are you?

CAROLAN:
      My name is Carolan and this is Bridget Cruise
      We took no part in the war:
      There are more important things than war
      All the things that nobody dies for

MAN:
    Neutral, Dick, but neutral on our side
    I never could mistake a Papist hide.

CAROLAN:
    Bridget, those men are gone now—
    I know you do not really mean what you say;
    I know a woman's nature. . . .

THE WAKE OF THE BOOKS
A *Mummery*

[In response to an editorial in *The Bell* July 1947 which suggested that an annual wake be held for the year's censored books]

Dramatis Personae
M.C. MASTER OF CEREMONIES
CHORUS (THE BLUE HUSSARS)
SEAN O'FAOLAIN
FIRST MILLIONAIRE
PATRICK KAVANAGH
A WOMAN
FRANK O'CONNOR
AN OLD PRIEST
A YOUNG PRIEST
AN EDITOR
A POET
AUSTIN CLARKE
SECOND MILLIONAIRE
AN ACTOR
AN ACTRESS
AN ALLEGED FILM DIRECTOR
YOUNG B.L.
YOUNG SOLICITOR
POLITICIAN

Prologue

This little drama that I introduce
Is no great lecher to excite my muse,
For howsoever I try I can't but feel
The censorship of books is not a real
Problem for the writers of this land:
There's much that's insincere in what is banned—
And time if left the corpse would bury it deeper
In ten years than our bitterest conscience-keeper.

Yet, as I have been asked to undertake
Master of Ceremonies at this comic wake
As I lead the characters in I'll try
To show the kernel of the tragedy—
The reality of bank and bake-house
Screeching unheeded round the writer's wake-house,
The inarticulate envy and the spleen
Echoing in the incidental scene
We call the Censorship.

        But before
My mummers enter by the imaginary door
I'd like to say a few words here—
(Not yet remove the draping from the bier)
Our greatest censors and worst enemies
Are those who gurgle praise—so soft to please.
The "last judgment" that William Blake demanded
Would leave nine-tenths of these rhymsters stranded.

It all adds up to native cultural life,
The whore's honoured as the chastest wife;
The journalists cheer loudly for all
The noblest verse and the stupidest doggerel.
        But I delay
You did not come to hear me, but a play.

The scene you must imagine is a square
Overlooked by windows, there, and there and there!
In the centre is the corpse, a coffin filled
With all the books the censorship has killed.
Here all the streams of society converge—
New Rich, Old Rich, purple and navy-serge;
Bishops, priests, nuns; art patrons who
Would run a brothel if it paid them to.
These last I would particularly like to send
To hell at once, for these pretend

More than all others that a man can serve
Not two but twenty masters. You shall have
The ordinary people surging round
As you imagine.

Let the gong sound
And now we bring the chorus in (some rousing airs)
And what better chorus than the Blue Hussars
Dressed for the show parade
And wearing yards of rich heraldic braid.
And what it symbolizes we don't know or care.
Now the chorus gallops round the evening square.

Chorus
        Horses, horses, horses, horses
        Cheer the hoof-marks of our race
        Horses, horses, horses, horses
        Since Finn McCoul have owned this place.
        Horse-faced women, horse-faced men—
        Horses, horses, horses, horses—
        The horse is mightier than the pen
        The stick of evil stirs the sources
        Of poetry and philosophy,
        Muddies the pool, but road necks bend
        Over true springs of gaiety.
        Burn all books, let no more be penned.

O horses, horses horses,
Are the things to run in verses,
On the course or in show ring
Let us hear their noble snoring. . . .

M.C.

Now the chorus goes and I shall call
Upon the servants to remove the pall.
That done I call on Sean O'Faolain's muse
To favour us with his peculiar views.

SEAN O'FAOLAIN

When I and O'Connor sauntered by the Lee
In the silver springtime of our Gaelic dream
We saw a people rising who did deem
The apotheosis of true liberty
To be the heart run wild in Nature's way—
Perhaps 'twas Munster we had in our minds—
We never thought that what frees also binds,
And I became the Hamlet of the play.
With yes, and no, and ifs and buts and maybes
The philosophic doubt that has no centre—
But the certainty that centered our great mentor
Filled his muse with poison worse than rabies.
Religion is it false or is it true?
Can one go picking berries in the procession?
Can the artist's pride survive a good confession?
These are the questions I am putting to you.

M.C.

This doesn't seem to make the play progress
You're leading us into a wilderness.
I want to see you lost in angry sadness
About the judgment on *Midsummer Madness*.

SEAN O'FAOLAIN

I wrote that book when I and O'Connor held
The fantasy of living warm in love;
There's faith in it and something born of
The intangible passion that has impelled
Young men to leave the cool paths of grass,
The luxury of April-furnished ditches
To be seduced by desert-wandering witches
And walk barefoot on broken, poisonous glass.
O may I lift this poor child of mine
Out of the coffin for one last look—
Ah me! I never wrote a better book—
A little bit Chekovian but—still fine.

M.C.

I draw your attention to that window there
The big bay window to the left of the square
Look straight I bid you with no artistic bias
And you will see three men wearing long pious
Faces; these three men are millionaires
They dance, they race—and always say their prayers.
Come here my smiling friend
A little nearer the window; there's no one here
Of whom corrupt Power has need to fear;
Dead ideas that once shocked are in the pillory
The writers are playing with their grandmothers' frillery.
Synge, Yeats and yesterday, the fiddle-faddle
As futile as the heroes of the saddle.
Come millionaire and let the people hear
About your road of fortune—
Now give ear.

MILLIONAIRE

Money! money!
Who measures success in money? I had imagined

194

That I was speaking to poets. Money! money!
Money has no interest for me, my ideal
Is my country prosperous, my workers paid
Each Friday evening. Since the day I fought
In nineteen-sixteen I had one thought:
Home industries, self-sufficiency, national fame.
I started as a poor man with an empty pocket
But with my ideal in my heart's gold locket.

VOICE FROM THE BACK
    Shite!

FIRST MILLIONAIRE (*Pointing*)
    Master of Ceremonies, there's a group down there
    Intriguing in that corner of the square.

PATRICK KAVANAGH
    Prosperity's purse is a heart that's hollowed,
    Virtue that's merely emptiness goes well
    With bishops sometimes . . . .

HYSTERICAL FEMALE VOICES
    Anti-clerical! anti-clerical!

M.C.
    Here enters from the big suburban houses
    A well clad woman who stops where Kavanagh browses
    Over the coffin where the condemned books lie:
    She's sniffing for some spicey ribaldry.

WOMAN
Forever Amber?

M.C.
    She pokes the bookish belly
    Expecting what is bawdy to be smelly.

KAVANAGH
>Madam, I have been a book reviewer;
>You'll find the novel you seek in any sewer;
>The novels in this literary coffin
>Are merely truth that you would find most shocking.

WOMAN
>Here's Kate O'Brien's lovely *Land of Spices*
>And *The Midnight Court* that nearly caused a crisis
>No wonder the library of the R.D.S.
>Is such a frightfully boring wilderness.

M.C.
>That's enough of that. Who's next?
>No, not O'Rahilly, he'll take Sterling as his text,
>Nor Seagrave Daly who has apples on the brain.
>Come Frank O'Connor, but please do refrain
>From getting angry over culture here
>It's not much better in England now I fear.

FRANK O'CONNOR
>I am not interested one way or the other
>Whether they ban or unban; we do not matter,
>Eliminated ourselves.
>The most immoral place of all
>Is the middle of the road. Neutrality
>Was our destruction.
>I saw the little English girls working
>In their pretty over-alls and I knew then
>That this was life with all the enthusiasms
>Of faith young in the world again.
>(*Sneers from several windows*)
>'Tis better to believe in something wrong
>Than to be blasé, cynical as here,
>Accepting every pious racketeer.
>We live skin deep. We lack the courage
>To lie close to life like the English.

Let them ban the books,
Let them ban the books,
You have your bishops and knights and rooks
And the pawns to be shifted about by crooks.
Haw, haw, I laugh at the silly tripe
As the dust of the town from my feet I wipe.
Banned or unbanned
I see no hope for this hopeless land.

AN OLD PRIEST

He has the enthusiasm of a lover in pain
No mind-frosted faith in the heart's rich vein.

A YOUNG PRIEST

If I had my way I'd never let him back
I'd stretch him and all scribblers on the rack.
He writes of priests as sinners; would you not ban
The blackguardly works of such a man?

OLD PRIEST

God did not breed Pegasus for a halter
In the fields of faith his gallop does not falter.

YOUNG PRIEST

He sneers at marriage, all these writers sneer
At the Sacrament of Matrimony here.

OLD PRIEST

Sneers!
In my parish for twenty years
There isn't a marriage to sneer at.
The old unmarried people sneer at life,
While every writer has at least one wife.
When I see the old maids
Coming along the country roads
To be confessed
I hear the blasphemy of the foul breast.

197

YOUNG PRIEST (*aside*)
>   Horrible old man
>   Country living has degraded him:
>   Bulls and cows
>   And immoral cocks in the hen house.

M.C.
>   An editor has been speaking, let us heed him
>   And then we will not need to read him.

AN EDITOR
>   We fought all censorships, tooth and nail,
>   We dared to print the Windsors' photo daily
>   And Princess Elizabeth's too.
>   We kept our Saturday poets going gaily.
>   We've got the reins of power now. The Taoiseach,
>   A man for whom I have the greatest *gradh,*
>   Is a decent man. But it remains to be seen
>   If the Gaelic child is worthy of the Da.

JEERING VOICES
>   Blah, blah, blah!

M.C.
>   It is about time to bring in the chorus again
>   A different chorus this time.
>   Will some man come and look down the street at the moun-
>   tains
>   And tell us what he feels.
>   A poet! All in rags, indifferent to convention.

A POET
>   The leaves are falling on the suburban roads
>   And red flowers in a garden look tired,
>   And there is a mist like a somber curtain on the Georgian
>   facades,

198

And the laugh of the poor is life that has not tired.
I feel as I look that we are waiting for
A new and surprising world that is coming round the turn
And the first years of Christendom. There's the same air
And the same strange hope exciting a life-sick world.
That gay young girl of fashion has a smile
That is virtue under the cloak of coquetry
And she is faith and hope in what is real,
And she has scorn for the empty musketry
Of pleasure that means nothing called to grow.
She dances now but seems to keep forgetting
The glide that is vain. Dance finished, she will not bow.

AUSTIN CLARKE
Derivative verse echoing the nineteenth century.

O'CONNOR
Destructive critic, nothing survives his breath
Greater enemy than the censorship.

CLARKE
Go back to B.B.C.

M.C. (*Like a radio commentator*)
Now around the corpse a brawl is taking place,
Poets, Essayists, Novelists, in-fight embrace,
With light of battle in his schoolboy face
Smyllie is there making a ring for the row.
Clarke is taking the count! No, he is lifted now
By one of the McManuses, I don't know which.
The millionaires from the windows look on
Filled with delight. O'Faolain takes no sides,
The Hamlet of the play is in two minds.
Now Smyllie rings a bell and thunders "Stop it!
Nemo me impune lacessit!"

The Independent's writing a headline:
"Disgraceful scenes at a literary wake."
Out of the confusion I now can see
Who's for life and who's for death:
Watch where the millionaires watch smilingly.

A SECOND MILLIONAIRE
　　'Tis wonderful to see the writers so free
　　From all convention. The only life that's beautiful
　　Is the poet's.
　　There are hundreds of poets in this city.

CLARKE
　　Many hundreds

O'CONNOR
　　Blasphemy!

THIRD MILLIONAIRE
　　There are a few there whom I would never trust
　　We'll have to prove them sinners or just mad.

FIRST MILLIONAIRE
　　No need. So long as we can keep the legend up
　　That there are hundreds of them, poets, writers,
　　We're safe. Let that be published in the press tomorrow
　　And plug the idea of milling geniuses
　　As common as dirt, the two-a-penny story.
　　The general bedlam will discredit all.
　　Off to the Scuttery to collect our wives.

M.C.
　　A group of actors has now arrived from the west
　　Bound for the Abbey and a film test.

AN ACTOR

Books! Such a lot of books. Who wrote all these?
Such trash! no *Captain Boycott* or *Green Years*.
Colum, I suppose. Those trampy men
Are writers? Very stupid-looking then.

AN ACTRESS

My mother said to keep away from writers
She said, they beetened to be very good
Or they'd be taken up by Hollywood.

KAVANAGH (*To an actress*)

Hello.

M.C.

She turns away from Kavanagh's queer virility
With all an upstart peasant's insultability.
And she speaks to one whom she takes for a film director
With a sigh, remembering her mother's "God protect her."

ALLEGED FILM DIRECTOR (*To actress*)

Come to my hotel. I want to give you an audition.
(*Sounds from the crowd*)

M.C.

Now cut the laughter! Poor Kavanagh's very sad
To lose such beauty to a brainless cad.
The Government Party arrives. My! How it swells
With young unemployed solicitors and B.L.s.

YOUNG B.L.

I think there's fifteen more years in the Party,
In that case I'd be fixed before I'm forty;
A District Justiceship would not be bad
If there was nothing better to be had.

The law's the last, at present not a crumb in,
Although I am the chairman of my Cumann.
My father, blast his sowl, he worked, instead
Of dying on the hills—he died in bed;
The bloody fool, he worked till old age got him
And so I have to climb from bed-rock bottom.

YOUNG SOLICITOR

My partner's gone to jail—embezzlement
Of moneys that were some old women's rent
But I came free
I hope it doesn't do me injury.
And I came here to join the howling mob
Of censors—it is one way to a job.

YOUNG B.L.

A simple tip, my friend, before we part—
Be seen at concerts and learn to talk of Art.
There's virtue in abstract painting—and Mozart,
But damn all native writers to perdition. . . .
Silence! Here comes a noted politician.

POLITICIAN

I love to see you literary boys
Raising our country in the world's eyes.

O'FAOLAIN

And yet you have the brazen cheek to ban us!

POLITICIAN

What does it matter what I in private feel?
There's such a business as the public weal.

M.C.

It seems to me another row is brewing,

Some nasty pens are busily reviewing
A book that tells of profits and of jobbery,
Government Gaelic screams: "*Ná h-abair é!*"
The reviewer writes: "these controversial matters
Are unworthy of the author's fine afflatus;
He lets us down in public. . . ."
   So in case
Further brawlings should our dead disgrace
We'll call in our poet to relieve
With the light of his imagination this make-believe.

POET

Sometimes I can see in these poor streets
A little village, and hear in the women's gossip
The talk of country women at a well
Echoing in the valleys.
The women selling oranges have a grip
On life that our Censorship
Would call obscene—
Life pressed in the gutter yields the gutter's dream
Of flowers.
I have no fear, new Aprils will be ours.

I see young boys climbing a wall
And little girls playing with a doll
Hell battles with heaven for every inch of ground
Yet nowhere do I see God losing a round.

And I know that poetry will never lose its courage
That men will always be moved to happiness
By the sun rising or the sun setting or the brown ivy
Or the wild swing of a young man in love
Going down the stone steps from his girl's hall door.
Let it be an October stubble field or a cluster of grey gables
Upon which the moonlight falls, our gasp will be the same

For something remembered, some intensity
Of clay transfigured in an innocent dream.
When I look down the river at the painted houses
And gaze in old alleyways I hear
The girl of the eighteenth century singing
"Cockles and Mussels." And I have no fear
For what is beautiful. The song will continue
And the children of the gods whose hearts are humble
Will hear, will hear.

M.C.

They're taking the coffin up. They're moving away.
Ah, writers too are living in yesterday,
Challenging the enemy that died last night,
For the spirit in travail now they have no sight
To see or ears to hear, or words to name
The lies that crowd around this day's life-dream.
Synge who drove people wild is now the vogue. . . .
But I must give way to the

Epilogue

The wake is over now and if my drama
Resolved itself into a panorama
The curtain woven from the passing day
Showed up the futile shadows of the play.
And showed up also, I sincerely trust
Spirits who fertilise the world's dust.

AFTER LOVE

You understand how easily I might have been lost
In the deep deceitful river, and kindly
Led me towards the shallows of sentiment where blindly
Lovers may spend their grief at a little cost.

You led me on till I laughed to find under
My feet the dry earth of reason. Now we can part.
Nothing has happened these past six months. My heart
Is sealed against you. I have felt no terror or wonder.
Was it that I was too cautious, too burned before?
Or too mean to accept the sacrifice? Did I calculate
The price of each drop of blood? The price of each breath?
And now the field of my love is empty and needs no gate;
Because I was careful and frugal I now am poor
Staring across the bare valley to cowardly death.

Today and tomorrow and the day after
I will day-dream dreams of daring, how I dared
The wildest floods of passion at your word
The poet gambles higher, rollicks dafter
Than the dumb children. In words he'll try
The farthest penance of love's ecstasy.

COMMON BEAUTY

I will forget all that was cultivated, all that was told
How to be beautiful: The sights that made
My companion point with his arm and cry "wonderful
The sweep of the land, the variegated shade
Of the mountain sides!" He knew that it must be
Beautiful, someone had said so.
                    To me
God's truth was such a thing you could not mention
Without being ashamed of its commonness:
First there is
A dark lane between a garden wall and a gable
A vegetable garden too, for yellow cabbage leaves
Sometimes are caught on the jutting spikes of masonry
And on top of nettles—

Ah, that lane, a short-cut to Clonsilla
Worn in the middle
Where a stream of dirty water ran
Its sloping banks grew broken bottles like grass,
My God baptised me there by the hands of John.
There is a cart-pass in Drumnagrella—
I could cry, almost, remembering its excitement in July
When moving with an old scythe the rushes that fringed the
    rim of the ruts
I learned how not to die.

AFTER FORTY YEARS OF AGE

There was a time when a mood recaptured was enough
Just to be able to hold momentarily November in the woods
Or a street we once made our own through being in love.

But that is not enough now. The job is to answer questions
Experience. Tell us what life has taught you. Not just about
    persons—
Which is futile anyway in the long run—but a concrete, as it
    were, essence.

The role is that of prophet and saviour. To smelt in passion
The commonplaces of life. To take over the functions of a god
    in a new fashion.
Ah! there is the question to speculate upon in lieu of an answer.

JUNGLE

Through the jungle of Pembroke Road
I have dragged myself in terror
Listening to the lions of Frustration roar,

The anguish of beasts that have had their dinner
And found there was something inside
Gnawing away unsatisfied.

As far as Ballsbridge I walked in wonder,
Down Clyde to Waterloo
Watching the natives pulling the jungle
Grass of Convention to cover the nude
Barbaric buttocks where tail-stumps showed
When reason lit up the road.

On Baggot Street Bridge they screeched,
Then dived out of my sight
Into the pools of blackest porter—
Till half-past ten of the jungle night
The bubbles came up with toxic smell
From Frustration's holy well.

JOAN RUSSELL

Joan Russell
Accept this clay vessel
As a token
Of the unspoken,

Within
You will find sin
But also you
May find what is true
And good
To be understood.

And pray
At the end of the day

With your pure heart
For him who walked apart
On the hills
Loving life's miracles
Of stone and grass
And the ecstatic caress
Of wind in the face.
Round the bends of old roads
He expected God's
Angels to appear.

And so my dear
Joan
He was mostly alone
And lonely and sad
On hill and road,
And so Joan Russell
He wanted to nestle
In the warm clay
Of Time's everyday

Maybe God will
Show him that miracle.

A VIEW OF GOD AND THE DEVIL

I met God the Father in the street
And the adjectives by which I would describe him are these:
Amusing
Experimental
Irresponsible—
About frivolous things.
He was not a man who would be appointed to a Board
Nor impress a bishop
Or gathering of art lovers.

He was not splendid, fearsome or terrible
And yet not insignificant.
This was my God who made the grass
And the sun,
And stones in streams in April;
This was the God I met in Dublin
As I wandered the unconscious streets.

This was the God that brooded over the harrowed field—
Rooneys—beside the main Carrick road
The day my first verses were printed—
I knew him and was never afraid
Of death or damnation;
And I knew that the fear of God was the beginning of folly.

THE DEVIL

I met the Devil too,
And the adjectives by which I would describe him are these:
Solemn,
Boring,
Conservative.
He was a man the world would appoint to a Board,
He would be on the list of invitees for a bishop's garden party,
He would look like an artist.
He was the fellow who wrote in newspapers about music,
Got into a rage when someone laughed;
He was serious about unserious things;
You had to be careful about his inferiority complex
For he was conscious of being uncreative.

GOOD BY LADIES

Here and now colloquially the hammer
I give to all these ladies and the glamour—

The baker's daughter—did I love her?
Her figure like a turn-over
She had a thousand pounds or two—
But Shakespeare put her with the rue.

The lunchtime lady that I meet
At one o'clock on Grafton Street
Must take this rhyme from me in lieu
Of rosemary, thyme or rue.

No screw is rattling in my heart
As I from Jo and Joan now part
The girl in brown with the girl in blue
Have left with me no lovely rue.

And many another dame un-used
To the mind of a writer smiled, bemused
Never knowing how ungentle
How brutal and elemental.

FORBIDDEN FRUIT

There is a Forbidden Fruit
Of that you may be sure
It grows on many different trees
Something that you will want terribly bad
That always evades you. And you say
If I had that I would be fulfilled.
And you never know all the time
About the invisible Guardian Angel.

Then some unlucky day all incidents
Co-ordinate into a perfect moment
You get what you want whatever it is
And you are cast down into eternal torment.
I know what I am talking about.

FILM CRITIC

For three years you have been watching pictures on a screen
So maybe you could tell us in verse
What cash of experience you earned,
What memories lie glittering in your purse.
Have Robert Taylor, Katherine Hepburn, Clark Gable,
Synthesised themselves into a fable?

I am as poor as when I started
There was no experience
To buy a rhythm's tension
All the glittering coins were made of wax.

For three years I have been watching pictures on a screen
And I will tell you frankly in verse
There is not as much as would buy a rhythm's tension
The coin was not even brass but melting wax.

THE ROAD TO HATE

He said: The road you are going will lead you to Hate
For I went down that way yesterday and saw it away
In the hollow a mile distant and I turned back
Glad of my escape.

                        But I said: I will persist,
For I know a man who went down the hill into the hollow
And entered the very city of Hate
And God visited him every day out of pity
Till in the end he became a most noble saint.

NO SOCIAL CONSCIENCE

He was an egotist with an unsocial conscience
And I liked him for it though he was out of favour,
For he seemed to me to be sincere,
Wanting to be no one but his own saviour.

211

He saw the wild eyes that are the Public's
Turned on the one man who held
Against the gangs of fear his ordinary soul—
He did no public service but lived for himself.

His one enthusiasm was against the hysteria,
Those dangerous men who are always in procession
Searching for someone to murder or worship—
He never qualified for a directorship or a State pension.

THE PADDIAD

OR THE DEVIL AS A PATRON OF IRISH LETTERS

In the corner of a Dublin pub
This party opens—blub-a-blub—
Paddy Whiskey, Rum and Gin
Paddy Three sheets on the wind;
Paddy of the Celtic Mist,
Paddy Connemara West,
Chestertonian Paddy Frog
Croaking nightly in the bog.
All the Paddies having fun
Since Yeats handed in his gun.
Every man completely blind
To the truth about his mind.
In their middle sits a fellow
Aged about sixty, bland and mellow;
Saintly silvery locks of hair,
Quiet-voiced as monk at prayer;
Every Paddy's eye is glazed
On this fellow. Mouths amazed
Drink in all his words of praise.
O comic muse descend to see
The devil Mediocrity,
For that is the devil sitting there,
Actually Lucifer.

212

He has written many Catholic novels,
None of which mention devils:
Daring men, beautiful women,
Nothing about muck or midden,
Wholesome atmosphere—Why must
So-called artists deal with lust?

About the devil's dark intentions
There are some serious misconceptions:
The devil is supposed to be
A nasty man entirely,
Horned and hoofed and fearful gory—
That's his own invented story.

The truth in fact is the reverse
He does not know a single curse;
His forte's praise for what is dead,
Pegasus's Munnings bred.
Far and near he screws his eyes
In search of what will never rise,
Souls that are fusty, safe and dim,
These are the geniuses of the land to him.

Most generous-tempered of the gods
He listens to the vilest odes,
Aye, and not just idle praise!
For these the devil highly pays.
And the crowds for culture cheer and cheer:
'A modern Medici is here,
Never more can it be said
That Irish poets are not fed'
The boys go wild and toast the Joker
The master of the mediocre.

'A great renaissance is under way'
You can hear the devil say
As into our pub comes a new arrival,
A man who looks the conventional devil:
This is Paddy Conscience, this
Is Stephen Dedalus,
This is Yeats who ranted to
Knave and fool before he knew
This is Sean O'Casey saying,
Fare thee well to Inishfallen.

He stands on the perimeter of the crowd
Half drunk to show that he's not proud
But willing given half a chance
To play the game with any dunce;
He wears a beaten bedraggled pose
To put the devil at his ease,
But Lucifer sees through the pose
Of drunken talk and dirty clothes;
The casual word that drops by chance
Denotes a dangerous arrogance,
Still sober and alive enough
To blast this world with a puff.

Every Paddy sitting there
Pops up like a startled hare,
Loud ignorings fill each face—
This behaviour's disgrace,
A savage intruding on our Monday's
Colloquy on trochees, spondees,
And whether Paddy Mist or Frog
Is the greatest singer of the bog.
Hypodermics sourpiss loaded
Are squirted at our foolish poet.
The devil sips his glass of plain
And takes up his theme again:

'My suggestion is for a large bounty
For the best poet in each county.
How many poems, Mist, can you spare
For my new anthology of Clare?
Ten guineas per poem is fair,
But they must definitely be Clare;
Some lyrics in your recent volume
Were influenced by Roscommon'

Conscience: 'I'm a Clareman more than Mist'
Mist, 'But essentially a novelist'
Frog: 'Essentially a man of prose
As any whole-time verseman knows.
I think that Paddy Connemara West
Is worth twenty guineas at least'
'I agree, Frog
West is one of the great singers of the bog—
I'll give him twenty guineas, so—'

'Oh, oh, oh,'
Conscience is going mad,
Tearing, raving, using bad
Language in the bar
Where the bards of Ireland are.
Now peace again, they've chucked him out.
Paddy Frog leaves down his stout,
Clenches his chubby grocer's fist,
Says: 'I disagree with Mist
That Paddy Connemara West
Is inferior to Stephens at his best—
A Catholic and Gaelic poet,
His last group of poems show it'
Devil: 'Paddy Connemara gets my vote
As the expressor of the Catholic note,
His pious feeling for the body
And rejection of the shoddy

215

Mystical cloak that Conscience trails
Places him among the greatest of Gaels:
In my last radio talk I drew
Attention to this Froggish view.

We must bring out a Collected Edition
The money's a minor consideration—
What most we want to bring success
Is an end to petty bitterness,
No more slashing notices in the press
But something broadly generous
We want an openness of heart—
No Olympian critics saying: depart
From me ye cursed pack of fools,
Only poetasters form schools.
You remember Paddy Conscience
'Count me out at mummers' rantings'

Here news has just come in that Paddy
Conscience lost his latest body,
Dead in Paris—
The devil sighs—'Shocking news—
I much admired all his views.
A man of genius, generous, kind,
Not a destructive idea in his mind.
My dearest friend! Let's do him proud.
Our wives will make a green silk shroud
To weave him in. The Emerald Isle
Must bury him in tourist style.

A broadcast on his work might be
A reading of his poetry.
The Government will give a grant
To build a worthy monument,
I know the Minister involved,
The cost will readily be halved.

Before we part let's make a date
To meet tomorrow night at eight
To make the final funeral plans,
For this will be Ireland seen by France.
This is the window of our shop.
Paddy Mist might do an ap—
Preciation on the general
Culture of an Irish funeral.'

All the Paddies rise and hurry
Home to write the inside story
Of their friendship for the late
Genius who was surely great;
Recall his technical innovations,
His domestic life, his patience
With humblest aspirant
On the literary bent.

All this hunger was imagined,
Never was a falser legend,
He could make whenever he chose
A fortune out of verse or prose.
Irish women spirituelle
Ran from race-tracks at his spell,
Left the beds of jockeys, actors—
These may be considered factors.

The group's dispersed. The devil stays,
Some discontent in his face.
Already he can see another
Conscience coming on to bother
Ireland with muck and anger,
Ready again to die of hunger,
Condemnatory and uncivil—
What a future for a devil!

THAT'S HOW IT WAS

Fragments

. . . But was it worth it? Have I not
Been very happy in my way
A queer fellow—hates the sight of work
Eccentric, they say.
But I've had women call on me who would
No more call on a businessman than on
A monkey in the zoo.
It was the weak will they loved
The smoker's, drinker's daydreamer's will,
I say to myself. My nature is to surrender.

I could hate like poison, it is true
But could I keep my hatred up?
No, it died—and every one you hated said that you
Were impulsive, egged on by some cute scoundrel.
As they left you poor without fear.

But now I will hate till my hate
Comes out the other side of the world as love,
Love in Australia.
I hope I shall not vacillate again,

Though the crop Men
Is cruel to the hands as broken glass
Among tufts of grass.

Listen to his talk:
"Pious children, you are good
I know you are good, for we are born to lead
Europe to the Cross again.
What's money?
One heathen child baptised is worth it all."
This man's a millionaire,

Director of three large companies:
Brother's a bishop,
Sister a Mother Superior.

"Pride is hate.
Last week
A writer in a paper called me enemy
Of the poor. Wicked fool
Today he walks the streets.
If he had learned
To pray as well as he had learned to write
He'd be a chief-editor this night.
Brain power!
It makes me laugh to hear these brainy men
Talk in their pride. A poor child's Hail Mary
Is worth all the poems of all the poets."

Take him away shadows till I tell
How this man claimed to be my friend, the friend
Of the spirit of the poet.
He buys pictures,
He hears music
He must now buy poems—or poets.

A job, I asked him for a job.
He thought and thought
Staring through a window.
Ought he? ought
He risk freeing me?
The gravel grind
Keeps humility in a writer's mind
Lift them up and they become
Impossible, they'll wreck the home
Destroy the family, send Christ back
To His manger—this he thought
While his mouth made other words.
There was no job that I could do

But would I take a five-pound note
A tiny token here in lieu
Of all the lovely things I wrote?
I took the five-pound note and laughed
All the way up the street
I thought I had touched something soft
Christ charity so very sweet.

A JOB AT LAST

Our language must have seemed among the learned
Cliches of the morning press, but we earned
Our eighteen pence a line and as time passed
On Dublin papers reporters became at last.
We climbed to art exhibitions, book reviewers
Wrote on the drama—technique that allures;
We discovered actresses, musicians too—
Every cliche on the scale we knew.
The film! We went to French and Russian pictures
Mixing with much praise some gobshite strictures.
And we often wrote on food;
We understood
Fancy foods and wines. We rose to glory
On scoops that caught our latest puerile story.
Old editors died out, went mad or sinned
And we applied to blow the smelly wind
Of the editorial gasbag.
          So came he
Who in this room before me you can see.
The editor stands back, others arrive
All showing hardness where my angles edge.
I am cussed, they say, I who seek the normal
Will not fit in no matter how I strive.

ADVENTURE NEAR WESTLAND ROW

Half drunk, he recited Longfellow—
There's poetry for you! He went on
To mutter about Owen Ruadh
And "The long-haired Bohemian"

Who, from what I could gather
Was a remarkable mixture—
Concocted by commerce synthetically—
Of painter, poet and musician.

Did it seem eccentric of me to feel
Hate oozing? The pimple
That laughed a malignant tumour?
Evil in what seemed quite simple?

Venom. Yet I was glad that I had drawn
This one for me, for not I
Was the object, but some spirit
Of unchanging morality

Of which I was the tool—
I idly said:
"The effigy looks authentic."
This drove him mad.

His hair ran down his face
He screamed a mult—
Itude of obscene words
At my "insult."

The face was volatile and there
Was history in that face
Of the unstable bog, the quaking scraw
Of a defeated race.

Then I realised that this race
Had assumed power:
Firbolgs dressed for a festival
Storming the ivory tower,

Staggering up to the gods
Trying to outlaugh the serene
Laugh at the monstrous Apollo—
What can his wild words mean?

ANTE-NATAL DREAM

I only know that I was there
With hayseed in my hair
Lying on the shady side
Of a haycock in July.

A crowd was pressing round
My body on the ground
Prising the lids of my eyes—
Open and you'll be wise.

The sky that roared with bees,
The row of poplar trees
Along the stream struck deep
And would not let me sleep.

A boortree tried hard to
Let me see it grow,
Mere notice was enough,
She would take care of love.

A clump of nettles cried:
We'll saturate your pride
Till you are oozing with
The richness of our myth;

For we are all you'll know
No matter where you go—
Every insect, weed
Kept singing in my head.

Thistle, ragwort, bluebottle,
Cleg that maddens cattle
Were crowding round me there
With hayseed in my hair.

TO BE DEAD

To be dead is to stop believing in
The masterpieces we will begin tomorrow;
To be an exile is to be a coward,
To know that growth has stopped,
That whatever is done is the end;
Correct the proofs over and over,
Rewrite old poems again and again,
Tell lies to yourself about your achievement:
Ten printed books on the shelves.
Though you know that no one loves you for what you have done,
But for what you might do.
And you perhaps, take up religion bitterly
Which you laughed at in your youth,
Well not actually laughed
But it wasn't your kind of truth.

TALE OF TWO CITIES

The streets of London are not paved with gold,
The streets of London are paved with failures;
They get up and move about when they are filled with drink
Just as in Dublin. Yesterday in Fleet Street

In a pub I met one. He shook my hand
And he was full of poisonous fellowship as he looked into my
    eyes:
I would have a double whiskey.
I was from Dublin, most wonderful spot on earth.

How was Harry Kelly, Jack Sullivan and Brady
And Galligan the greatest Dubliner of them all?
I'll tell you the name of the greatest living poet, he muttered,
He lives near Manchester and will be heard of yet.
What about Auden, I interrupted. He ignored me—
Yeats was second-rate, not a patch on Higgins—
I was back in Dublin as I listened.
You certainly must have another double whiskey, he cried
And once again he gripped my hand in his
And said there was no place like Dublin.
His friendship wounded, but I dare not complain
For that would seem boorish. Yet it was this
Insincere good-nature that hurt me in Dublin.
The sardonic humour of a man about to be hanged.
But London would not hang him; it laid him horizontal
To dream of the books he had written in liquor
Once again he would return to Dublin.
Where among the failures he would pass unnoticed,
Happy in pubs talking about yesterday's wits,
And George Moore's use of the semi-colon.

SPRING DAY

O come all ye tragic poets and sing a stave with me—
Give over T. S. Eliot and also W. B.
We'll sing our way through Stephen's Green where March has
    never found
In the growing grass a cadence of the verse of Ezra Pound.

The University girls are like tulip bulbs behind
More luxurious than ever from Holland was consigned,
Those bulbs will shortly break in flower—rayon, silk and cotton
And our verbal constipation will be totally forgotten.

Philosophy's graveyard—only dead men analyse
The reason for existence. Come all you solemn boys
From out your dictionary world and literary gloom—
Kafka's mad, Picasso's sad in Despair's confining room.

O come all darling poets and try to look more happy,
Forget about sexology as you gossip in the cafe;
Forget about the books you've read and the inbred verses there
Forget about the Kinsey Report and take a mouthful of air.

The world began this morning, God-dreamt and full of birds,
The fashion shops were glorious with the new collection of words.
And love was practising phrases in young balladry—
Ten thousand years must pass before the birth of Psychology.

O come all ye gallant poets—to know it doesn't matter
Is imagination's message—break out but do not scatter.
Ordinary things wear lovely wings—the peacock's body's common.
O come all ye youthful poets and try to be more human.

BANK HOLIDAY

Nineteen fifty was the year
The August Bank Holiday that I am here
Sitting in my room alone
Conscious of a season gone;
Ultimate failure straggling up
Through the barren daydream crop.
I must not defer a date
For a meeting with my fate.

There he comes your alter ego
Past the Waterloo and Searson's
With a silly gaping mouth
Sucking smiles from every slut,
Sure that this is Heaven's high manna—
God is good to Patrick Kavanagh,
Building like a rejected lover
Dust into an ivory tower.

In the pubs for seven years
Men have given him their ears,
Buying the essence of his heart
With a porter-perfumed fart.
Make him turn his pockets out
And his seven harvests count.
Spread out the vain collection—
Not a penny of affection.

Knock him to the ground for he
Is your sister Vanity,
Is your brother Clown
Exhibited for a sneering town.

He's your son who's named Tomorrow,
Kill him, kill Remorse your mother,
Be the father of your fate
On this nineteen fifty date.

ADVENTURES IN THE BOHEMIAN JUNGLE

A simple man arrived in town,
Lover of letters; more than that
A true believer in the mystical
Power of poets. Moral, yet
Willing for a well-made song
To let the poet choose his own.

The fruit would justify the rape
Of blossoms, though he might regret
The virgin pink of May—
And thus he came to get
A peep into the temple of
The Muses. He was full of love.

A bearded man who wore a cloak
He sighted. To himself, he said,
This is my man. He introduced
His plan. The bearded man replied,
I'll lead you through the world of art
Where beats a universal heart.

SCENE:

This is the entrance to the bohemian jungle which lies on the perimeter of Commerce.

From the depths of the rotten vegetation can be heard the screams of drunken girls.

The gabble from Schools of Acting, Painting, Music.

A stream of large cars passes in.

In one of these cars sits Count O'Mulligan, wealthy father of Sheila O'Mulligan, the star of 'Cardinal Error.'

Count O'Mulligan brings with him two gross of gold, diamond-studded replicas of the Ardagh Chalice as Cups to be competed for at the Drama Festival.

Above the stinking weeds, whose life is derived from the moonlight, rises the phallic tower of Bohemia's temple, The Theatre.

The Catholic Cultural League in procession headed by its Chaplain, Father John, who is loaded down with two gross of rosary beads for presentation to the performers, moves slowly through.

The fantasy reminds the Countryman of the nighttown scene in *Ulysses*, or Dante's Hell or something out of John Bunyan.

Through the railings is visible an apartment in which a wild

227

bottle party is in progress. Young women are being led from the main room into bedrooms. One of these girls the Countryman recognises as the highly—as he imagined—respectable daughter of a highly respectable doctor.

In the foyers of several theatres can be seen a number of early middle-aged women who are talking about actors and musicians while trying to sow a catch-crop of passion in this favourable climate.

Other sights are: politicians carrying flags, the women correspondents of several newspapers, radio commentators, the President of the Travel Society. This man is showing some Americans around and explaining to them that Necessity Number One is not unavailable in this country. Snatches of the conversation came over:

American:
If there's no Sex, what good is my shillelagh?

Travelman:
The situation is improving daily.

Guide:
Here's where we go in—
Throw it away, throw it away, throw it away.

Countryman:
Throw what away?

Guide:
The cold disgust upon your face,
The Ussherine Refusal,
The cut-and-dried opinions—
See life as just amusing.

See life as newspapers show it
Without a moral judgment,
The bank Integrity
Holds but a beggar's lodgement.

Truth's what's in power to-day,
The lie's what's in the breadline
So take your Gospel straight
From the morning headline.

Bow down to fools in office,
Keep yourself in practice,
Admire the successful,
But damn the between rackets.

Anticipate the failure,
His smile when out of place
Can blast your life. Have no
Memory for Failure's face.

Simply reverse the manner
By which you've lived till now;
Life is not a heifer
But a great-uddered cow.

They join the bottle-party where there is a constant shuffling and
poking of heads through the crowd as if everyone wanted to
speak to someone else.

Countryman:
Show me some authors.

Guide:
You saw the look they gave you, that was you
Being their conscience
Hide that mirror,
Have a drink.
(To barman) Mick,
A ball.
(To a man) How is Des?

Countryman:
You know them all.
Have I to go through all this to find
The world of Art?
Guide:
For success, yes.
They will not accept
The man not broken and remade
To the formula.
The real is too unpredictable.
Have another drink . . .
Mick!

Countryman:
This is a wonderful world.
(To a girl half-tight)
How about me kissing you?

Before he has time to organise his courage there is a commotion
near the door as the crowd rushes forward to catch a glimpse
as Father John, Chaplain to the c.c.l., passing by with Sheila
O'Mulligan on his arm.

Guide:
She's the Adjudicator at the Festival.

Countryman:
She looks a good thing.
There's something to be said for the common bitch,
She has not virtue's jealous-gripping power
Such
As the good woman who can devour
A man's mind and entrails, spit
His chewed-up personality out on to the grass
While her hungry thought goes screaming, howling wildly
For a soul, a soul to fill a gaping space.

For here is the stuffed tiger of Desire
With nylon fur and wire-recorded roar
The flashing fangs like Instinct's, yet quite safe,
Quite safe . . .
And what a bore!

Angry faces are turned in the speaker's direction. A young man
with a frustrated grin, seizes the Countryman by the shoulder.

The Man:
Sheila's performance in 'Cardinal Error' was aesthetic
The Catholic World by its readers' vote
Acclaimed her outstanding Catholic of the year . . .
So if you want your dial defaced—

Guide returns and explains that Countryman is a friend of his.

Countryman:
A thug!

Girl (whom he had tried to kiss):
Well, Jack's a friend of mine. See?
Come on, Jack, the curtain's going up;
Mummie's too tight to leave the (appropriate word) car.
Who was that bullock in the china-shop?

The Guide leads the Countryman out to get sick. Around them
they see bodies in varying states of futile lechery. The President
of the Travel Society and the American are judging a Beauty
Competition. A woman reporter is present eagerly listening.

Travelman:
How do girls here compare . . . ?

The Guide and the Countryman move away to where Count
O'Mulligan is standing talking to Father John.

Father John:
This is the great Art patron, Count O'Mulligan,
Sheila's father, the motor salesman.
Who's your friend?

Guide:
A man from the mythical land of Simple Country
Learning about life, about Art.

Chaplain:
Has he a grudge against life?
Why is he so sour?

Guide:
He is difficult, he sees life as morning in a field of dewy
    grass.
He is shocked at the corruption through which all must pass
To arrive at knowledge
He will not take the world as it runs
I fear he will suffer for his denial
Of what Is.

Guide follows Countryman who has moved away.

Guide:
Why did you insult the great O'Mulligan?
Richest man in town, worth knowing.

Countryman:
I know him;
He once employed a poet in his factory
At thirty bob a week
And gave ten thousand pounds to the C.C.L.
He has never committed rape or bigamy it is true
Goes to Mass every morning in fact,
A good beginning to the businessman's day

God nicely in His place, card-indexed,
His stomach comfortable on golf dreams
The Bishop calling round to have dinner to discuss
With him the problem of the city's poor.
A charitable man is Count O'Mulligan
Chairman of the Christian Beggars' Guild
Benign, bountiful—evil.

There is further commotion as the Players made up for the verse-play pass by.

Countryman (musingly):
Sorcerers,
Mediaeval monks,
Ancient Abbesses,
Necromancers,
Alchemists.

Guide:
Culture on the march, join in.
Oh, here's the Count again.
Be nice to him.

The Count:
The greatest of the Arts is music—
Mozart, Beethoven, Kreisler, Menuhin;
After music, the art of the actor—
Olivier, Crosby, Barry, Ireland's droll—

Chaplain:
And McCormick, Ireland's soul.

Newspaper photographers push Guide and Countryman aside to get shots of the Count and Father John. They interview Sheila O'Mulligan.

Interviewers:
What's your opinion of the atomic bomb?
Should it be outlawed by the United Nations?
What is the future of the film industry?
Will Television pay still higher wages?
What's your opinion of the American Theatre?
Who is America's outstanding mind?
What is your message to the Irish people?
Are we still the spiritual leaders of mankind?
Is religion still the force in Filmland?
Did the Cleaner Films and Rosary Crusade
Bring further customers to the Cinema?

Countryman:
O God! O God! O God!

Guide:
This is the world of Art,
Of Love.
You dream of romantic sin, the Seven
Are the locked doors of the idealistic Heaven.

Countryman:
I dreamt of sin and it was fire
A May-time-in-the-fields desire,
Violent, exciting, new,
Whin-blossoms burning up the dew;
Sudden death and sudden birth
Among the hierarchies of the earth;
Kings that ruled with absolute power
If 'twas only for an hour;
Trees were green, mountains sheer
And God dramatically clear.
But here in this nondescript land
Everything is secondhand:
Nothing ardently growing,

234

Nothing, coming, nothing going,
Tepid fevers, nothing hot,
None alive enough to rot;
Nothing clearly defined . . .
Every head is challenged. Friend,
This is hell you've brought me to.
Where's the gate that we came through?

Guide:
Simply imagine the nightmare's ended,
And you're already outside the gate
Watching the patrons, players, playboys
Worshipping the second-rate
That's Hell's secret, to be the mirror
For a mixture of truth and error.

At this point the satire explodes in a burst of wild cheering as
the Countryman joins a group of Crumlin gurriers who are
betting on a competition for who can urinate the highest. The
Countryman wins, but is later arrested and charged with com-
mitting a public nuisance.

THE ROCKY PRESENT

A girl came in my door
And because I loved her she changed me.
She said:
Read me something you have written,
Read to me how you saw
Beauty in the world. I read to her
Of narrow gaps bright with streaming straw,
Like part of the moonlight.
Of cabbages I read and how the clay
Under the broad leaves is so cool
But she pressing her bosom against the humped shoulders of
the writer

Said: You must leave all that behind you
For the day that is here is so beautiful.
You could write of a dress like mine
With its dyes, you said, stolen from the September seas.
Yesterday you praised the city
Where faces hurry past windows.
I listened knowing how right she was:
All that was rooted in clay, me,
Must be remembered no more, lamented no more.
The rocky present
Edges me into the fight for existence.

IRISH POETS OPEN YOUR EYES

(After Yeats)

Irish poets open your eyes,
Even Cabra can surprise;
Try the dog tracks now and then—
Shelbourne Park and crooked men.

Could you ever pray at all
In the Pro-Cathedral
Till a breath of simpleness
Freed your Freudian distress?

Enter in and be a part
Of the world's frustrated heart
Drive the golf ball of despair,
Superdance away your care.

Be ordinary,
Be saving up to marry.
Kiss her in the alleyway,
Part—"Same time, same place" and go.

Learn repose on Boredom's bed,
Deep, anonymous, unread
And the god of Literature
Will touch a moment to endure.

GOD IN WOMAN

Now I must search till I have found my God—
Not in an orphanage. He hides
In no humanitarian disguise,
A derelict upon a barren bog;
But in some fantastically ordinary incog:
Behind a well-bred convent girl's eyes,
Or wrapped in middle-class felicities
Among the women in a coffee shop.
Surely my God is feminine, for Heaven
Is the generous impulse, is contented
With feeding praise to the good. And all
Of these that I have known have come from women.
While men the poet's tragic light resented,
The spirit that is Woman caressed his soul.

NINETEEN FIFTY-FOUR

Nineteen fifty-four hold on till I try
To formulate some theory about you. A personal matter:
My lamp of contemplation you sought to shatter,
To leave me groping in madness under a low sky.
O I wish I could laugh! O I wish I could cry!
Or find some formula, some mystical patter
That would organize a perspective from this hellish scatter—
Everywhere I look a part of me is exiled from the I.
Therefore I must tell you before you depart my position;
Making the statement is enough—there are no answers

To any real question. But tonight I cannot sleep;
Two hours ago I heard the late homing dancers.
O Nineteen Fifty Four you leave and will not listen,
And do not care whether I curse or weep.

EPIC

I have lived in important places, times
When great events were decided, who owned
That half a rood of rock, a no-man's land
Surrounded by our pitchfork-armed claims.
I heard the Duffys shouting 'Damn your soul'
And old McCabe stripped to the waist, seen
Step the plot defying blue cast-steel—
'Here is the march along these iron stones'
That was the year of the Munich bother. Which
Was more important? I inclined
To lose my faith in Ballyrush and Gortin
Till Homer's ghost came whispering to my mind
He said: I made the Iliad from such
A local row. Gods make their own importance.

ON LOOKING INTO E. V. RIEU'S HOMER

Like Achilles you had a goddess for mother,
For only the half-god can see
The immortal in things mortal;
The far-frightened surprise in a crow's flight
Or the moonlight
That stays for ever in a tree.

In stubble fields the ghosts of corn are
The important spirits that imagination heeds.
Nothing dies; there are no empty
Spaces in the cleanest-reaped fields.

It was no human weakness when you flung
Your body prostrate on a cabbage drill—
Heart-broken with Priam for Hector ravaged;
You did not know why you cried,
This was the night he died—
Most wonderful-horrible
October evening among those cabbages.

The intensity that radiated from
The Far Field Rock—you afterwards denied—
Was the half-god seeing his half-brothers
Joking on the fabulous mountain-side.

WHO KILLED JAMES JOYCE?

Who killed James Joyce?
I, said the commentator,
I killed James Joyce
For my graduation.

What weapon was used
To slay mighty Ulysses?
The weapon that was used
Was a Harvard thesis.

How did you bury Joyce?
In a broadcast symposium.
That's how we buried Joyce
To a tuneful encomium.

Who carried the coffin out?
Six Dublin codgers
Led into Langham Place
By W. R. Rodgers.

Who said the burial prayers?—
Please do not hurt me—
Joyce was no Protestant,
Surely not Bertie?

Who killed Finnegan?
I, said a Yale-man,
I was the man who made
The corpse for the wake man.

And did you get high marks,
The Ph.D.?
I got the B.Litt.
And my master's degree.

Did you get money
For your Joycean knowledge?
I got a scholarship
To Trinity College.

I made the pilgrimage
In the Bloomsday swelter
From the Martello Tower
To the cabby's shelter.

PORTRAIT OF THE ARTIST

I never lived, I have no history,
I deserted no wife to take another,
I rotted in a room and leave—this message.

The morning newspapers and the radio
Announced his death in a few horrid words:
—A man of talent who lacked the little more
That makes the difference
Between success and failure.

The biographer turned away disgusted from
A theme that had no plot
And wrote instead the life of Reilly.

Great artist, came to town at twenty-one.
Took a job,
Threw it up,
Lived a year with Mrs. Brown.

Wrote a play,
Got the pox,
Made a film,
Wrote the incidental music.

Left his Mrs.
Took another,
Lived in Paris
With a mummer.

His critics were
Denounced as monsters,
Jungle beasts
Who hated Art

Great artist, great man, the pattern was perfect
And the biographer recorded it with enthusiasm.

INNOCENCE

They laughed at one I loved—
The triangular hill that hung
Under the Big Forth. They said
That I was bounded by the whitethorn hedges
Of the little farm and did not know the world.
But I knew that love's doorway to life
Is the same doorway everywhere.

Ashamed of what I loved
I flung her from me and called her a ditch
Although she was smiling at me with violets.

But now I am back in her briary arms
The dew of an Indian Summer morning lies
On bleached potato-stalks—
What age am I?

I do not know what age I am,
I am no mortal age;
I know nothing of women,
Nothing of cities,
I cannot die
Unless I walk outside these whitehorn hedges.

AUDITORS IN

I

The problem that confronts me here
Is to be eloquent yet sincere;
Let myself rip and not go phoney
In an inflated testimony.
Is verse an entertainment only?
Or is it a profound and holy
Faith that cries the inner history
Of the failure of man's mission?
Should it be my job to mention
Precisely how I chanced to fail
Through a cursed ideal.
Write down here: he knew what he wanted—
Evilest knowledge ever haunted
Man when he can picture clear
Just what he is searching for.

A car, a big suburban house,
Half secret that he might not lose
The wild attraction of the poor
But proud, the fanatic lure
For women of the poet's way
And diabolic underlay;

The gun of pride can bring them down
At twenty paces in the town—
For what? the tragedy is this
Pride's gunman hesitates to kiss:
A romantic Rasputin
Praying at the heart of sin.

He cannot differentiate
Say if he does not want to take
From moral motives or because
Nature has ideal in her laws.

But to get down to the factual—
You are not homosexual.
And yet you live without a wife,
A most disorganised sort of life.
You've not even bred illegitimates
A lonely lecher whom the fates
By a financial trick castrates.

You're capable of an intense
Love that is experience.
Remember how your heart was moved
And youth's eternity was proved
When you saw a young girl going to Mass
On a weekday morning as
You yourself used to go

Down to church from Ednamo.
Your imagination still enthuses
Over the dandelions at Willie Hughes'
And these are equally valid
For urban epic, a peasant ballad.
Not mere memory but the Real
Poised in the poet's commonweal.
And you must take yourself in hand
And dig and ditch your authentic land.

Wake up, wake up and compromise
On the non-essential sides
Love's round you in a rapturous bevy
But you are bankrupt by the levy
Imposed upon the ideal:
Her Cheshire-cat smile surmounts the wall.
She smiles 'Wolf, wolf, come be my lover'
Unreal you find and yet you never
Catch on. One cannot but feel sorry,
For the ideal is purgatory.
Yet do not be too much dismayed
It's on your hand, the humble trade
Of versing that can easily
Restore your equanimity
And lay the looney ghosts that goad
The savages of Pembroke Road . . .
Bow down here and thank your God.

II

After the prayer I am ready to enter my heart
Indifferent to the props of a reputation:
Some feeble sallies of a peasant plantation,
The rotten shafts of a remembered cart
Holding up the conscious crust of art.
No quiet corner here for contemplation,
No roots of faith to give an angry passion

Validity. I at the bottom will start
Try to ignore the shame-reflecting eyes
Of worshippers who made their god too tall
To share their food or do the non-stupendous,
They gave him for exploring empty skies
Instead of a little room where he might write for
Men too real to live by vapid legends.

Away, away away on wings like Joyce's
Mother Earth is putting my brand new clothes in order
Praying, she says, that I no more ignore her
Yellow buttons she found in fields at bargain prices.
Kelly's Big Bush for a button-hole. Surprises
In every pocket—the stream at Connolly's corner
Myself at Annavackey on the Armagh border
Or calm and collected in a calving crisis.
Not sad at all as I float away away
With Mother keeping me to the vernacular.
I have a home to return to now. O blessing
For the Return in Departure. Somewhere to stay
Doesn't matter. What is distressing
Is waking eagerly to go nowhere in particular.

From the sour soil of a town where all roots canker
I turn away to where the Self reposes
The placeless Heaven that's under all our noses
Where we're shut off from all the barren anger
No time for self-pitying melodrama
A million Instincts know no other uses
Than all day long to feed and charm the Muses
Till they become pure positive. O hunger
Where all have mouths of desire and none
Is willing to be eaten: I am so glad
To come accidentally upon
Myself at the end of a tortuous road
And have learned with surprise that God
Unworshipped withers to the Futile One.

LEAVE THEM ALONE

There's nothing happening that you hate
That's really worthwhile slamming;
Be patient. If you only wait
You'll see time gently damning

Newspaper bedlamites who raised
Each day the devil's howl
Versifiers who had seized
The poet's begging bowl

The whole hysterical passing show
The hour apotheosised
Into a cul-de-sac will go
And be not even despised.

JOYCE'S ULYSSES

The fabled daughters of memory are all pastiche,
God born-clean we desire;
But thoughts are sin and words are soiled
And Nietzschean blood is syphilitic.

The children take delight in levelling the city,
Violently tear down the walls,
Screeching from the steps of a ruin
Where a broken milk bottle rolls.

THE DEFEATED

Always in pubs I meet them, the defeated,
With a long sweep of the face crying;
Ridiculous the idea that you have stated—

I lived ten years in that city, and you are lying
To say that houses with slate roofs exist,
With windows, wooden floors and rooms upstairs;
A dream, dear friend, there's no bed gives such rest
As a straw bed evenly spread. There are no powers
Greater than this most ancient barnyard knows.
And you'll come back, come back, come back—
They always do—in ten years or a score
And find this pig-sty for your pig's broad back,
And in it all religion, literature, art—
I know, I know the secret of your heart.

Drink up, drink up, the troughs in Paris and
London are no better than your own,
Joyce learned that bitterly in a foreign land.
Don't laugh, there is no answer to that one!
Outside this pig-sty life deteriorates,
Civilisation dwindles. We are the last preserve
Of Eden in a world of savage states.
With a touch more cunning and a touch more nerve
You'd establish at the trough your own good place;
Meet all the finest sows if you would just
Not damn each hog you meet straight to his face;
They're all your friends if you but knew. Please put
Your skyward turned snout unto the ground
And nuts that Africa never knew you'll find.

Remember Colum and his fair-green promise,
Young maidens' laughter on a midland lane
A greater singer far than Dylan Thomas
Phrase-maker innocent as April rain.
And see O'Casey lost in English Devon
Who never wrote another line worth reading
Since he left St. George's Pocket in 'twenty-seven
Weaving in vain an alien material.
The blue and rapturous phrase, the brave banner

Of a man's own people shabby and torn
Strained on the thorn of the English manner
Lost is the man who thinks that he can scorn
His parish mother's paps. The greatest sage
May not reject his people's heritage.

Around you, don't forget is genius which
Walks with feet rooted in the native soil
Don't sweep them from your path or say that such
Are merely drunken talkers without mind.
The poet's task is not to solve the riddle
Of Man and God but buckleap on a door
And grab his screeching female by her middle
To the music of a melodeon (preferably), roar
Against the Western waves of Connemara
Up lads and thrash the beetles. This tradition
Is what the stranger comes to buy or borrow
What you would leave to chase a worthless mission.
Leave Christ and Christlike problems and you'll be
The synthesis of Gaelic poetry.

I went away and thought of all the answers
But there were none that killed his ghastly smile
Which said to me: life has no enchantment,
Art is no more than Sancho Panza's Isle;
A phrase made up to crown a pint of beer,
A paragraph for a gossip columnist,
A group of idle men and women or
Anything temporary, sensationalist—
Shakespeare and Blake, where are they now, or Keats?
Drink up your drinks, get yourself a job . . .
O God, I cried, these treats are not the treats
That Heaven offers in the Golden Cup.
And I heard the demon's terrifying yell:
There is no place as perfect as our hell.

PLAY

The scene is a country lane
With massed banks of primroses and violets
A thick thorn hedge behind,
White and red butterflies in the air
And midges filling the mouth of a low culvert.
It is a scene that makes us sad
As we try to hold it in our memories;
We should be like children and not try to possess it
And that way it will be ours forever.
On the grass margin of this country lane
The hero of the play who is also the author
Sits waiting for something to happen
And how it should happen
And he is convinced that it can happen
That it is no mere illusive ideal.
That belief is the basis of tragedy
Waiting for this other life
Which eventually is Eternal Life.
A girl comes up,
Daughter of a small-town merchant, perfect type
Of the best natural selection, tall, full-bosomed—
Imagination cloistered in morality.
He speaks to her, comments upon the weather.
He knows she fits the pattern to a detail;
She has the self-sacrificing courage of women
Who are less materialistic than is sometimes said.
He does not act, he is imprisoned
In the chamber of reflection.
He must go out and take an interest in people
And not be the central character of the play
If what happens to him is to be important
It must be seen as the importance of others.
Bring in the girl and let her speak.

ROAD TO THE CITY OF GOD

I was in the town of Mallow
And in Charleville
And now I name these names
Hoping for a miracle
By incantation to recover
The serenity of a successful lover.

Scattering ideas, organising
Themselves once more
To fight their way out of the chaos
We went through Tramore
And from the top of the hill
Still no miracle.

I talked to men who lived
By a satisfactory creed
But there was no answer in their answer
To my need.
And in Waterford
I was crying Lord, Lord.

On the Rock of Cashel I looked
Through the ruined roof
Of a splendid cathedral
For some inkling of
The order that brings fruit
Up from the darkened root.

I went through Tipperary
To Thurles and Clonmel
Seeking the enchanted moment
Where I again might dwell
In sonorous repose
Beyond the power of those

Enemies of the heart.
What are they?
Hurry on, hurry on,
To Kilkenny. This way
Is a mirage, no road
To the City of God.

VALLEY OF SENSATION

As I walked in the Valley of Sensation
A place not definable with precision,
I saw the fantasy as a Blake-like vision—
The feast of sultry Sloth was the occasion.
The gambler was there caressing degradation
Venturing madly for an ultimate shame
And he was the normal man with the responsible name
Among the business world's population.
The attitude that gave routine protection
On shopping expeditions, public living
Had dropped—and *there* was Murder in this section,
And Suicide her lily-white throats waving,
And in every class of home cannibals
With the trophies of the orgy on their walls.

NEW WORLD

I made a new world last summer
A well equipped world where everything was fresh
New beasts that only performed for one rhymer
And waters living with exclusive fish,
Everything. I was Adam. I could wish
And that was mine. Bad neighbours roared insults
And shouted loud my age where women were
Had no effect.

IF EVER YOU GO TO DUBLIN TOWN

If ever you go to Dublin town
In a hundred years or so
Inquire for me in Baggot Street
And what I was like to know.
O he was a queer one,
Fol dol the di do,
He was a queer one
I tell you.

My great-grandmother knew him well,
He asked her to come and call
On him in his flat and she giggled at the thought
Of a young girl's lovely fall.
O he was dangerous,
Fol dol the di do,
He was dangerous
I tell you.

On Pembroke Road look out for my ghost,
Dishevelled with shoes untied,
Playing through the railings with little children
Whose children have long since died.
O he was a nice man,
Fol dol the di do,
He was a nice man
I tell you.

Go into a pub and listen well
If my voice still echoes there,
Ask the men what their grandsires thought
And tell them to answer fair.
O he was eccentric,
Fol dol the di do,
He was eccentric
I tell you.

He had the knack of making men feel
As small as they really were
Which meant as great as God had made them
But as males they disliked his air.
O he was a proud one,
Fol dol the di do,
He was a proud one
I tell you.

If ever you go to Dublin town
In a hundred years or so
Sniff for my personality,
Is it Vanity's vapour now?
O he was a vain one,
Fol dol the di do,
He was a vain one
I tell you.

I saw his name with a hundred others
In a book in the library,
It said he had never fully achieved
His potentiality.
O he was slothful,
Fol dol the di do,
He was slothful
I tell you.

He knew that posterity has no use
For anything but the soul,
The lines that speak the passionate heart,
The spirit that lives alone.
O he was a lone one,
Fol dol the di do
Yet he lived happily
I tell you.

KERR'S ASS

We borrowed the loan of Kerr's big ass
To go to Dundalk with butter,
Brought him home the evening before the market
An exile that night in Mucker.

We heeled up the cart before the door,
We took the harness inside—
The straw-stuffed straddle, the broken breeching
With bits of bull-wire tied;

The winkers that had no choke-band,
The collar and the reins . . .
In Ealing Broadway, London Town
I name their several names

Until a world comes to life—
Morning, the silent bog,
And the God of imagination waking
In a Mucker fog.

RETURN IN HARVEST

We went in by the Conras Lane,
The upper end of the Mucker Lane,
And as is usual with my imagination
I only saw a flat rock that surfaced the lane
Near McCann's—
And I remembered a summer evening
And I was cycling home from Dundalk
Happy at the heart of simple worries,
Did the cow take a notion to calve when I was gone?

Nearly a mile from home yet foreign country.
Far away on my left a quarter mile
Was Ardglass
That I walked through as a small boy.

Was I going home?
And where is home
I asked my self and speculated
Can a man return
And lie again within the womb?

I thought of myself walking along the hedge
Between ourselves and Wood's back hill;
Through the hedge I could see the school, the railway,
And schoolchildren leaning over the bridge wall,

And the pink railway gate beside the bridge.
Sufficient to name these things
That knew the immortal part of me.

IDEAL PLEASURE (Fragment)

All his life he believed that a man could achieve
The ideal pleasure; often he had observed it in the offing
A young woman with eyes that spoke the old mischief
A riotous abandon dammed up for an ultimate loving.

WOMEN

If any man says his view was limited to landscape
Tell them they're fools.
Above all, it was woman as the luxuriant
Rotting of souls
Coming down to ruin him as he needed for growth.
O stinking life that has no use for a bath.

In twos and threes, for such was their necessity
For the holy orgy
God pity him for what he could look back at
Last word in torture
All to be present with each other at a deflowering.
O rapturous love, O holy whoring!

WET EVENING IN APRIL

The birds sang in the wet trees
And as I listened to them it was a hundred years from now
And I was dead and someone else was listening to them.
But I was glad I had recorded for him
 The melancholy.

HAVING CONFESSED

Having confessed he feels
That he should go down on his knees and pray
For forgiveness for his pride, for having
Dared to view his soul from the outside.
Lie at the heart of the emotion, time
Has its own work to do. We must not anticipate
Or awaken for a moment. God cannot catch us
Unless we stay in the unconscious room
Of our hearts. We must be nothing,
Nothing that God may make us something.
We must not touch the immortal material
We must not daydream to-morrow's judgement—
God must be allowed to surprise us.
We have sinned, sinned like Lucifer
By this anticipation. Let us lie down again
Deep in anonymous humility and God
May find us worthy material for His hand.

NARCISSUS AND THE WOMEN

Many women circled the prison of Reflection
Where he lay among the flashing mirrors
Hoping somewhere to find some door of Action
By which he might be rescued from his errors.

INTIMATE PARNASSUS

Men are what they are, and what they do
Is their own business. If they praise
The gods or jeer at them, the gods can not
Be moved, involved or hurt. Serenely
The citizens of Parnassus look on
As Homer tells us, and never laugh
When any mortal has joined the party.

What happens in the small towns—
Hate, love, envy—is not
The concern of the gods. The poet poor,
Or pushed around, or to be hanged, retains
His full reality; and his authority
Is bogus if the sonorous beat is broken
By disturbances in human hearts—his own
Is detached, experimental, subject matter
For ironic analysis, even for pity
As for some stranger's private problem.

It is not cold on the mountain, human women
Fall like ripe fruit while mere men
Are climbing out on dangerous branches
Of banking, insurance and shops; going
To the theatre; becoming
Acquainted with actors; unhappily
Pretending to a knowledge of art.

Poet, you have reason to be sympathetic—
Count them the beautiful unbroken
And then forget them
As things aside from the main purpose
Which is to be
Passive, observing with a steady eye.

THE HERO

He was an ordinary man, a man full of humour,
Born for no high sacrifice, to be no marble god;
But all the gods had failed that harvest and someone spread the
    rumour
That he might be deluded into taking on the job.
And they came to him in the spring
And said: you are our poet-king.

Their evil weakness smiled on him and he had no answer to it,
They drove him out of corners into the public gaze;
And the more he tried to defend himself the more they cried,
    O poet
Why must you always insult us when we only want to praise?
And he said: I wish you would
Pick on someone else to be your god.

They laughed when he told them he had no intention of dying
For virtue of truth—that his ideal would be
As a mediaeval Sultan, in a middle-class setting enjoying
Many female slaves—where Luxury,
All joyful mysteries,
Takes Wisdom on her knees.

Thinking of the mean reality of middle-class life
They saw the normal as outlandish joy
And all of them embittered with a second-hand wife,

Growing literary, begged him to die
Before his vision became
The slightest bit tame.

He advised them that gods are invisibly cloaked by a crowd,
Mortality touches the conspicuous;
They had the wrong ideas of a god
Who once all known becomes ridiculous.
—I am as obvious as an auctioneer
Dreaming of twenty thousand pounds a year.
At this they roared in the streets and became quite hysterical
And he knew he was the cause of this noise—
Yet he had acted reasonably, had performed no miracle,
Had spoken in a conventional voice,
And he said: surely you can
See that I am an ordinary man?

But instead they rushed off and published in all the papers
And magazines the photograph of their poet genius, god;
And all the cafés buzzed with his outrageous sayings—
He feared he was beaten and might have to take the job
For one day in the insincere city
He had an attack of self-pity.

He looked in the shoe-shop windows where all the shoes were
    toys.
Everything else similarly scaled down;
The hotels were doll's houses of doll's vice—
He was trapped in a pygmy town.
Vainly on all fours
He tried the small doors.

Crowds of little men went in with smooth authority
To settle this and that at boardroom tables;
Sometimes they looked up and imagined him Morality,
The silenced bishop of some heathen fables,
The ruler of the See
Of monstrous Anarchy

259

Yet he found out at last the nature and the cause
Of what was and is and he no more wanted
To avoid the ludicrous cheer, the sick applause—
The sword of satire in his hand became blunted,
And for the insincere city
He felt a profound pity.

THE ROWLEY MILE

As I was walking down a street
Upon a summer's day
A typical girl I chanced to meet
And gathered courage to say:
'I've seen you many, many times
Upon this Rowley Mile
And I'm foolish enough to believe you love
Me for you always smile.

Well, she gathered herself into a ball
Receding all the time.
She said: 'I beg your pardon,
I do not know what you mean.'
I stammered vainly for the right word
I said: 'I mean to say
I'm not trying to get off with you
Or anything in that way.

The street was full of eyes that stared
At something very odd.
I tried to imagine how little means
Such a contretemps to God.
I followed her a few slow yards
'Please just one moment stop'
And then I dashed with urgent tread
Into a corner shop.

As I walked down that sunny street
I was a broken man
Thanks to an Irish girl
Who smiles but is true to the plan
Taught her by Old Gummy Granny—
You must try out your power with a smile,
But come to the test hard reality must
Make the pace on the Rowley Mile.

I HAD A FUTURE

O I had a future
A future.
Gods of the imagination bring back to life
The personality of those streets,
Not any streets
But the streets of nineteen forty.

Give the quarter-seeing eyes I looked out of
The animal-remembering mind
The fog through which I walked towards
    The mirage
That was my future.

The women I was to meet
They were nowhere within sight.

And then the pathos of the blind soul,
How without knowing stands in its own kingdom.
Bring me a small detail
How I felt about money,
Not frantic as later,
There was the future.

Show me the stretcher-bed I slept on
In a room on Drumcondra Road,
Let John Betjeman call for me in a car.

It is summer and the eerie beat
Of madness in Europe trembles the
Wings of the butterflies along the canal.

O I had a future.

ON READING A BOOK ON COMMON WILD FLOWERS

O the prickly sow thistle that grew in the hollow of the Near
    Field
I used it as a high jump coming home in the evening—
A hurdle race over the puce blossoms of the sow thistles.
Am I late?
Am I tired?
Is my heart sealed
From the ravening passion that will eat it out
Till there is not one pure moment left?

O the greater fleabane that grew at the back of the potato pit:
I often trampled through it looking for rabbit burrows!
The burnet saxifrage was there in profusion
And the autumn gentian—
I knew them all by eyesight long before I knew their names.
We were in love before we were introduced.

Let me not moralize or have remorse, for these names
Purify a corner of my mind;
I jump over them and rub them with my hands,
And a free moment appears brand new and spacious
Where I may live beyond the reach of desire.

SONG AT FIFTY

It came as a pleasant surprise
To find experience
Where I feared that I
Had no such currency,
Had idled to a void
Without a wife or child,
I had been looking at
Field, gates, lakes, all that
Was part and parcel of
The wild breast of love.
In other fellows' wives
I lived a many lives
And here another cries:
My husband I despise
And truth is my true
Husband is you.

So I take my cloak of gold
And stride across the world
A knight of chivalry
Seeking some devilry
The winter trees rise up
And wave me on, a clap
Of falling rock declares
Enthusiasm; flares
Announce a reception committee
For me entering a city
And all this for an unthrifty
Man turned of fifty;

An undisciplined person
Through futile excitements arsing
Finds in his spendthrift purse
A bankbook writ in verse

And borrowers of purity
Offering substantial security
To him who just strayed
Through a lifetime without trade,
Him, him the ne'er-
Do-well a millionaire.

CYRANO DE BERGERAC

She kicked a pebble with her toe,
She tapped a railing idly—
And when we met she swerved and took
The corner very widely.
I thought that could be love; I know
The power of the male,
But without an introduction
The thing, she knows, will fail.

And so I planned for many a day
A ruse to soothe convention:
Stare up at numbers over doors
And some doctor mention;
Or get myself invited to
Some party where she'd be—
But all these things went down the drain
Of anti-dignity.

And then one day we actually
Did meet by introduction
And I told her with a laugh or two
She had been my distraction.

IRISH STEW

Our ancient civilisation—and—
This Christian State of Ireland!

He said to open his oration
With protective incantation.

Then, all in the Name of God
He turned on me a beaming broad

Face that twitched with a restive hate,
And this is what that man did state:

You're far too great a genius to
Talk of steak and onions or a stew,

Luxury would ruin your sublime
Imagination in no time.

And domesticity, wife, house, car,
We want you always as you are.

Such things don't fit into the scheme
Of one who dreams the poet's dream.

Your wildness is your great attraction,
You could not be a man of action.

Now, you'll never have to worry how to live—
A man who has so much to give.

My cousin dabbles in verse? but he
Has not your spark of poetry;

Unlike you he has not nobly strained—
But in economics he is trained;

He has a politician's mind
To deal with an ugly world designed;

Knows how to handle you great men,
Artists and masters of the pen,

Can run an office, plan a series
Of lectures for the Cork O'Learys

Or Jesuits of Clongowes College
Because he's got the practical knowledge

And that is why he has been sent
To travel on the Continent

To bring back the secret of great arts
To Kerry and remoter parts.

To spread in Naas and Clonakilty
News of Gigli and R. M. Rilke.

Our last art emissary whored
And that's one reason we can't afford

To risk an important man like you
In the dangerous European stew.

THE CHRISTMAS MUMMERS

Apology

This is the stuff of which I was made,
The crude loud homespun bagging at the knees,
The primitive but not simple barbarities,
The casual labourer with an unskilful spade.
Unsimple ignorance was our only trade;
Our minds untrained to tensions would not seize
The string and stretch it till sincerity's
Tune to the pain-nobled end was played.

We shouted on mountains, but no god gathered
The wise sayings and the extraordinarily pure notes;
All went for nothing, a whole nation blathered
Without art, which is Character's city name.
And that is the story, the reason for the trailing coats;
The unmannerly bravado is the bluff of shame.

The Roomer
Room, room my gallant boys and give us room to rhyme,
We'll show you some activity coming on this Christmastime;
We act the rich, we act the poor, the simple and the critical,
We act the scenes that lie behind the public and political
We bring you noble statesmen and poets loused with song
And actors who make stacks of money making fun,
And if you don't believe me and give in to what I say
I'll call in Seamus O'Donavan and he'll soon clear the way.

Seamus O'Donavan
Here comes I Seamus O'Donavan—against the British menace
I fought when I was younger in the War of Independence;
Encouraged the national language, too old myself to learn it—
And if I got a pension who says I didn't earn it?
In days when 'The Emergency' was no poor cow in labour
But war most awful threatening the world and our neighbour
I took my musket down and joined young men who were no
    moochers
But soldiering nobly for the land into congenial futures;
My face as you can see is clear-marked old IRA,
An Irish face good-natured, Catholic, liberal and gay
My hair is turning whitish (though in youth severely mauled,
Oddly, no man who ever fought for Ireland goes quite bald).
For the good name of my country I am most insanely zealous
And of comrades who got richer I am not the least bit jealous
And if you don't believe me and give in to what I say
I'll call in a Successful Statesman and he'll soon clear the way.

Successful Statesman

Here comes I a Successful Statesman, from the people I am
  sprung
My father a National Teacher learned in Gaelic rune and song;
My mother was of ancient stock and early taught to me
The fear of God and daily toil and common poverty.
By the worthy Christian Brothers my character was shaped
And we prayed for Mother Erin when by Saxons she was raped;
I played my part in the struggle—played football for my county
And won an All-Ireland medal when I was barely twenty.
And I never deserted poetry—God be good to poor Owen Roe!
And the thousand Kerry poets who were slaughtered by the foe.
And if you don't believe me and give in to what I say
I'll call in Sean Og O'Gum and he'll soon clear the way.

Sean Og O'Gum

Here comes I Sean Og O'Gum, seven pounds have I
Retainer from the Government for writing poetry:
I write about tinker tribes and porter-drinking men
Who shoulder-shove their minds into the handle of my pen.
The clans are scything song again on rebel-ripened hills
And reason screams for mercy at the stratching of our quills.
We know a hundred thousand ways for saying 'Drink your
  liquor'
When we toss the coin of language ne'er a ha'penny comes a
  sticker.
No truck have we with pagans or the foreign-backside licker.
I set my boat's proud prow to sea and hoist my ballad sails
And chant on decks of destiny for the all-too-silent Gaels
And if you don't believe me and give in to what I say
I'll call in a Famous Actor and he'll soon clear the way.

Famous Actor

Here comes I, a Famous Actor of films stage and radio,
I was born the son of a peasant in the county of Mayo;
I am the man they call on to speak the verse of Sean

And other Gaelic poets, and lately I have done
A lot of work in English that's well out of the groove—
The popular taste in culture we are aiming to improve;
And last week when adjudicating at a Drama Festival,
I found that Irish audiences liked Eliot best of all.
I've escaped the grind of daily toil and cabins dirty, smelly
And I'm married to the daughter of Senator O'Kelly,
And if you don't believe me and give in to what I say
I'll call in Senator O'Kelly and he'll soon clear the way.

Senator O'Kelly

Here comes I Senator O'Kelly a simple businessman,
I make no claims to culture though I do the best I can
To foster our great artists and though business presses so
I go to exhibitions and I spend a lot of dough.
And one thing most I do regret, a thing to me most shocking
And that is certain critics who are far too fond of knocking
The men who make their country known throughout the artistic
    sphere
Earning dollars with the pictures at which these fellows sneer.
As a common or garden businessman this attitude I deplore
But I thank God for our vigilant Press which shuts on them its
    door.
And if you don't believe me and give in to what I say
I'll call in a Leading Editor and he'll soon clear the way.

Leading Editor

Here comes I a Leading Editor who knows the Irish dream,
I'm open to every idea that fits in with the regime:
The Liberal Opposition who complain of bishops' mitres
And the rising cost of turnips and the censorship on writers.
The Press is free, the radio gives them a free debate,
New Statesmanism is essential to every well-run state.
These are not Lilliputian cranks as destructive critics scream
They are the Official Liberal Opposition and part of the regime.
And if you don't believe me and give in to what I say
Go to the bogs or Birmingham or Mountjoy right away.

The custom of Mummers or rhymers going around before Christmas per-forming in rural kitchens still lives on in some parts of Ireland. Each Mummer re-presents some historical or nonsensical character. The formula is exactly as in this piece.

The Hitler war was known officially in Southern Ireland as 'The Emergency'.

Owen Roe. Owen Roe Sullivan was in the front rank of the ten thousand Irish poets of his day. The standing army of Irish poets seldom falls below this figure.

Football prowess in Ireland, as in Hungary today, has always been a path to political success.

Contrived, manufactured verse with its necessary lack of any passionate impulse or belief is what passed for poetry among the Gaels. Phrase-making. The poet was a romantically wild man who was seldom sober, was a devil for the women. Dylan Thomas brought this bogusity to the English who thought it new and wonderful.

New Statesmanism. The *New Statesman* is the name of an English radical weekly.

Mountjoy is the principal Dublin jail.

Working on the turf bogs in Ireland is equivalent to salt-mining in Siberia.

The surplus Irish population who cannot get into the B.B.C. work in Birmingham where they are to be seen high up in the sky painting gasometers.

THE SON OF GOD

He said, "Art thou the Son of God?" expecting
"Thou has said it"—or some such words
From a humble man ashamed to admit
That he too would shoot down Pleasure's singing birds.
But I took my heart in my hands and showed it
Constricted by selfish muscles and I denied
That I was prepared to die for the sins of men;
And he tore the dust of death that was his hair and said I lied.

270

"He's great, he's God" he ran through the streets telling
Everybody that would listen. I was enticed
To accept. But I dashed over the hills when they hammered the
  cross—
The Christ that won't die is a mean Christ.

Out beyond Calvary I found myself a house
And lived there in comfort. But I could hear
Often on summer evenings from the deserts of the heart
Of man the cry for the blood of God's only Son.

GREY LIFFEY

Having read Spenser who could stop the Thames
To hear his Prothalamion—and no wonder!
I fell back defeated from the miracle.
The Freudean river clinical
Is grey with silt
To high romance inimical—
Grey Liffey run less sadly with my guilt.

Auden knows all the answers, and the question
Is where can we find a question to ask.
We ring all the changes on the emotions
Re-weave and re-weave the shoddy
Vary the tilt
Of the dead body—
Grey Liffey run less drearily with my guilt.

SERENE

The world seeks to destroy
That serenity
The moralising sphynx

That is never softened by drinks
That seems so near and yet
Far away as a sunset,
That seems as sweetly kind
As a lovely woman's mind
Exciting the lust of power
Break the neck and remove the flower,
And claws reach out—then voices
Scream helpless prejudices
At the monstrous chaste unchaste
In a veil of mystery cased.

Questions roar in the road:
Tell us are you God?
And the smile that is queerly obscene
Sneaks near the serene
Watching an opening to touch
That which they fear so much,
Which if 'twere destroyed their fame
Would not be an inner shame
In failure's desperation.
They swear by the sacred nation
Or as fans of a football team
Organized to defeat the dream,
And the devil their master drives
Without mercy their baseless lives.

And the serene with its pity close hidden
Laments for the forbidden
Who cannot for worldliness see
The Mosaic wand on the tree,
Humility that makes the rock spout
Bloody tears from Compassion's redoubt.
On his face he would lie this erstwhile
Sphynx of remoteness and guile,
Beg of the earth for permission

To act—like a muscular Christian,
Let the world know
He's not to be trifled with so.
No more to be dedicated,
Aloof, alone, hated

INSCRIPTION FOR THE TOMB OF THE
UNKNOWN WARRIOR

Passers-by on the Bridge of your Charity
Forget that my least sin was my vulgarity,
For underneath the motley I affected
A nasty piece of goods might be detected.
Sometimes I assumed the role of clown
With the intention of knocking talent down,
Or with a fund of anecdotal wit,
Parrotted from all sources, I was It.
Genius, if it happened to appear
I saddle-marked with some belittling smear.
The technique I employed to blast the serious
Was laugh it in the face, go quite delirious.
If someone were to say "God's Good" I'd answer
"His tongue is in his cheek, the bloody chancer."
When another ventured to speculate
Too earnestly about man's ultimate fate
To his cunning peasant background I did draw
Attention with an organized "Haw, haw,"
That rascal who deserted pick and shovel
"Ephemeral trash" was what he called my novel.
When the Friends of Civil Liberty I joined
He said all liberty was in the mind
And that it would be hard from any section
To pick a more illiberal collection.
Forgive the temper that I seem to show
In this long aside about my final foe.

He said a pea-size thought would burst my gizzard—
I ultimately perished in his blizzard.
All that I did while posing as a man
Was dictated by a eunuch's bitter plan.
But I am dead, pray God that so I stay,
And Dublin free to be sincere and gay.

PRELUDE

Give us another poem, he said
Or they will think your muse is dead;
Another middle-age departure
Of Apollo from the trade of archer.
Bring out a book as soon as you can
To let them see you're a living man,
Whose comic spirit is untamed
Though sadness for a little claimed
The precedence; and tentative
You pulled your punch and wondered if
Old Cunning Silence might not be
A better bet than poetry.

You have not got the countenance
To hold the angle of pretence,
That angry bitter look for one
Who knows that art's a kind of fun;
That all true poems laugh inwardly
Out of grief-born intensity.
Dullness alone can get you beat
And so can humour's counterfeit.
You have not got a chance with fraud
And might as well be true to God.

Then link your laughter out of doors
In sunlight past the sick-faced whores

Who chant the praise of love that isn't
And bring their bastards to be Christened
At phoney founts by bogus priests
With rites mugged up by journalists
Walk past professors looking serious
Fondling an unpublished thesis—
'A child! my child! my darling son'
Some Poets of Nineteen Hundred and One.
Note well the face profoundly grave,
An empty mind can house a knave.
Be careful to show no defiance,
They've made pretence into a science;
Card-sharpers of the art committee
Working all the provincial cities,
They cry 'Eccentric' if they hear
A voice that seems at all sincere.
Fold up their table and their gear
And with the money disappear.

But satire is unfruitful prayer,
Only wild shoots of pity there,
And you must go inland and be
Lost in compassion's ecstasy,
Where suffering soars in summer air—
The millstone has become a star.

Count then your blessings, hold in mind
All that has loved you or been kind:
Those women on their mercy missions,
Rescue work with kiss or kitchens,
Perceiving through the comic veil
The poet's spirit in travail.
Gather the bits of road that were
Not gravel to the traveller
But eternal lanes of joy
On which no man who walks can die.
Bring in the particular trees

That caught you in their mysteries,
And love again the weeds that grew
Somewhere specially for you.
Collect the river and the stream
That flashed upon a pensive theme,
And a positive world make,
A world man's world cannot shake.
And do not lose love's resolution
Though face to face with destitution.

If Platitude should claim a place
Do not denounce his humble face;
His sentiments are well intentioned
He has a part in the larger legend.
Dwell upon how once you prayed:
"Holy Mary Mother of God"
And visualize her as a happy
College girl in a cafe.

Remember well your noble brother
Whose constant heart embraced no other
But you, and when love's arteries harden
Evoke the image of the Front Garden,
Yellow with sunlit weeds, and there
You are the hound and he the hare,
And round and round you run and laugh.
This moment is immortal stuff.
Name his name, beloved name Peter
And only regret that words must fail
To tell that marvellous brotherly tale.

So now my gentle tiger burning
In the forest of no-yearning
Walk on serenely, do not mind
That Promised Land you thought to find,
Where the worldly-wise and rich take over
The mundane problems of the lover,
Ignore Power's schismatic sect,
Lovers alone lovers protect.

FAILURE OF A KIND

No I will never speak in the third person
About my failure to take chances—
And sometimes I feel I've about had it, arsing
Around among the ever-rising antes,
Small-time auctioneers standing nattily
Up at the gleaming bar holding on to a gin,
Policemen's sons who've made it glance around at me
Penny-pricing the duds I'm standing in.
They cannot see my mind gyrating wittily
Compassionate me gagging my laughter's sin.

But they have the last word—the scarlet Jag,
House in Foxrock and wife and kids;
My only home is in a poetry mag
And hell! I still have got those laughing fits.

MATTHEW MEERS: OR ART HAS NO MEANING

There was a man who had a clock, his name was Matthew Meers,
He counted every tick and tock for eight and eighty years;
And then one day he found the seconds turned to things
That you could work like puppets with imagination's strings.
And he who had been eighty-eight switched back to twenty-nine
About to be joined in wedlock to a woman half-divine.
Now when the men of ninety saw this miracle so strange
They all bought clocks and counted tocks and waited for the
    change.
But they couldn't get the secret from this man called Matthew
    Meers
And the moral of his marvel in no history appears.

POEM FOR FIVE FRIENDS

O my Five Friends whom I won out of the indifferent
Crowds rushing to their appointed stations.
It is autumning again over my Pembrokeshire
And I need more than ever the consolations
Of those who care like prayer; with easy eyes
Smooth down the jittery nerves; with unselfish ears
Give him hope and home and family ties
What never he did have through all his years.
O my Five Friends pray with me to the end of the rhyme
And I will in your name absorb
The poignancy of the yellow leaves coming down again
And I who thought that before now I would disturb
The relentless cycle of my character
And live beautifully as God promised me
Walk down Pembroke Road alone
Still dragging on his cursed predestined chain.
O my Five Friends, O my Five Friends,
Thank you ever so much for all you've done.

WISDOM

His conscience asked him: Are you wise?
Have you had experiences
That make it essential you write or speak?
Have you a message for the weak
Whose insane hate at Serenity glares
From the corner of a pub beneath the stairs
Wanting to bash the confident face
Of one too calm in a great madhouse?
Can you show sick heart where purpose lies
Pregnant with all possibilities
So that a man no longer requires
To be fed daily madness by uncomforting liars?

The answer to this is that there is none,
No answer, no message from experience won,
Advice forever explores the banal
So let us walk along the banks of the canal
On this summer evening and realise
This was the water that mirrored our childhood eyes
And this grass and these reeds
Can give the protection the soul needs.
Isn't it extraordinary to have discovered
That a man who has read, thought, suffered
More than many and has met
Thousands of interesting people yet
Can only offer to the hungry mass
Unkempt water and the immortality of grass.

Knowledge does not take the stage
At the prompting of an age.

A RIDICULOUS CELT

In the Duke of Wellington as the evening grew darker
In 1954 I met George Barker:
Smug he was and confident of his latest vision—
Greatest English poet since Auden went on the Foreign Mission.
Hard was the heart that I tried to influence
For all that I got was a patronising glance
Unknown to the Sunday reviewers how sad I felt!
Just another rather ridiculous Celt!

THE HOSPITAL

A year ago I fell in love with the functional ward
Of a chest hospital: square cubicles in a row
Plain concrete, wash basins—an art lover's woe,
Not counting how the fellow in the next bed snored.

But nothing whatever is by love debarred,
The common and banal her heat can know.
The corridor led to a stairway and below
Was the inexhaustible adventure of a gravelled yard.

This is what love does to things: the Rialto Bridge,
The main gate that was bent by a heavy lorry,
The seat at the back of a shed that was a suntrap.
Naming these things is the love-act and its pledge;
For we must record love's mystery without claptrap,
Snatch out of time the passionate transitory.

HOUSE PARTY TO CELEBRATE THE DESTRUCTION OF THE ROMAN CATHOLIC CHURCH IN IRELAND

Her book was out, and did she devastate
The Roman Catholic Church on every page!
And in Seamus's house they met to celebrate
With giggles high the dying monster's rage.

When Seamus gazed upon this woman he
Reflected on one absolute disgrace
Outside the bounds of every decency—
'A female replica of Cromwell's face'

Was how some rural savage had described
This noble woman—she was not blotched
Her wart was a beauty mole. He had been bribed
To rhyme his sneer. Some Bishop had been touched.

So terrible was Seamus's emotion
The sherry glass was dancing in his hand—
The Jansenistic priesthood of the nation
Had perished by this woman writer's hand.

With fighting admiration in his eyes
He could not see his wife but only Her
He stammered: 'You did more than satirise.
Great artist! The Irish Voltaire.'

The reviews were coming in by every post
Warm and fulsome—Seamus read extracts:
'The Roman Catholic Hierarchy must
Be purple now with rage. She states the facts

With wit, and wit is what they cannot bear'.
In far off parishes of Cork and Kerry
Old priests walked homeless in the winter air
As Seamus poured another pale dry sherry.

A FUTURE (Fragment)

Will you wait for me while I do some messages
I was sent out at birth to grow up and marry
And have eight children who would grow up in Kerry
All so beautiful, intelligent, none would be hostages
To fortune or to fame. Do you think I leave it late
No, that's a newspaper view that makes me see yellow.

They tabulate everything to please the idiotic fellow
Who plans to retire at sixty or even fifty-eight.
One must not be depressed at these people and their need to
    hurry;
It is all over by forty, they must take it easy then
They cannot rise above time and time's worry
They watch the television while I run
To catch a damsel caught up in branches
Of a tree conventional—astonishes.

A LETTER IN VERSE

Dear Paddy as George Barker does,
Letter in rhyme pleaseth us.
Here am I in old New York
With drinking as my daily work.
I see the Farrellys regular,
At present this is how they are:
John's right hand is paralyzed
The radial nerve he was advised.
Dede is well and I'm sure the same
And nothing sorry that I came.
A year ago was Lecture Time
An orgy out of reality.
(To hell with rhyme)
It was something that happened like a great
Love affair or an accident of fate
And we were involuntary players
At Olympian affairs.
Elizabeth Smart Barker called
Much news of London she told
How you were raging
Over the bolloxy paging
In *Nimbus*. By the lord Harry
George Barker is superior at this carry-
On in rhymed letter.
But I'll be better.
A defect in USA society
Is the absence of that moiety
Of persons who can make the province
A Parnassian metropolis.
Provincials all.
I hear that Cronin is engaged
On life of Joyce—good man himself.
I hope your Onagh and the baby
Are doing fine. I'll soon be back

About May and I may go via London
By air and see you there.
New York floats on whiskey.
The Arts Council I hear
Are publishing the Lectures,
They are in print.
Of course they are not the actual script
Though my praise of Barker is in.
I called it the Forgiven Plough
From Blake's line, you know:
"The cut worm forgives the plough."
The audience is the cut worm,
Cronin gave me the idea.
As I mentioned at the top of this page
No consecrated bishops of the Muse
Are here to confer orders:
All look to London or to some vague Otherwhere.

OCHONE! OCHONE!

It is long ago
Since was heard such a tale of woe,
Banker says we've spent the fag
End of our Hanover money bag.
At last the game is up
We'll have to work for bit and sup,
We'll have to sell our only cow
Nothing for the children but water now.
The landlord pushes us for the rint,
My arms ache, my back is bint,
My husband's delicate, not his fault
The daily diet of praties and salt,
Not counting heavy doses of malt.
I haven't a change of skirt or shift
Perhaps we might get an idea from Swift

Sell the bairns for butcher's meat
So hang on to Seventy-Second Street.
Bless us, but that's the way
Rise early, even before noonday.
If the luck's not with you all's no use
If you had the wealth of Morgan House.
No vacation for John or I
Little George will get no prize
Except Kavanagh's kind when he shuts his eyes.
Elizabeth too
Will have some reason to be christened Boo.
A couple of grand would do the trick.
Which isn't much when you say it quick.
We'll leave all to God, trust in prayer
To draw out money that isn't there.

DAILY BREAD

Touch and go. What ever was it but touch
And go? Meanwhile we must keep up appearances,
Though they, grown tight and shady, do not become us,
Depend a lot on the time of day
And the company. These two get harder to handle,
Don't seem to meet the way they used to;
At least the tow-path idling here
With all its leaves for walking on,
Must wait a while for night to call,
Wait for the wine and the laughter.
Two swans keep the lock
One dives, deep in the drift; that other lovely neck
Will follow, surely. Now we have feet, great tails and feet
Keeping themselves to themselves. . . . Busy, is it?
Making a living out of this water?

LAST NIGHT

So be it, so be it,
I have made her and she walks high
In the genuflecting sky
And cries my eye
Get drunk and run
Amoke among the crowds of words
The divvle davvle
Wisdom I
Heard spoken till everyone went asleep.
We are away on business where no challenge has priority
If I say yes there is no no. If I say piety
Means sitting with a primrose on my lap
You cannot take me up or say what crap!

Wow wow with the wai and the woa
And the smell of Edward Lear or Plymouth the Hoe

With the bluff take off
Will the bluff come off
If the bluff takes off
If the bluff comes off
It is airborne love
And the genuine stuff

Woa wai with the wai and the wy
And the stink of Lewis Carroll and London Cry.

That's the way it goes
There's a lull in the line
And a rift in the lute
A hole in the ballad
Page out of the book
But sense will keep intruding
However high she flies

Give my love to John Barrow
And every best wishes
But remember to be warned
Of the criss-crossing prayers
And the priest of the Popmen
Take your partners out of doors.

Oh oh, tell me was I drunk last night. I remember
Not a single thing, how I got home or where I
Ended up. Tell me the truth was I very
Silly. I have made promises time out of number
To keep a log of my movements and the times
I was wherever I was. Was there a woman on a high stool
  speaking rhymes
You were tight to be sure and you kept using
Terrible language in the presence of ladies
You pissed in your trousers and you were puking
On the floor and knocking over drinks on tables
And you called yourself the master of the knowers
Took off your shoes and called us bloody bores.

In the beginning I came
To name
With comic disinterestedness the course
Of this my life in lightsome verse.

I remember the first woman I met. . . . Yes I know
But the women have to be in it again. Yes
Fifteen she was and I lusted for her more than I could now.
Her plump young body tantalising in a gym dress.
And she told me her story. "I have been touched
And you wouldn't want me". And I said, "By whom?"
He was a dedicated holy man who had bunched
My dreams of having this young maidenbloom
He who had vowed to celibacy the wretch
Why could he not contain himself within

286

The coffin box of listening-unto sin.
I took what he had left without a stitch
Of lining and cried sexual-salted tears
But in the end she repaid my sex with sneers.

IS

The important thing is not
To imagine one ought
Have something to say,
A raison d'être, a plot for the play.
The only true teaching
Subsists in watching
Things moving or just colour
Without comment from the scholar.
To look on is enough
In the business of love
Casually remark
On a deer running in a park;
Mention water again
Always virginal,
Always original,
It washes out Original Sin.
Name for the future
The everydays of nature
And without being analytic
Create a great epic
Girls in red blouses,
Steps up to houses,
Sunlight round gables,
Gossip's young fables,
The life of a street.

O wealthy me! O happy state!
With an inexhaustible theme
I'll die in harness,
I'll die in harness with my scheme.

TO HELL WITH COMMONSENSE

More kicks than pence
We get from commonsense
Above its door is writ
All hope abandon. It
Is a bank will refuse a post
Dated cheque of the Holy Ghost.
Therefore I say to hell
With all reasonable
Poems in particular
We want no secular
Wisdom plodded together
By concerned fools. Gather
No moss you rolling stones
Nothing thought out atones
For no flight
In the light.
Let them wear out nerve and bone
Those who would have it that way
But in the end nothing that they
Have achieved will be in the shake up
In the final Wake Up
And I have a feeling
That through the hole in reason's ceiling
We can fly to knowledge
Without ever going to college.

FREEDOM

Take me to the top of the high hill
Mount Olympus laughter-roaring unsolemn
Where no one is angry and satirical
About a mortal creature on a tall column.

REQUIEM FOR A MILL

They took away the water-wheel,
Scrap-ironed all the corn-mill;
The water now cascades with no
Audience pacing to and fro
Taking in with casual glance
Experience.

The cold wet blustery winter day
And all that's happening will stay
Alive in the mind: the bleak
Water-flushed meadows speak
An enduring story
To a man indifferent in a doorway.

Packaged, pre-cooked flakes have left
A land of that old mill bereft.
The ghosts that were so local coloured
Hiding behind bags of pollard
Have gone from those empty walls.
The weir still curves its waterfalls
But lets them drop in the tailrace
No longer wildly chivalrous.

And with this mention we withdraw
To things above the temporal law.

LOVE IN A MEADOW

She waved her body in the circle sign
Of love purely born without side;
The earth's contour, she orbited to my pride,
Sin and unsin.
But the critic asking questions ran

From the fright of the dawn
To weep later on an urban lawn
For the undone
God-gifted man.
O the river flowed round and round
The low meadows filled with buttercups
In a place called Toprass.
I was born on high ground.

YELLOW VESTMENT

Lately I have been travelling by a created guidance,
I invented a Superintendent, symbol henceforth vaster
Than Jupiter, Prometheus or a Chinese deity in alabaster.
For love's sake we must only consider whatever widens
The field of the faithful's activity. See over there
Water-lilies waiting to be enchanted by a folk song chanted.
On the road we walk nobody is unwanted;
With no hate in his heart or resentment each may wear
The arrogant air that goes with a yellow vestment.
Do not be worried about what the neighbours will say,
Deliver your judgment, you are independent
Of the man in the pub whose word is essential to happiness,
Who gives you existence. O sing to me some roundelay
And wear with grace the power-invoking habit.

COME DANCE WITH KITTY STOBLING

No, no, no, I know I was not important as I moved
Through the colourful country, I was but a single
Item in the picture, the namer not the beloved.
O tedious man with whom no gods commingle.
Beauty, who has described beauty? Once upon a time
I had a myth that was a lie but it served:

Trees walking across the crests of hills and my rhyme
Cavorting on mile-high stilts and the unnerved
Crowds looking up with terror in their rational faces.
O dance with Kitty Stobling I outrageously
Cried out-of-sense to them, while their timorous paces
Stumbled behind Jove's page boy paging me.
I had a very pleasant journey, thank you sincerely
For giving me my madness back, or nearly.

MISS UNIVERSE

I learned, I learned—when one might be inclined
To think, too late, you cannot recover your losses—
I learned something of the nature of God's mind,
Not the abstract Creator but He who caresses
The daily and nightly earth; He who refuses
To take failure for an answer till again and again is worn.
Love is waiting for you, waiting for the violence that she chooses
From the tepidity of the common round beyond exhaustion or
   scorn
What was once is still and there is no need for remorse;
There are no recriminations in Heaven. O the sensual throb
Of the explosive body, the tumultuous thighs!
Adown a summer lane comes Miss Universe
She whom no lecher's art can rob
Though she is not the virgin who was wise.

THE ONE

Green, blue, yellow and red—
God is down in the swamps and marshes
Sensational as April and almost incredible the flowering of our
   catharsis.

A humble scene in a backward place
Where no one important ever looked
The raving flowers looked up in the face
Of the One and the Endless, the Mind that has baulked
The profoundest of mortals. A primrose, a violet,
A violent wild iris—but mostly anonymous performers
Yet an important occasion as the Muse at her toilet
Prepared to inform the local farmers
That beautiful, beautiful, beautiful God
Was breathing His love by a cut-away bog.

OCTOBER

O leafy yellowness you create for me
A world that was and now is poised above time,
I do not need to puzzle out Eternity
As I walk this arboreal street on the edge of a town.
The breeze too, even the temperature
And pattern of movement is precisely the same
As broke my heart for youth passing. Now I am sure
Of something. Something will be mine wherever I am.
I want to throw myself on the public street without caring
For anything but the prayering that the earth offers.
It is October over all my life and the light is staring
As it caught me once in a plantation by the fox coverts.
A man is ploughing ground for winter wheat
And my nineteen years weigh heavily on my feet.

WINTER

Christmas, someone mentioned, is almost upon us
And looking out my window I saw that Winter had landed
Complete with the grey cloak and the bare tree sonnet
A scroll of bark hanging down to the knees as he scanned it

The gravel in the yard was pensive, annoyed to be crunched
As people with problems in their faces drive in in cars
Yet I with such solemnity around me refused to be bunched
In fact was inclined to give the go-by to bars.
Yes, there were things in that winter arrival that made me
Feel younger, less of a failure, it was actually earlier
Than many people thought; there were possibilities
For love, for South African adventure, for fathering a baby
For taking oneself in hand, catching on without a scare me, or
Taking part in a world war, joining up at the start of hostilities.

THE SELF-SLAVED

Me I will throw away.
Me sufficient for the day
The sticky self that clings
Adhesions on the wings
To love and adventure,
To go on the grand tour
A man must be free
From self-necessity.

See over there
A created splendour
Made by one individual
From things residual
With all the various
Qualities hilarious
Of what
Hitherto was not:

A'November mood
As by one man understood;
Familiar, an old custom
Leaves falling, a white frosting
Bringing a sanguine dream
A new beginning with an old theme.

Throw away thy sloth
Self, carry off my wrath
With its self-righteous
Satirising blotches.
No self, no self-exposure
The weakness of the proser
But undefeatable
By means of the beatable.

I will have love, have love
From anything made of
And a life with a shapely form
With gaiety and charm
And capable of receiving
With grace the grace of living
And wild moments too
Self when freed from you.
Prometheus calls me on.
Prometheus calls me: Son,
We'll both go off together
In this delightful weather.

CANAL BANK WALK

Leafy-with-love banks and the green waters of the canal
Pouring redemption for me, that I do
The will of God, wallow in the habitual, the banal,
Grow with nature again as before I grew.
The bright stick trapped, the breeze adding a third
Party to the couple kissing on an old seat,
And a bird gathering materials for the nest for the Word
Eloquently new and abandoned to its delirious beat.
O unworn world enrapture me, encapture me in a web
Of fabulous grass and eternal voices by a beech,

Feed the gaping need of my senses, give me ad lib
To pray unselfconsciously with overflowing speech
For this soul needs to be honoured with a new dress woven
From green and blue things and arguments that cannot be
    proven.

LINES WRITTEN ON A SEAT ON THE GRAND CANAL, DUBLIN, 'ERECTED TO THE MEMORY OF MRS. DERMOT O'BRIEN'

O commemorate me where there is water,
Canal water preferably, so stilly
Greeny at the heart of summer. Brother
Commemorate me thus beautifully.
Where by a lock Niagarously roars
The falls for those who sit in the tremendous silence
Of mid-July. No one will speak in prose
Who finds his way to these Parnassian islands.
A swan goes by head low with many apologies,
Fantastic light looks through the eyes of bridges—
And look! a barge comes bringing from Athy
And other far-flung towns mythologies.
O commemorate me with no hero-courageous
Tomb—just a canal-bank seat for the passer-by.

DEAR FOLKS

Just a line to remind my friends that after much trouble
Of one kind and another I am back in circulation.
I have recovered most of my heirlooms from the humps of rubble
That once was the house where I lived in the name of a nation.
And precious little I assure you was worth mind storage:
The images of half a dozen women who fell for the unusual,
For the Is that Is and the laughter-smothered courage,

The poet's. And I also found some crucial
Documents of sad evil that may yet
For all their ugliness and vacuous leers
Fuel the fires of comedy. The main thing is to continue,
To walk Parnassus right into the sunset
Detached in love where pygmies cannot pin you
To the ground like Gulliver. So good luck and cheers.

THINK A WORLD INTO EXISTENCE

Now I have to sit down and think
A world into existence; you cannot borrow
Anyone' else's; you will take to drink
To fill the huge emptiness of sorrow.
I will have to try to manufacture
A colony of interesting people
Of every sort of mentality and stature,
The stumpy stumpy and the steepy steeple.
I will stay in tomorrow to introduce
Myself to all these people, admire the girls,
Listen to men's political views,
And be the pig who snouts among the pearls,
And have to hear no more the tired mood
Of fools in pubs and all that laughy lewd,
And I will also make many kinds of friends
Picked casually from my people; they will never talk
Poetry to me; co-ordinate my odds and ends
And when I am tired of them talking they will take a walk.

COOL WATER UNDER BRIDGES

Once more to walk in summer along the canal
Where the original weeds and reeds are never banal
Once more to look at the cool water under the bridges

And be excited to meet old acquaintances such as
A branch in the water and a cocksfoot of this year's growth
And be able to say I knew your father and your mother both.
Be able to compare how I felt then and the way my shoulder
Responds to the turf now that it is a year older
And not be sad that a year has passed without showing
Me any further into the future to which I am going
But just to stand with the eternal which has no regrets
The thrilling immortal grass and those sunsets
That look back at me from Crumlin. And once again
To walk with someone immortally as mortally when
We walked arguing the immemorial dispute.
A face is being slapped forever and a voice "You brute"
Is heard by two men on bicycles on the opposite side.
The evening is lifted up and in Eternity poised.

ALONG THE GRAND CANAL

As I walked along the Grand Canal
One summer evening lately
I thought about myself and did
Not admire my talents greatly.

And isn't it remarkable
I said that for a song
I only have the reeds and weeds
And grass remembered long
And chewing withered cocksfoot
I'm in the race and young

And as I walked along I met
A girl who inquired
The recipe for happiness
I said that I was tired
But if she'd join me on a seat
I might become inspired.

We sat upon the seat and I
I fear was acting badly
She said that what I had to say
And did was rather sadly
What every fool tries every day
And old fools try most madly.

And so she vanished in the crowd
A most depressing bevvy
Of smile a-once and good-by Pat
Who pays the human levy;
I choose for choosing sake and am
Head light and spirit heavy.

I've paid the price, I've paid the price
I try to cry aloud,
But happiness, say your head
Is bloody well not bowed
With Auden I was forced to bless
What is, whatever be its dress
I sat me down upon the grass
And asked what have I paid for this
Why should I be allowed?

MY POWERS

I will take a walk this summer evening through places
High up among the seven great wonders—
Light, clay, grasses,
And the four unnamed privileges, the unplundered
For the man with no meaning, the resentful
Art lover frantic in his woman's presence.
Monstrous emperor learned in all lecherous reasons
Producing a miracle for every necessity. . . .
And it is to sample such imperious

Possessable powers (as well as a modest felicity)
That I walk through this evening ignoring wild kyrios.
For I simply choose to name
Something not hitherto involved with time.

As simple as that. It's a question
Of recognising the invisible
In the awful average greenness, amid the swishing
Ashplants of men tossing the grass for some prizable
Advantage that they dropped coming over the rocks of Yes
And they can never find it, that is one sure five;
There is nothing we possess unless
We have manufactured it out of the day's habitual purile.
O only free gift! No need for Art any more—
Come with me, come with me, and take the mad chance
As Authority speaks from the far end of the bar
For should you lose, just accept the dread position
This is a gambler's theme. . . .

                                        He runs, he runs
To join a poor man's poet loud in session.

LOVE NOT REASON

I ran away from reason and immediately
Qualified for the Olympic games, those on the original venue
And it was remarkable how much Greek wisdom my Celtic pen
   knew
And I searched through the caverns of Coleridge and repeatedly
Left my know-all critics eating their morning words
And they left searching frantically for the Franz Stampl
That had brought me on by such leaps and bounds.
Reason's tail went swishing, he'd had enough as the sounds
Of pure music whizzed up from the ground. I scampered.
I stood on the rostrum collecting my lovely gold medal
Being worshipped by models from beaches and heiresses flush

With money and looks and beautiful abandon
Who would stand by me in spite of or because of a newspaper
    scandal.
Some said a great artist, others ambiguously, a fiddle
But I was away in a hack over river and bush.

WHAT TO OFFER?

I walked along the Grand Canal
In the summer of Fifty-five
The summer we will all remember
As long as we're alive.

And as the heat came crashing down
With guarantees of more
And the listening water asked the reeds
Will it ever again downpour?
I was faced with a serious problem
And my quietest conscience strove
To deny the world's claim
That a man has no right to rove.

Out of a summer evening
Merely to name the water
And the reeds and the weeds. For his journey
What has he got to offer?

OUR LADY'S TUMBLER

My verse though light I hope is not
A trivial thing facetious or
Inclined to doggrel at times.
I come to you with verse's chimes
For Easter's sake when tulip time

In Stephen's Green is yours and mine;
Once more, deck chairs and all the knowledge
That's learned in summer's sunny college,
The grass to lie on by the gate
Where we can see down Grafton Street
And get to know new blades of grass
Particular personal visions as
You last year on the Grand Canal
Got to know the mystical
View of Leeson Bridge, the view
That happened to no one else but you.

I come to you to verse my thanks
To parks and flowers and canal banks
I bring you this verse interlude
Our Lady's Tumbler's gratitude.

MOMENT ON THE CANAL

Hold it, hold it by its slippery tail
This moment as you lie on the Canal bank
In hot summer weather:
Although you have occasional twinges of pain
You are not unhappy and are entitled to thank
God that the grass you lie on is exactly
The same grass that meant so much to you years ago,
The same feel. O mother
Grass, mother me the poet's faculty
Of loving to the heart of any ordinary thing
And sitting there by the cool Pierian spring.
On the Strand the horses gallop
Commonplace sight.
Up here on a green plateau we move about,
Row of bookies
Tents,

A man leaning against a tent-pole drinking beer
For some reason this day is lifted to delight.
Is the Tide
Coming in,
Going out a woman says.
Bet you ten
It's coming in
Says a very violent man.

THE WONDERS OF LOVE

It takes half a lifetime to learn
To be abandoned, to yearn
For no respectable fame:
The wild is trained from the tame.
Rush out and bring in roses
To the Joycean laugh that imposes
No restrictions on the word
Promethean, uproarious, absurd,
But still and for all that, airborn
Above the weeds and the thorn
Of beginning, middle and end
And idiot verbs that perpend.

Do not delay, for the moon
Will be round at our back window soon
And we will see the cool sheaves
Of wheat with its golden believes
And plenty of room for a prayer
As gay and as wild as we are.
It is not a joke that I make,
I labour for happiness sake
And I ask you to dance with your thought
For all other pleasure is not.
Bring in a theme of enthusiasm.
All that intensely amuses them.

Talk of the poems of Tom Hood
And the funny spirit he had,
Not facetious, for that is just coarse,
But gay at its ultimate source.
Come friend, O come into my house
And our talk will be wildest carouse,
I only advise you of
The wonder of holy love.

LIVING IN THE COUNTRY:
Opening

It was the Warm Summer, that landmark
In a child's mind, an infinite day
Sunlight and burnt grass
Green grasshoppers on the railway slopes
The humming of the wild bees
The whole summer during the school holidays
Till the blackberries appeared.
Yes, a tremendous time that summer stands
Beyond the grey finities of normal weather.

The Main Body
It's not nearly as bad as you'd imagine
Living among small farmers in the north of Ireland
They are for the most part the ordinary frightened
Blind brightened, referred to sometimes socially
As the underprivileged.
They cannot perceive Irony or even Satire
They start up with insane faces if
You break the newspaper moral code.
'Language' they screech 'you effing so and so'
And you withdraw into a precarious silence
Organising in your mind quickly, for the situation is tense,
The theological tenets of the press.

There's little you can do about some
Who roar horribly as you enter a bar
Incantations of ugliness, words of half a syllable
Locked in malicious muteness full of glare.
And your dignity thinks of giving up the beer.

But I, trained in the slum pubs of Dublin
Among the most offensive class of all—
The artisans—am equal to this problem;
I let it ride and there is nothing over.

I understand through all these years
That my difference in their company is an intrusion
That tears at the sentimental clichés
They can see my heart squirm when their star rendites
The topmost twenty in the lowered lights.
No sir, I did not come unprepared.

Oddly enough I begin to think of Saint Francis
Moving in this milieu (of his own time of course)
How did he work the oracle?
Was he an old fraud, a non-poet
Who is loved for his non-ness
Like any performer?

I protest here and now and forever
On behalf of all my peoples who believe in Verse
That my intention is not satire but humaneness
An eagerness to understand more about sad man
Frightened man, the workers of the world
Without being savaged in the process.
Broadness is my aim, a broad road where the many
Can see life easier—generally.

Here I come to a sticky patch
A personal matter that perhaps

304

Might be left as an unrevealed hinterland
For our own misfortunes are mostly unimportant.
But that wouldn't do.
So with as little embarrassment as possible I tell
How I was done out of a girl,
Not as before by a professional priest but by
The frightened artisan's morality.

It was this way.
She, a shopgirl of nineteen or less
Became infatuated by the old soldier,
The wide travelled, the sin-wise.
Desdemona-Othello idea.
O holy spirit of infatuation
God's gift to this poetic nation!

One day her boss caught her glance.
'You're looking in his eyes' he said.
From then on all the powers of the lower orders—
Perhaps all orders—were used to deprive me of my prize
Agamemnon's Briseis.
It soured me a bit as I had
Everything planned, no need to mention what,
Except that it was August evening under whitethorn
And early blackberries.

In many ways it is a good thing to be cast into exile
Among strangers
Who have no inkling
Of The Other Man concealed
Monstrously musing in a field.
For me they say a Rosary
With many a glossary.

POEM TO THE NEW FORMULA

The gardener is coming with his spade and rake,
Darling, listen to the dying weeds,
Where shall we listen for old time's sake?
Darling, listen to the dying weeds.

The sun is shining in the whitethorn tree,
Darling, listen to the coloured birds,
This is our own infinity
Darling, listen to the coloured birds.

Down the lane where we walked as lovers
Darling, stand in your old footprints,
This is the past the poet recovers,
Darling, stand in your old footprints.

Have we a thought we might here insert
Darling, that would suggest a real
Passion pulsing in this great inert,
Darling, if only we were real.

THE GAMBLER: A BALLET WITH WORDS
EXPLANATION

Here we have a work of fiction, purporting
To portray the ways of the poet-artist,
It has gone wrong in places, missed
The secret of love—the gift
Of the poet's knowledge that is subject to no sporting
Chance on a wheel. The idealist
Is a man sick for art's panacea, courting
Remote beauties. But the poet's snorting
Is for schoolgirls or large women full of drive.
Roulette life is for fools. Being alive—
Surprisingly quite rare— is a solid factor,
But we must conventionalise for the actor
And play the artifices to show the true.

For the artifice cold and implacable
Has an inhuman beauty for our pleasure
The dancers are a variable treasure
In a world so noisily cackable.
From a normal viewpoint they are untackable
Stylised sex sinful but inbackable
Essentially as toys meant
Unlike Annie Besant
Whose backside was quite whackable
When we want to be withdrawn they are the answer
To many problems in a television society.
You are in a low pub reading the paper
And you see in the monstrous mirrors the sleething dancer
Who demands of you no emotional moiety
Or your attention as he capes his caper.

THE GAMBLER: A BALLET

Here we go round the mystic wheel
Dancing a wild Gaelic reel
Gambling on the ideal.

I have nothing to announce
On any subject yet once
I was full of bounce

At what I can't say
At this time of day
But it was all felt violently

By god and by guss
It's not that but this
Like Wyndham Lewis.

The theme here invented
And by me patented
Psychology bended

Is about a poor hero
Who gambled on Zero
There's no rhyme but Nero.

Happiness can be achieved
This hero believed
As the roulette wheel revved.

And so it can
Happen to a man
That's the tan—

Talising thing
We nearly made it sing
Great glory to the king.

This sad fool
Knew he could scoop the pool
Of the beautiful

Have a beauty of vast sexuality
And brutality
Not the ideal but the actuality.

Such is our act
Not quite divorced from fact
By fate we are racked.

He danced with the red
Even money to bed
But no maidenhead

He danced with the black
Who will fall on her back
For a twopenny smack

While he plays his high jinks
It's much later than he thinks
He'll be alone with his drinks.

There's only eighty years at most
And he cannot see his own interest
Tawdry marriage at best.

Zero is just
A thin aspect of lust
O huge thighs, enormous bust

And see the schoolgirls
Repugnant to morals
Wait by the pillars

The key of all treasure
The secret of pleasure
Is what you can measure.

He plays for disaster
Some slow and some faster
I am Fate and the master

I am Art and not life
I will give him a wife
And a houseful of strife.

She roars in my rhyme
I want him him
To rip me in twain.

Unmaiden me with ferocity
There's nothing like audacity
For a virgin's capacity
On no ceremony stand
You've the whip in your hand
I'm at your command.

The croupier Fate
Is in quite a state
When I tell him to quit.

I the king
Decide everything
Dancers you've had your fling.

I choose
A sixteen year old muse
For my idealist. Here's news
Disperse, die fade
Fool, unmaid
Zero
Hero
You've the tools of the trade

There's really nothing one can say
Useful we all mess up our play
And fail any old way.

NEWS ITEM

In Islington for the moment I reside
A hen's race from Cheapside
Where Tom the peeping sun first eyed.

Where Gilpin's horse had bolted
All the traffic halted
The man on board was malted.

And in these romantic lots
I run into Paul Potts
Noticing the pull of roots.

I have taken roots of love
And will find it pain to move.
Betjeman, you've missed much of

The secrets of London while
Old churches you beguile
I'll show you a holier aisle—

The length of Gibson Square
Caught in November's stare
That would set you to prayer.

Dickens—all the clichés
Revert to the living species
Ideas with the impact of Nietzsche's.

I walk in Islington Green
Finest landscape you ever seen
I'm as happy as I've ever been.

A SUMMER MORNING WALK

The sun is hot, long days, yet summer
Finds me very little dumber
Than last winter in grey old London

Lying on a bed in a basement, unable
To lift my sickness to a fable,
Hating the sight of a breakfast table.

On Christmas Day stretched out, how awful
Not heeding the Church's orders lawful
While everyone else is having a crawful.

It is black all round as terror stricken
I climb stone steps, trying not to weaken,
My legs are taking a terrible licking.

To the King Edward, empty of pudds
Two friends and I in crumpled duds
Go to talk with John Heath-Stubbs.

O Charles Dickens with your Scrooge
I would gladly have taken refuge,
I was as sick as the devil's puke.

I try to be merry those three lit hours
Then back to the subterranean fires
Drinking whisky to the sound of lyres.

Odd how such things six months later
Leap up as laughter's instigator
From the depths of that Paddington crater.

I must avoid being unfrank
The plain truth is that I drank
More than would kill a New York yank.

And verse that can redeem a soul
And make a body beautiful
I did not work at it at all.

O there is a Muse not good and gracious
But long suffering, and tenacious
She will not have a man stay stocious.

I hope I am not being clammy,
The whisky bottle I loved like mammy
The curse of drink! let's not get hammy.

I just want to assure all
That a poem made is a cure-all
Of any soul-sickness. Toolooral!

Today in the street I was astonished
The years had left me so unpunished,
I was in love with women—honest!

The Word is the messenger of the eye.
The old canal is as full of blue sky
As a year ago and so kind to I.

That Grand Canal into which I was pushed
At wetting me must have surely blushed.
The men who did the job were cursed:

I had praised it in many a sonnet
And the dear swans that lived upon it—
So for the grudgers to hell or Connaught!

Now I must speak to people but keep intact
The virginal knowledge, converse about fact
Newspaper news of some international pact.

It is only twelve o'clock noon
And I have experienced about one
Millionth of a day begun.

I meet a man whom I once had pumped
With ideas, he was sad and humped
Like a market that had downward slumped.

The ideas I had upon him forced
Were gone and left him much worse the worst
And to think how amusingly he had discoursed.

Very nearly a poet complete with irony,
Knowledged in every literary joinery,
He used to dress in poetic finery.

And then he leaked and although I strove
To fill him with the breath of love
The fatal puncture still blew off.

It was sad to see the empty bag
Blown about like a dirty rag.
But let us be humble and never brag.

The way things were going he thought my stuff
Contained far too much Parnassian guff,
As a businessman he had enough.

So I went on my way carrying the flame
On to the ultimate Olympic Game
Where no one belonging ever gives in.

Out of weakness more than muscle
Relentlessly men continue to tussle
With the human-eternal puzzle.

There were gulls on the pond in St. Stephen's Park
And many things worth a remark.
I sat on a deck-chair and started to work

On a morning's walk not quite effectual,
A little too unselectual
But what does it count in the great perpetual?

I revert once more to those limpid arses
Which for me can give the ideal catharsis,
But the memory of what's lost saddens and embarrasses.

I must be content with the roses—
But sitting in deck-chairs Holy Moses!
University girls here in roly-poses.

I certainly enjoyed myself thoroughly
Rambling idly and rather amorally
For a whole hour. Now surely

I can lie on the grass, feel no remorse
For idling, I have worked at verse
And exorcised a winter's curse.

A BALLAD

O Cruel are the women of Dublin's fair city
They smile out of cars and are gone in a flash,
You know they are charming and gay in their hearts
And would laugh as vivaciously buried in chaff
As they would underneath a pink shower of confetti.

I knew one in Baggot Street, a medical student
Unless I am greatly mistaken is she;
Her smile plays a tune on my trembling psyche
At thirty yards range, but she passes by me
In a frost that would make Casanova be prudent.

It's the same everywhere—the wish without will,
And it tortures, yet I would not change it for all
The women from Bond Street right down to The Mall,
For wealth is potential, not the remedies at call,
I say as I walk down from Baggot Street Bridge.

POETRY

When I was growing up and for many years after
I was led to believe that poems were thin
Irrelevant, well out of the draught of laughter
With headquarters the size of the head of pin.
I do not wonder now that my mother moaned
To see her beloved son an idiot boy;
He could not see what was before his face, the ground
Tremulous with living, infinite as Cleopatra's variety.
He stumbled on the secret door that leads to the heaven
Of human satisfaction, a purpose and did not know it.
An army of grass blades were at his call, million and million
Kept saying to him we nearly made Whitman a poet.
Years after in Dublin in summer past midnight o'clock
They called to him vainly from curb stones on Bachelor's Walk.

A CHRISTMAS CAPER

To all my Journal friends and others
Who're bound by ties as strong as tethers
A Happy Christmas, sisters, brothers,

For all who work upon the paper
I cut this poetic caper
And wishing well to my baddest neighbour:

There's none of them would see my cow
Sunk in a bog-hole anyhow
Or interfere with my old swing plough.

God Grant you His indemnity
From every serious calamity
And here's a health to Paddy Jemmety.

And see how I begin to remember
Many a Twenty-fifth of December
Christmas with its star-high number.

In Inniskeen coming up high steps
Besides the graves of the native septs
I was young and healthy and holy—perhaps.

There was no electric light
But candelabras from a height
Dropping grease. O Blessed sight!

And the harmonium worked by bellows
Blaring Adeste for us fellows—
The tenor voice was John McNello's.

Then it was Dingle, love-lost years later,
The lovely lady I could not get her,
She gave me the brush-off—the creature!

And I drank my grief but it would not sink,
In love there is no double think
For nights I could not sleep a wink.

But I have memories with Sean a' Cota
Walking to Ballyferriter, botha
Little drunk and somewhat tuatha.

Later New York, Mid-town Manhattan
Long way from Inniskeen and Drumcatton
With St. Patrick's congregation frattin.

Back to the Algonquin looking in
At Arthur Godfrey advertising gin,
Ringing up friends—call round at ten.

I remember too with a crust of bread
Bust and forgotten on Pembroke Road.
But the past is dead, let us look ahead

But cheers, cheers, may jolly holly
Christmas blossom from all our folly.
Things aren't too bad actually.

THE OLD TIME CHRISTMAS STORY 1960

O children of the television era
I wish that you had known
The Christmas number of the *Weekly Freeman*
Our Boys and *Ireland's Own.*
Cartoons by Gordon Brewster. Dear a
Dear! The Flintstones are only lumps of stone.

There was kissing under the mistletoe
In the oldtime Christmas story,
And bells were ringing across the snow
And the stars glittering in glory.
There was homecoming. The trap had to go
To meet the train in a hurry
For after twenty years in the States
And dressed all in dollar green
Sheumas comes home to her who waits,
His own faithful Kathleen:
They hug by the dresser of shining plates—
O happy, happy scene.

There are scores of children in brightest crayon
Playing with red and green toys.
This is Christmas Day and friends all stray in;
And now a young girl's voice
Singing praise of Erin, and freedom's in
The hearts of girls and boys.

Round the dining room the family sit
Grandma and grandpa are there,
And all are radiant, all are lit
I am not being cynical, dear,
For I read these stories as a kid
In a country bleak and drear.

And our kitchen floor of pot-hole clay
Was changed as we read
To a carpeted room on Christmas Day.
Romance was in every head.
A brandy-flamed pudding came in on a tray
Carried high by a well-off dad.

PUZZLE

The rhyme's the thing, I assure you I will stake
My reputation on this most plain assertion
And those who know me I'm not the person
To back a horse that can't accelerate.
A rhyming dictionary is far more valuable
Than the inspiration of sweet thirty-seven.
There's heaven, Devon, Kevin, half-eleven,
A scholar's puzzle that is never soluble.
And there's in Blancherstown hospital John Jordan
About to decode these verses, this bamboozle
Which is not as much as it seems. I whistle
I twiddle the knob and wait till something's turned on.
No good, no go, I lose my bet and burden
And all that I have left is a barefaced puzzle.

LITERARY ADVENTURES

I am here in a garage in Monaghan.
It is June and the weather is warm,
Just a little bit cloudy. There's the sun again
Lifting to importance my sixteen acre farm.
There are three swallows' nests in the rafters above me
And the first clutches are already flying.
Spread this news, tell all if you love me,
You who knew that when sick I was never dying
(Nae gane, nae gane, nae frae us torn
But taking a rest like John Jordan).
                              Other exclusive
News stories that cannot be ignored:
I climbed Woods' Hill and the elusive
Underworld of the grasses could be heard,
John Lennon shouted across the valley,
Then I saw a new June moon, quite as stunning
As when young we blessed the sight as something holy . . .
Sensational adventure that is only beginning.

For I am taking this evening walk through places
High up among the Six Great Wonders,
The power privileges, the unborn amazes
The unplundered
Where man with no meaning blooms
Large in the eyes of his females:
He doesn't project, nor even assumes
The loss of one necessary believer.
It's as simple as that, it's a matter
Of walking with the little gods, the ignored
Who are so seldom asked to write the letter
Containing the word
O only free gift! no need for Art any more
When Authority whispers like Tyranny at the end of a bar.

HAVING TO LIVE IN THE COUNTRY

Back once again in wild, wet Monaghan
Exiled from thought and feeling,
A mean brutality reigns:
It is really a horrible position to be in
And I equate myself with Dante
And all who have to live outside civilization.
It isn't a question of place but of people;
Wordsworth and Coleridge lived apart from the common man,
Their friends called on them regularly.
Swift is in a somewhat different category
He was a genuine exile and his heavy heart
Weighed him down in Dublin.
Yet even he had compensations for in the Deanery
He received many interesting friends
And it was the eighteenth century.

I suppose that having to live
Among men whose rages
Are for small wet hills full of stones
When one man buys a patch and pays a high price for it
That is not the end of his paying.
"Go home and have another bastard" shout the children,
Cousin of the underbidder, to the young wife of the purchaser.
The first child was born after six months of marriage.
Desperate people, desperate animals.
What must happen the poor priest
Somewhat educated who has to believe that these people have
    souls
As bright as a poet's—though I don't, mind, speak for myself.

JULY EVENING

It's really marvellous this evening the first day of July
Nineteen-sixty-two, eight in the evening, you haven't to try

For meanings; all you have to do is to state
A few facts: the corn is shot out
And the swamp by Caffreys is a forest of yellow flaggers.
O Muse, today you cannot call us beggars,
Every man his own poet, walks down the lane
Ennumerate the same old things again
And they are not old at all, they only arrived
A few hours ago. How wonderful to have lived
To see these miracles, to feel the power
Of Pope or Milton living at this hour.
And gather round me fathers, mothers, daughters, sons
And let us celebrate the plentitude as once
When we were twenty-two.
O let us just take notice from our pew.

QUESTION TO LIFE

Surely you would not ask me to have known
Only the passion of primrose banks in May
Which are merely a point of departure for the play
And yearning poignancy when on their own.
Yet when all is said and done a considerable
Portion of living is found in inanimate
Nature, and a man need not feel miserable
If fate should have decided on this plan of it.
Then there is always the passing gift of affection
Tossed from the windows of high charity
In the office girl and civil servant section
And these are no despisable commodity.
So be reposed and praise, praise praise
The way it happened and the way it is.

LECTURE HALL

To speak in summer in a lecture hall
About literature and its use

I pick my brains and tease out all
To see if I can choose
Something untarnished, some new news

From experience that has been immediate,
Recent, something that makes
The listener or reader
Impregnant, something that reinstates
The poet. A few words like birth-dates

That brings him back in the public mind,
I mean the mind of the dozen or so
Who constantly listen out for the two-lined
Message that announces the gusto
Of the dead arisen into the sun-glow.

Someone in America will note
The apparent miracle. In a bar
In Greenwich Village some youthful poet
Will mention it, and a similar
In London or wherever they are

Those pickers-up of messages that produce
The idea that underneath the sun
Things can be new as July dews—
Out of the frowsy, the second-hand won . . .
Keep at it, keep at it while the heat is on
I say to myself as I consider
Virginal crevices in my brain
Where the never-exposed will soon be a mother.
I search for that which has no stain,
Something discovered vividly and sudden.

THE POET'S READY RECKONER

Nothing more to be done in that particular
Direction, nothing now but prayer—

Watching, regarding, piecing together a new curricula.
An un-angry enumerator
Handling all sorts of littleness as it has to be handled
As if it were in the eyes
Enormous as an English biographer's tittle-tattle
All held low so gossip can settle
Close in the nest
I brooding must itemise
Consider every colour and marking
Search out for letters
Pretend I am interested in important writers.
  That's not the game no more,
  We have no game no more
Must catch that rhyme that up there I left parking

  We have no game no more
  Some one stole our game
  And left us high and dry
  On a beliefless shore
  But it ain't no shame
Plainly the only thing is not to be a bore
To ourselves; no more to it than that
I have to live here in the country till I get a flat.

When first walking along these roads
Nobody but myself walked there
But wait a minute, an hour a day
There are men and women behaving
There are girls in troubled love
And all that I need to do is weave the action
And many may do things quite valuable.

Form.
Life At Work—Do not Disturb.
I am independent now.
I know what I must write if I can
This is the beginning of my Five Year Plan
Concerned am I with the activities of my own man.

And a week ago I idled,
That is to say I roared and cursed over the position
Broke, I had a good excuse for not caring
Arts Council croppers harvesting and sharing
And my deserted village all ill-faring
Activity on every front
And nought for the poor bastard who bore the brunt
Of the day's battle—blood and sweat and grunt
Satire a desert that yields no——
As I have mentioned on many an occasion
Living in the country is a hard old station.

In the pubs everyone talks about age
My age, they know it to a day
No use lying on that score
I could get away from it all if I had a motor.
I must remember to absorb
Like a sponge, not disturb
By projecting my knowledge
It's hard work at Experience's college.

When drawn into involvement with the barmaid
By sharp-nosed fellows from the Assistant Mountains
Of Castleblaney
I will let the embarrassment run its course
Be rather glad
A little of this is good.
To be always protected by a bodyguard
Of reserve, remoteness—putting them in their place
With a word from There
Is quite unhard
But no use when you return to a vacant room.
Now that I've cottoned on to holy hoarding
Pelman himself could not increase my wording
To take it at its least value

I never suffer from malnu-
Trition. Or need for grog
I make a product I can easily flog
I am a small country exporting
The pill of meaning to those
Whom the condition is hurting
At this moment I can make spells
Whatever I say goes
Come London-Irish to me your voided souls
Shall not be left unfilled
I am more than a pub or club
I am the madhouse that spilled,
Spills, the true reason
The abandoned laughing of the free
You were Behaned in Egypt
And the alien-milled
Corn had no vitamins of hope
You're ill poor folks and suffering from gripe.

And all this is a mere side-product. Into me never entered
Care for you. I am self-centered
But bunch of bums
I throw you these bewitching crumbs
I give you the womb
Of the poem.

In the disused railway siding
(O railway that came up from Enniskillen)
A new living is spreading
Dandelions that grow from wagon-grease
I stand on the platform
And peace, perfect peace
Descends on me.

I said to Maggie a most purist maid
Can you explain the modern parade

Of tycoons sultaning it with shabby whores
Notorious nobodys in a world of bores
She said that that was twentieth-century play
As we lay together on an ex-railway

She said all public heroes were the same
From pimp descended and the poxy dame
Glittering in dinner dress in brass tiaras
No poet could be interested in those arses
I saw that this was probably the case
Private beauty and green happiness
Demand much courage. And I recalled
Being asked by poor fellows if I willed
Their right to enjoy a picture say or book
So glad when I gave the green light were those folk
They had enjoyed that most uproarious play
And were so glad that they had laughed.
                    Away

Begone dull care thou has not got a chance
The rapturous eagles soar us up from Hence
                    To Thence
                    From Sense.

My love lies at the gates of foam
The last dear wreck of day
And William H. Burroughs collages the poem
As the curfew tolls the knell of Gray.

SENSATIONAL DISCLOSURES!

(KAVANAGH TELLS ALL)

Kavanagh tells all,
Lays bare his soul

For the good of his neighbours
And the Sunday papers.
Patiently he labours
To advise and warn
Poets soft in the horn.
Rising from his own dirt
He sends this sensational report:

He frittered away
A talent that could flay
D. J. Enright—say;
He could disburse
A fabulosity of verse,
Could swallow without dodgery
Ted Hughes' menagerie,
He often spat forth
Lions of more wrath.

But Kavanagh, the dog,
Took to the grog
Leaving Larkin and Logue
Manufacturing fog,
And even MacNeice
Making ground in the race.

But he'll have the last laugh
On Davie and Hough
For as he went wandering
In a valley, deep thundering
From long-muted fellows
Conspired in some hello's
To halt him as he rambled,
Drank brandy and gambled:

O Kavanagh repent
And start to invent

An amenable myth
Of everyday width
To meet every condition
Outside genuine passion.
Learn to shovel:
A bulldozer novel.
Make critical works
Like those industrious jerks
Who don't even relax
When they go to the jakes.

Gladden our days
With musical plays—
And profoundest believer
Write prayers for the Beaver.
And then of the sum
Make a megaton bomb.

So he sailed up the Cydnus
To Chatto and Windus
And with one cannonade
Wrecked the critical trade.

Rumble and roar
In the poetry war.
American bums
Change the angle of thumbs
And get on the blower
To find out the score
(Post Spanish Civil War.)
Oscar Williams is sore
Screaming to harass
The heart of Alvarez,
Starts to eat till he'll founder
The files of *Encounter*.
'Why wasn't I told
Of new gallups polled?'

The battle is on,
There are gasps from Thom Gunn
Elizabeth Jennings
Suspends all her pennings,
To meet new assessments
Edith burns her vestments.

And that's how it was
When Kavanagh uprose
From his dosshouse of filth
In vulgar good health.
Next week he'll reveal
All about the smell
From Soviet poets who rebel
Against what is dead,
Reminiscent of Hampstead.

Tame, tame, tame, tame,
Kavanagh lifts the lid of same
Exposes all the guilty men,
The selectors of the team.

MERMAID TAVERN

No System, no Plan,
Yeatsian invention
No all-over
Organisational prover.
Let words laugh
And people be stimulated by our stuff.

Michelangelo's Moses
Is one of the poses
Of Hemingway
Jungle-crashing after prey

Beckett's garbage-can
Contains all our man
Who without fright on his face
Dominates the place
And makes all feel
That all is well.

Yet without smuggery
Of the smirk of buggery
Or any other aid
We have produced our god
And everyone present
Become godded and pleasant
Confident, gay—
No remorse that a day
Can show no output
Except from the gut.

In the Name of The Father
The Son and The Mother
We explode
Ridiculously, uncode
A habit and find therein
A successful human being.

ONE WET SUMMER

Another summer, another July
People going on holiday, women in light dresses
How I once jealously feared for them under the printed cotton
Limp unresisting to any man's caresses.
I would have one of my own
And then like other men I could make cynical remarks
At the dangers they ran and never be worried about summer
And what happens in the shelter of parks.

As it is I praise the rain
For washing out the bank holiday with its moral risks
It is not a nice attitude but it is conditioned by circumstances
And by a childhood perverted by Christian moralists.

IMMENSE EVENT

O immense event
I am standing at a hospital window
That has a fine view of the Dublin mountains;
Not now, there is a heavy mist
Of February over a landscape of houses that were built
About eighteen-seventy—
Sad homely little houses particularly from the back
Where the clothes lines swing without shame
Contented people, I'd venture to say,
Lived in those houses—watching a television play.
But the thing is
That I am at this window.

THE TAP ROOT

I tapped, tapped on every rain stone
For the mystery message hidden under
That would prove for me alone
Long life, long love, long roll of sexual thunder
Like Chaplin, Picasso or Goethe.
I tapped and I tapped and recited a most sensational litany
    O scrabbled scroll
    O message for my soul.

KEY TO THE DOOR

Yes, at the last word in Ulysses I open score
At the most wise word known to the tongue

Yes, the key to the door
Of love even though it makes an old-fashioned song.
Yes, you young. . . .

AN INSULT

I came to a great house on the edge of a park
Thinking on Yeats' dream Great House where all
Nobility was protected by ritual
Though all lay drunk on the floor and in the dark
Tough louts and menial minds in the shrubberies lurk
And negative eunuchs hate in an outer hall.
The poet and lover is sage though from grace he fall
Temporarily. The Evil Barbarian dare not work
The servile spell, the insult of a fool
To which there is no answer but to pray
For guidance through the parks of every day
To be silent till the soul itself forgives,
To learn again there is no golden rule
For keeping out of suffering—if one lives.

FROM THE MEATH HOSPITAL

O Muse—Deirdre, Judy,
Who asked me for my autograph,
Would it be possible at this juncture
To bring me down some green lane
Of youth and health?
Not a cure, a revival
But just the sensational
Start of a May day.
I will certainly not let this chance go to waste.
I shall stay out all the time and play
Without analysing the movement of the legs

That run. Take everything for granted
The kiss wildly in my mouth planted.
O Muse! You are understanding as all beautiful girls are
So please remember my most dearest prayer.

JULY 1959

Will I ever forget the Candlefort Lane
In nineteen fifty-nine's July
With the clegs lighting on me at every bare point
And drawing blood with avidity.
It is curious that the six years that have passed
Since that sultry afternoon have just enabled
Me to look at myself at that particular time
Quite young, quite young and quite sexually fabled.

Could I have lived the moment? Is it possible
To experience ourselves as the Beatles seem to do?
The Now exploited and the wild squeals of teenagers
Improvising youth for us. Well, I failed to

Achieve myself walking at fifty-three.
There were cries for me to come through the hedge
But it was no use, I just couldn't manage
The ability to being One Now and not the aftermath grudge.

Still there were those promiscuous flies
And the steamy lane and the green briary hedges
And I did walk it up the hill and then down to the village
And that the bonus on this six year pledge is.

LEFT

Here with my whisky in front of me
I think of the successful with their houses

334

And their wives and children and motor cars
And a job in the city paying thouses
And I am genuinely envious when the normal
Thing is to gloat over one's own free existence
But with the race running out there is no consolation
In being left at the post by a distance.

WINTER IN LEEDS

To take something as a subject, indifferent
To personal affection I have been considering
An ancient saga for my instrument
To play on without the Person suffering
From the wearing years. But I can only
Tell of my problem without solving
Anything. To rewrite a famous tale
Or perhaps to rewrite again of midnight calving
On midsummer night. This cow sacred on a Hindu scale.
There it is my friends. What am I to do
And the void growing more awful every hour.
I lacked a classic discipline. I grew
Uncultivated and now the soil turns sour,
Needs to be revived with a great story not my own
Of heroes enormous who do astounding deeds
Out of this world. Only thus can I attune
To despair an illness like winter alone in Leeds.

THUS A POET DIES

I am here in my own acres again
Looking around me, thinking
Thoughts that have no life
Though it is mid-summer I've
No wish to rhapsodise,
Thus a poet dies.

335

And yet once upon a time
These days could inflame
And I'd throw loving charms
At my two stoney farms
That I'd sell at no price,
Thus a poet dies.

I'm practising hard
At finding the word
That when it is said
I will rise from the dead
In a field of surprise,
Thus a poet never dies.

By the laws of Oray
I cantate. I make a display
On the top of small hills
That are zipping with drills
And my public raise cries
As their poet undies.

AT THE END OF OUR TETHER

I have nothing to announce
On any subject, yet once
I was full of anger
A tyrannical ganger
Satirising immortality
With savage impartiality.
When sad poets I welted
It was I who felt insulted
Going off in a huff,
Too well I knew that two-timing stuff;
Dublin's thousand and one
Sad poets blackened my name

With landlords, bankmen and the like.
Still, for years I was rearing to strike
But for what and against what I don't know,
It all seems too long ago.

I have changed now and try
To have charity
For myself. O hell!
To be here with nothing to tell!
To have learned after
Fifty years so little of laughter,
How the infinite absurd
Alone can contain the live word.
Give me an excuse to stop
Go out to the pub for a scoop.

And that is all—
Isn't it enough to appall
Samuel Becket
Or other demons of the last decade:
All that we learn from living
Is—if we can be forgiving
To ourselves. Invent techniques that lift
Vacuums into a gift
Till we reach the final free get-together
At the end of our tether.

FOR MY NIECE

Keelin at 250 East 30th Street
Strained her small face to smile
At me when I said "hello" in my usual greet—
Ing. I was sad and worried. I'll
Note that May morning many a mile.

I gazed out the window at Kipp's Bay
A shopping centre non-descriptly vulgar
But Keelin's smile out-shone Second Avenue's ray
And Italians, Greeks and perhaps a Bulgar
And Puerto Ricans living high hugger-mugger.

Keelin you cried for a hour when I was babysitting
And I was afraid you had a pain but then I remembered
That sick children don't bawl, you were just getting
Your will and being bad-tempered—
Then you fell asleep in the end like Lady Humbert.
(A most imaginary lady, I may tell you).

And then there was that jet journey to Chicago
Out to Madison by maddening propeller
You didn't bother your head about Henry Rago
But just sucked your Similac like sago.

And you looked calmly down at Wisconsin
The cows and corn, the rolling plains of pride
And you never had a thought for President Johnson
You saw large tractors in the fields deployed
And took in all the Mid-west unalloyed.

IN THE BEGINNING

Starting from nothing I have a job on hands:
To get a couple of things fixed into position—
A condition, and more than that, a theme
With steps and turnings, happenings that teem
From a life of eagerness and activity.
An intellectual battle waged
Exuding the aura of a spirit outraged:
I did it once and thought it at the time
Important, but apparently I was out on a limb

Wandering over the outback where words like "central"
"Spurtive," "umo," were not present to give parental
Authority. Poor bastard without a birthright
Among its own who laughed hidalgoishly in cafes blue painted
Swopping each other's powers to keep them brilliant
And I out of it all.
But it won't be so this time for I shall create many manys
Who will circulate with me not copper but gold gold pennies.

NO POETIC AUTHORIZATION

I come to advise you on the moral position
For nobody is more cognizant of the awful fate
Of him who is a nobody in his own mind
With no poetic authorization.

I GRABBED AN EDUCATION

I wish I could be solemn as John Wain
Making the matter-of-fact pay up and look fairly
Adequate copy for a new book, thoughtfully plain
So many words well put together squarely.
I wish I'd grabbed an education early.

Similarily when over Ted Hughes' work I pore
I am astonished at his animal knowledge
That Billy Smart would pay good money for;
He'd be an asset to a veterinary college.
Has Howard got a faculty in Dulwich?

One of these days I'm going to study hard
Save up a heap of words and spread them squarely
A shelf of poem books by the robot bard
And John will not review my works unfairly.
I grabbed an education late but barely.

MY NATIVE VILLAGE

Exiled in the village of my birth
Where everyone is old and rude without mirth
And I am thirty light years from the earth.

They mention football games I played somewhere
The words I said and when I strive to care
They think that I am putting on an air.

When I am gelded by great cowardice
Afraid of the sound of my own voice;
All winter I lived well—on bitter rice.

Some people stare in wonder, and vague hints
Remind them that I am not he who once
Climbed little hills with them and tossed halfpence

On summer crossroads. They tell anecdotes.
I laugh tears, laugh and someone almost quotes
"Besides, this man is dead," of Eliot's.

LOVER

Something to forget the failures and the things lost
Books and letters are merely images
They were burned somewhere unwittingly or fell in the gutter
And though I lament these bits of my past, I am thinking,
I am brooding, I am breaking my heart.
And that is why I must turn forward and thus positioned
Observe the past unlost: Nuala and Sheila, Mary and Deirdre
And the time itself beautifully composed

And the moral-brake sickness in me from some lie
Believed by my mother before I was born.
No, I was always anything but queer, abnormally normal

And I probably had more women who loved me than Byron
And pure ones all. The wild, wild explosions of the innocent
Most of the famous women-men one hears of
Were very easy to please; it was all the same
The second-hand or the fiftieth-hand. But I was the true roman-
  tic,
Too far in that direction perhaps.

REFLECTIONS ON A SUMMER MORNING WALK No. 2

It is not my purpose to preach
The curse of drink or any such
Street corner morals, it is this:
To assure all
That the Poem alive is a cure-all
The only panacea for the soul.

Yesterday I was astonished
That time had left me so unpunished
I was alive and woman-haunted
Watching turning on spikey heels
A young woman's backside. O these thrills
Can pay back us for many ills.

It has always been in my mind
To praise woman's rotating behind
God's loveliest blessing for mankind.
Yet I leave it at that, there is much to see
Water and grass and light in a tree
On this June day so kindly to me.

The word is the messenger of the eye
The old flax-pit scummed with yellow fly
Gives me my life youth bloomingly.
I must talk to some humans yet keep intact
The virginal moment and here comes Jack
A charming chap with a curious lack.

This man that I in my need had pumped
With enthusism was sad and slumped,
The tire was soft and he thumped and bumped
He leaked and though I strove
To fill him with the air of love
The fatal puncture still blew off.

I was far too absolute he said
For the solid man with a business head
For this poetry business will not wed
With commonsense. He couldn't afford
To go by me and still make a hoard—
That was the gist of his windless word.

So I went on my way carrying the Flame
On to the ultimate Olympic Game
Where no one belonging ever gives in.
There were gulls on the pond
And I was healthy as I waved my wand
To versify from Here to Beyond.

RAMPAS POINT

On Rampas Point I stood for a time,
An imaginary place as you may have gathered
Except that here I gathered in my prime
All sorts of simple shepherd
From whom all the accumulated habits had fallen
Thirty years of them—and I was greedy
For thought adventures. I would dwell in
The heart of a terrible city with a terrible lady
And I would not be afraid of taking pot-luck
Without pride, that mean-faced accountant, checking every
    move.
O Pride, what a bore you have been,

A messer-up of the simplicities of love. Protecting my pence
From the rich robbers. Sin,
That's what I've shed on Rampas Point this time.
Say Hello. "Hello, hello, you're really in your prime."

KEELIN KAVANAGH

I'll miss you Keelin in a week or more
When I'll be left New York. The air you wore
When you had German measles. In mother's arms
With sick frizzled face you kept your charms.
And I will remember you at six months old
I held you to be photographed, your rashed legs recalled
The desperate sickness that lasted a week.
We were all terrible to find you sick.
I'm being a bit ridiculous I know
But I just want you in twenty years to glow
With amusement when you read what your uncle P.
Wrote about his six months niece Keelin K.

AUTOBIOGRAPHY

Here I am in London and fairly glad
To have my air ticket paid
To drive thousands mad.

For verse
Is born of a curse
That not even a New Moon Carnival can disperse.

Personally my party piece is usually
Lord Ullin's daughter rendited boozily
With the audience cursing me prosily.

For the thing I have learned from Forte's caffs
Is that discomfort is preferred to laughs:
Eating from a window sill pays off.

And many people would sit high gravely
Being bored by the verse of Donald Davie
Likewise Grand Opera and My Fair Lady.

The key to success is this
Bore and bore, you can't go amiss—
Humour is just disastrous.

It will drive you out of any flat
And keep you from the gravy that
Long faced rogues are lapping up.

'Twill bring you to heaven if there is such
A place which I doubt very much,
But it certainly won't make you rich.

And here I am in London talking
About my only way of working
Casual, sure, but never joking.

I yet may learn how to bore
Until your arses are red and sore
Sitting listening to my score.

If you are waiting for the denoument
The message in my personal song
Then I must say you're damn well wrong.

I have no message, no one has
Except that dullness will always pass
Bad singers, bad writers whose gold is brass.

So I cannot come to the point of my rhyme
Except that humour's the major crime
And art's the swindle which calls the tune.

So here in this gorgeous Albert Hall—
If I may do a MacGonagall—
I'll give you nothing, yet give you all.

AUTOBIOGRAPHY CONTINUED

Last year I went to America
To take part in a symposium on WBY
And I met a lot of idiotic professors
Who were teaching creativity
In writing and other arts
To girls mainly, and many
As far as I could see
They were making a fair penny
And all of them at some time
Came to Europe to preach on
Some particular writer
Who would run away screeching
And they would write down what he had
For his breakfast and dinner
And supper
And whether he got fatter or thinner.

Last autumn I went to Rome
And at a cocktail party
Locked myself in the lavatory
Of the Yugoslav Embassy.

Two months ago I was in the rats,
Alcoholic poisoning. That's
Nothing to laugh about. My legs
Buckled at the knees

My stomach groaned up its last dregs
And I had hallucinations.
There were people in my bedroom
Shouting at me and I ran twisted
Literally, to a sittingroom
Crowded with visitors.

I cried, there are people down there
Who have given me a scare.
But as I wobbled on my legs
Someone said, you're just in the jigs.
And all that night in bed
With the waving pictures of the dead
Over my head
I said: Kavanagh, you've drunk
A barrel of whisky in the last month
From my rural redoubt
Most loathsome spot
I shout and I shout
Let me out, let me out.

SHANCODUFF

Tom Brennan with a cart
Sow on hill
Carts overturning
The Griffith valuation
Good drop of turnips
Mowing light corn with a mist on the ground.
The rushy field
The scythe
The knapsack sprayer
The flail
Hard work
Put on four barrels
Filled with a porringer tin.
So does a poem bring a world alive in my mind.

We return to simplicity
The right way is wrong as Rock and Roll and the Beatnicks see.
Virtue of necessity. The ballad Monaghan
The long day's journey into night and day the same day.

TRUE LOVE

I wish you could have heard them cheer me
A hundred girls as I passed the school
In my native village. This was real fame,
This was love. This was the poet who succeeded
Paddy
Paddy
Paddy
They screamed delightedly.

I waited by the wall while they innudated
My neglected emotions with full-grown gifts
With the whole of Sex's gladness that has no stopping
The uninhibited facing life.

MAKING A REPUTATION

Resistance to—
Sales talk
C.P. Snow
Golding Lord of the Flies
In a small place everybody knows everybody else
Harder to make a genuine reputation
Ireland parochial not provincial
Provincial worries over what others think
Parochial doesn't care
Scores of Kinsellas
Putting poems together word by word
Can be taken down and re-assembled
Interchangeable.

ON THE CENTENARY OF THE BIRTH OF M.P. SHEIL

John, you've asked me to write a poem on M.P. Sheil
And I am doing it for you off the reel
And although I've never read a line he's written
I'll masticate the bite that off I've bitten
Because of James' Street in Thirty-eight
And you my only literary mate.
Sheil was then the ruler of Redonda
And you a duke. How many a weary tundra
Have we not traipsed since then through streets as fleet
And fleeting as the loves that we would meet
Before we met again in Westbourne Grove
To piece the past together just to prove
That success can be constructed out of loss—
Youth naturally gone, and the stone with no green moss
Is ours equally. Yet I feel
Through all this something that our M.P. Sheil
Would have accounted a portion of sad glory—
Sharing with Yeats and Kipling his centenary.

YEATS

Yeats, it was very easy for you to be frank
With your sixty years and loves (like Robert Graves).
It was thin and in fact you have never put the tank
On a race. Ah cautious man whom no sin depraves
And it won't add up at least in my mind
To what it takes in the living poetry stakes.
I don't care what Chicago thinks, I am blind
To college lectures and the breed of fakes.
I mean to say I'm not blind really
I have my eyes wide open as you may imagine
And I am aware of our boys such as Ben Kiely
Buying and selling literature on the margin.

Yes, Yeats, it was damn easy for you protected
By the middle classes and the Big Houses
To talk about the sixty-year old public protected
Man sheltered by the dim Victorian Muses.

THE SAME AGAIN

I have my friends, my public and they are waiting
For me to come again as their one and only bard
With a new statement that will repay all the waitment
While I was hitting the bottle hard.
I know it is not right to be light and flippant
There are people in the streets who steer by my star.
There was nothing they could do but view me while I threw
Back large whiskys in the corner of a smokey bar
And if only I would get drunk it wouldn't be so bad
With a pain in my stomach I wasn't even comic
Swallowing every digestive pill to be had.
Some of my friends stayed faithful but quite a handful
Looked upon it as the end: I could quite safely be
Dismissed a dead loss in the final up toss.
He's finished and that's definitely.

THANK YOU, THANK YOU
Epilogue to a series of lectures given at University College,
Dublin

. . . Particularly if yourself
Have been left as they call it on the shelf
All God's chillun got wings
So the black Alabaman sings.

Down Grafton Street on Saturdays
Don't grieve like Marcus Aurelius

Who said that though he grew old and grey
The people of the Appian Way
Were always the same pleasant age
Twenty-four on average.

I can never help reflecting
Of coming back in another century
From now and feeling comfortable
At a buzzing coffee table,
The students in 2056
With all the old eternal tricks.

The thing that I most glory in
Is this exciting unvarying
Quality that withal
Is completely original.

For what it teaches is just this
We are not alone in our loneliness,
Others have been here and known
Griefs we thought our special own
Problems that we could not solve
Lovers that we could not have
Pleasures that we missed by inches.
Come I'm beginning to get pretentious
Beginning to message for instead
Of expressing how glad
I am to have lived to feel the radiance
Of a holy hearing audience
And delivered God's commands
Into those caressing hands,
My personality that's to say
All that is mine exclusively.
What wisdom's ours if such there be
Is a flavour of personality.
I thank you and I say how proud

That I have been by fate allowed
To stand here having the joyful chance
To claim my inheritance
For most have died the day before
The opening of that holy door.

ABOUT REASON, MAYBE

The day I walked out on Reason—that old plodder
(But you didn't)
Was the best day of my life; it would take years
To tell of the dirty he did on me, the love-fodder
That other bulls backchewed for me in several gears.
(Catholic peasant)
It is too embarrassing to talk about love misses
And pleases those we ought not entertain.
She gave herself! Oh no! There were only kisses
The listener cannot endure the possible gain.
To tell the tale is needless repetition
But they did come with all heroic violence
(For that I'll vouch
On any couch)
But Reason always intruded on the session
Or perhaps it was the conscience of cold climates.
(Unwilling saint,
A moot point)
Well, call it what you like.

THAT GARAGE

The lilacs by the gate
The summer sun again
The swallows in and out
Of the garage where I am.

The sound of land activity
Machinery in gear
This is not longevity
But infinity.
Perhaps a little bit
Too facilely romantic
We must stop and struggle with
A mood that's getting frantic
Getting Georgian
Richard Church and Binyon
O stand and plan
More difficult dominion.

IN BLINKING BLANKNESS: THREE EFFORTS

I

I am here all morning with the familiar
Blank page in front of me, I have perused
An American anthology for stimulation
But the result is not encouraging as it used
To be when Walter Lowenfel's falling down words
Like ladders excited me to chance my arm
With nouns and verbs.
But the wren, the wren got caught in the furze
And the eagle turned turkey on my farm.

II

Last summer I made a world fresh and fair,
(As the daughters of Erin) completely equipped
With everything for the full life. A wealth of experience
Of every kind waiting to be tapped.
I had a story, a career
Shaped like a stateman's for the biographer.
I had done all things in my time
And had not yet reached my prime.

III

Nature is not enough, I've used up lanes
Waters that run in rivers or are stagnant;
But I have no message and the sins
Of no red idea can make me pregnant.
So I sit tight to manufacture
A world word by word-machine-to-live-in structure—
That may in any garden be assembled
Where critics looking through the glass can lecture
On poets—X, Y and Z therein entempled.

JUVENILIA

The following verses are taken from a family Commonplace Book used by the Kavanagh family between 1923-1927. Much of it is jocular and nonsensical. More serious attempts at writings were made on single sheets of paper now lost.

CARRICKMACROSS FAIR

The carts and lorries up and down
The main street dash like thunder
The dreadful noise our voices drown
And so we gaze in wonder.
It seems to me that Hell let loose
Was preparing for a battle
And who would of them ask a truce
When guns began to rattle.

Beside the corner house there stood
A few brave stalward boys
Keeping up the walls as best they could
In spite of all the noise.

And an apple seller too was there
In her good old woolen shawl
How she stood the noise and blare
I cannot tell at all.

Variation:
On market days and fair days the march begins in style . . .
'Tis a pleasant old street a short smiling street
A street full of nice little houses
A happy new street where on fair days you'll meet
Bobbed hair ones with lovely silk blouses.
It is here that the world famed ass fair takes place
Beside those nice cast-iron fountains
And tis there you will see many a hard looking case
'Mong the wild men that come from the mountains.
Do not mix with the asses except first insured
Against black eyes or pecuniary loss
For dreadful the pains that must be endured
If struck by an ass dealer from Cross.

INNISKEEN PIPERS BAND

The band turned out at early morn
Upon St. Patrick's Day
Down the old Bog Road they march
In wonderful array
And to the rolling of the drum
The pipes begin to play.

Oh! Though I live one hundred years
I never can forget
That we owe to that pipe band
An un-repayable debt;
For they wiped off the sad salt tears
That long our cheeks had wet.

And down they marched that dusty road
With fond hearts tried and true
Playing the *Dawning of the Day*
The only tune they knew.
And eggs with ne'r a chicken in
Found lots of work to do
And dogs that never howled before
Howled at this marching crew.

INNISKEEN VOLUNTEERS

On the whin covered slopes in fierce battle array
Stood the Inniskeen men at the close of the day
With their guns on their shoulders and their banners on high
Waving proudly yet gently in the evening's wind sigh.
And fiercely they gazed o'er the flower decked plains
Those warriors bold from the banks of the Fane.
There were ominous signs in the village that night
That something would happen that wouldn't be right.
The spirit of war with its dread and its thrills
Was permeating the breeze that came down from the hills.
And we thought of the terrors that came in its train
And fervently prayed for the boys from the Fane.

And now once again my sad eyes I cast
On the bray where I saw them a few minutes past,
And their ranks are in order and the word of command
Rings through the ranks, and to attention they stand.
They march and like demons sweep down to the plains
To fight for old Erin on the banks of the Fane.

By Lucy Kavanagh:
Patrick Kavanagh, you're a foolish boy
You seem to be related to Cod Malloy,
So try no more rhyming if you wish people joy
And shut your mouth, my decent boy.

Reply by Patrick Kavanagh:
When the hide of a gannet is lovely
And the tide at Cross does come in
I'll say you are lovely, dear Lucy,
But at present a falsehood is sin.

A DESCRIPTION OF JOSEPHINE KAVANAGH AT 13 YEARS

She is a stout little girl with a very fat face
Who is truly the pride and the star of this place
She wears a red jumper and a very broad nose
Which keeps straight before her wherever she goes.
It grieves me to say she is sour as gall
And proud as a peacock till pride got its fall.
She cries at the least thing and when she's asleep
Like a hedghog she rolls herself up in a heap.
With all her great faults and her ignorant ways
She sometimes comes in for real well-earned praise.

INNISKEEN VILLAGE

My own dear village fair
When I gaze upon thee now
I would that I could share
The sunshine of thy brow.
I wish that I forever
In this sweet glen could stay
Where the Fane, broad gentle river,
Flows on its winding way.

Now when I cast my eyes
Across the land, in pride
I see an old round-tower rise
The old churchyard beside.

Just as in the days gone by
It stands erect today
Beneath the sunny April sky
Whence the smooth Fane winds its way.

There's a mound that rises high
Tree covered o'er the clay
Of heroes great who peaceful lie
There for many a day.
And near it old and lowly
A few bare stone-walls grey
A relic of an Ireland holy
Where the smooth Fane winds its way.

Tripping down with footsteps light
The footpath I could see
A dozen maids all smiling bright
At everyone but me.
I didn't want their winning smile
If they but only knew
I wish that I could leave this hall
That I a fool came to.

The sun through the window is shining
The dark gloomy night faded away
And I on my pillow reclining
Am praising the lord for the day.

For night is the dread of the sick and the weak

I sit up in bed and fondly stare
Through an hospital window green hills fair,
And ponder on joys that I cannot share
Out in the bracing morning air.

And I hear the wild birds sweetly singing
And I hear the church bells faintly ringing
While love on the morning breezes fly.

The moon is now shining to light them to war,
The war and destruction quiet people abhor,
They know what war is who are from Inniskeen
And God help them for many a battle they've seen.
They can tell by the scent on the air if a train
Is being held up and raided by the boys from the Fane.

As I roved down through Carrick town
One stormy winter's day
I met a maid all dressed in brown
With eyes so sweet and gay.
I smiled at her just as we met
And she too smiled on me
And her smile I'm sure I'll ne'er forget
For all eternity.
There are lilies in the valley
There's a mossy bank by the old borheen,
Where the fairest flowers grow
There's a spot in the little meadow green
Where modest violets blow.
But the lilies I know in no field doth grow
For she lives in a little town
A maid so fair with black curled hair
All dressed in a suit of brown.
When plodding down life's highway
Through brightness or through gloom
Two little eyes are beckoning me
To lure me to my doom.
Two burned holes in a blanket
That never will forsake me
Are owned by that fair maiden
Her name is Mary Wakely.
And though I try to avoid her
The eyes still stare me through
And I run about like a madman,
Sure what else can I do.

When these two . . . . are staring me
I am feeling woeful shakey,
And wish to run forever from
My darling Mary Wakely.

The sun was sinking in the west
A fiery golden ball
And a glorious thrill shot through my breast
When I heard the battle call
Being sounded by the fifers in the old Parochial hall.

For long I gazed in joy and pride
At those brave Irishmen
Who long the tyrant power defied
On hill and silent glen.
And didn't fear or flinch to march at freedom's call again.

And proud was I to march with them
Beside the Fane's broad river
No foe however great could stand
A crowd of men so brave
Who marched to break the slave's chain or fill an honoured grave.

THE CHUNK

If poor old Carson would come back
And see the old deserted shack
With not a window broke at all
Or not a mark upon the wall
Nor smell about that once gay place
From some familiar Chunk-boy's face
I am sure he would feel sad and strange
And say that time brings many a change.
O fair Inniskeen!

I am sitting on a bag of oats on the loft; the sun is shining most
   beautiful on me, the 8th May 1923.
I know you are an earwig
Of lovely curly hair,
And I know some other things
To speak I wouldn't dare.
There's gallant boys in Carrick
And gallant girls too
Though I wish to love them all
I can only love a few.

A daffodil waves in the garden today
But my joy will be turned to sorrow
For its beauteous gold leaves will be lifeless and grey
When I stand in that garden tomorrow.
When it is faded no perfume it gives
Like the little strewn leaves of the rose. . . .

My dearest Mary Shannon
With a bursting heart I write
A few short verses hoping
That they may find you right.
I'm sure you still are living
Devoid of grief or care
In that nice row of houses
Beyond the cattle fair.
You're still at school I'm thinking
For lately I have seen
A charming photograph of yours
With one from Inniskeen.

In Gushers the dance of the season
Was held in that gentleman's hall
And to every boy there 'twas real pleasin'
To see every lass with her shawl.

THE SHOEMAKER

Oh see the boots being cobbled while the cobbler sings a song
About the pleasures of the time when he was young and strong,
When he could make a pair of boots in less than half a day
But now his hands are getting stiff and his hair is turning grey.
But his heart is light as ever it was in youthful days gone bye
He takes the world easily and makes grief look like joy.
Now light and fast upon the last he makes the hammer fall,
Then leaves it down upon the ground and then takes up the awl,
To sew some patches on the boot, 'twill keep someone's foot
    warm
To walk through bogs he won't need clogs to keep out cold and
    storm.

There were fifty scoffers in a row
When the Irish class began
With enthusiasm the girls were aglow
In their baiting for a man.
All thought it was a clever plan
To make a really Gaelic show
Even if they joined the K K clan
The men would never know.
Their plans before that year did pass
Were dashed unto the ground
They learned that at an Irish class
A husband wasn't found.

The lobby where Jackson lived long years ago
To my grief has succumbed to its formidable foe
Poor Betty and Jordan and Jackson today
Are sour old creatures that one time were gay.
O'er the chunkers the chunk and the boys did fall
For politics, politics holds them in thrall.

As you sow you shall reap
And if you sow bad seeds
Of evil bad deeds
You shall live to weep
And live to reap
A harvest of bad weeds.
The seed may grow up slowly

But still they do
But if in God's own ground you sow
In early youth
The seeds of truth
Into a holy tree will grow
And smoothly your river of life will flow
'Twill heal the bite of Satan's tooth.

MIKE MC TIGUE VERSUS BATTLING SIKEE

From the Giant's Causeway to the Lee
There is not a Gael should cheer Sikee,
Sure I myself would run a league
If that would help bold Mike McTigue.
To show that though a black is tough
An Irishman is better stuff.
O may he beat Sikee in fight
When he meets him on St. Patrick's night

MUCKER

The poplars grow in splendour there
The fields are white as snow
With posies bright and proud and fair
Their beauties are beyond compare
When they bend their tresses to and fro
In March when stormy winds do blow.

If we could only see that life is but a dream
And we are here but for a little while
How very foolish would our wisest actions seem
And with terror we would look on sin and crime
We will awaken in another land
Where this dream of sin and crime will be no more.
'Tis death alone can make us understand
The wonders of that near yet distant shore.

I am writing everyday very foolish things
In this book so that it may go down
To posterity, so that it may bring
Honour and renown.
But my words seem so foolish, they
May say it was from some wise man
The words came down, and there they may
The seeds of honour fan.
Today I see in my mind's eye

A shadow of the days gone by
A shadow of the Trenche's great
Pass slowly through the convent gate,
Those haters of the Celtic race
Who lived to see their own disgrace
And lived to see a convent grand
Beneath the roof where oft they planned
Destruction for the weak and small
Who dared to break the landlord's thrall
When by the cruel Agent led
He flung the sick from off their bed
And threw the cabin o'er their head
And cared not how the sick or old
Found shelter from the winter's cold.
But God has willed a wondrous change
And nothing gets beyond its range
And even they with all their might
Have faded like the shades of night.

INNISKEEN

That riotous little village
That never was surpassed
For shooting, loot and pillage
Is peaceful now at last.
All the roads around are clear
For those who aren't blind
Too well we see the fighting here
Has left its mark behind.
And at many turns in the road
Old trenches can be seen
Pitfalls for topers with their load
Of beer from Inniskeen.
The tree is felled that shaded me
On many a summer's day
The men are dead that raided me
And mouldering in the clay.
Some fought like heroes even when
Their fighting days were o'er,
They died the death of Irishmen
And now they fight no more.
But if Ireland ever breaks the chain—
The half-smashed one I mean—
There's none can say they died in vain
Who fell near Inniskeen.

Give me your hand, I will give you my heart
For I love you as no words can tell
And never my dear from you can I part
For I have succumbed to Cupid's sharp darts
Which has placed me under a spell.
I love you as I have loved none before
With pleasure, with sorrow, with pain
Which has struck at once at my hearts very core
When I think of the joy that love has in store
And the trouble it brings to my brain.

THE CHUNK

The Chunk has gone down in distress and dishonour
Her friends once so many now seem to be few
Why did they leave her, when death came upon her
Alas of the Chunk boys how many were true.
Where are those heroes that raised her to fame
Are they dead like all true men today
Or did they not think it a scandal and shame
To leave her and ramble away.
In the height of her fame there were men to defend her
They supported her then, yes, when she was young
But when she was old was there one to attend her
Too many support you if you should be strong.

Twelve months ago on St. Patrick's night
When at the dance until daylight
Where splendid blarney roses grew
And bells of every shade and hue
'Tis only now I think upon
The days which now are past and gone
And the roses which we held so tight
And stole away on that same night.
'Twas lucky that you went away
For since you left I am the prey
Of jeers such as I never knew
When codding round the roads with you
But when I think upon the joy
I had in those bright days gone by
And the fun I had inside that shed
Does greatly help to cool my head.
The scene can never be forgot
Of that secluded little spot
Such beauties since I never saw
As I on that lovely rick of straw.

Sure that is all about the past
How are you since I saw you last?
Well, one thing certain that I know
You are a man no matter where you go.
Another thing I know quite well
How some on English beef did swell
They almost did the government rob
When in the Scrubbs they got a job
To boil the pots and cook the meat
Twas them that got enough to eat
Sure they are Erin's pride and hope
Who eat while others teased the rope
When the English beef falls off their jaws
They will surely banish foreign laws.
This doesn't apply to a man like you
So now I'll say a fond adieu.

I was down by the Lagan in summer last year
And what I was doing you are going to hear
I was shooting and looting with comrades so gay
And beating my enemies out of the way.
Oh! Murder, destruction and many a raid
Was performed last year by the muffler brigade.
An Irish class used to meet every night
Till we beat them and smashed them and put them to flight
We erased from our mist every Papist away
And burned their homes on that very same day.
Of course for our duties we had to be paid
For we were the men of the Muffler Brigade

I did my duties the same as the rest
At putting all those in the Falls to the west.
What better thing could any man do
To show all the traitors that he was true-blue.
The Papists of course from our midst would all fade
If I got my way in the Muffler Brigade.

Of course all the boys fought on bravely
But they said that no one was half brave as me.
I am now a great man my laurels I've won
My actions last year put them all in the shade
And the boys made me chief of the Muffler Brigade.

THE BLOATER April 20th 1925

To the Patients of the Murray Ward, Monaghan Co. Infirmary
My dear friends,

On an old sheet of foolscap, I am writing these feeble lines
to you, an attempt to express my affectionate regard for you.
Four days may seem a short time in which to form a lasting
friendship, and yet in that short period I formed an attachment
with true and noble men, the memory of which will ever remain
with me. I am expressing my feelings in the shape of Odes which
I hope may help Dr. Hall's medicine to exterminate you all root
and branch.

Pat Kavanagh

FRANK MULLEN

A statesman, if ever there was one:
Consigned to dark oblivion,
In a hospital ward he rests, and blows
His windy eloquence through his nose.

A philosopher preaching his ethics pure
Out through the keyhole of the dure:
O spirit of Plato thou hast given
The loan of your brain to Francis Mullen.

PETER HUGHES

A man that doesn't boast his wit
And still has heaps and heaps of it.
Nobleness on his heart is writ,
With heavenly art.

A second Orpheus is he,
Although he ne'er did draw a tree
By music sweet; yet he drew me
Unto his heart.

His very presence gave me joy:
But now in Inniskeen I sigh,
Dark clouds have darkened all my sky
    Since we did part.

PETER

He doesn't know that thing called blush,
It was poor Adam's folly:
And still he wouldn't make a rush
At Katherine or Molly:
He dies in bed and never knows
That beds are made for two,
That when he dies he'll cock his toes,
And oh! 'tis then he'll rue.

McARDLE

A chap with a smiling face,
A joy in any place,
    I never heard him snarl:
Like a billy goat snores at night,
Doesn't waken until daylight—
    Little Owen McArdle.

BOBBY CHAPMAN

I looked on Bobby Chapman as he lay full length in bed,
I looked at him, and puzzled like I scratched my mighty head.
And I says, it's mighty hard to know the working of your brain,
So I'll lave you where you are, until we meet some day again.

SAM

Sam was a very quiet fellow
That wouldn't give his thoughts away
If he had such a thing as thought
For certain I can't say.

THE UNKNOWN WARRIOR

I hardly could say I knew him, like Sam he was too deep
To tell to us the things he knew; he's sooner let us sleep;
For that was his great hobby, a perfect sleeper was he
Slainte will come to the man I'm sure, who sleeps so perfectly.

TOAL

Toal was accursed: the last and the worst:
    And perhaps the best of all.

FIRST PUBLISHED VERSE (*Weekly Independent* 1928-1929)

FREEDOM

Now I am freed from first love pain
She's back with them that sent her,
My love, who will not come again
But why should I lament her?

She was too cruel and too proud
For winged little Cupid;
I was alone amid the crowd
Unhappy, strange and stupid.

369

Oft did I look into her eyes—
That were of greyish splendour—
To catch their secret lover-wise
And crush their proud defender.

Away to dreamy places I
Would steal at sundown's gleaming
To smother a deep bosom's sigh
And live my life a-dreaming.

Now she is gone and may she be
Forever waiting for me
While I'll be free and full of glee
Let it be fair or stormy.

SUMMER

Red summer looked
With eyes of flame
On a world old,
And cold and tame.
And all who slept
And they who wept,
Looked up when they heard his name.

Pale faces he changed
To husky brown
In the sun-starved lanes
Of every town.
Fair dreams awoke
As the thrall was broke
When summer came striding down.

THE PESSIMIST

The word rose to my lips
And there it died,
I could not speak my soul
And I've so tried,
Through days and years of gloom
Visioning Beauty's doom
When nothing fair shall bide.

O break, cold heart! Thou'rt lost
For want of wine.
Why doest thou beat when I
Have given the sign?
That love has perished now,
And pallid is his brow
Whose darkened soul is mine.

THE FAERY LAND OF SONG

I joined my hands
And turned mine eyes
Towards faery lands
Beyond sunrise
Where Beauty stands
Among the wise

She stands among
Her children fair
A wreath of song
Upon her hair.
The way is long
But I'll go there.

Today I'll go
On golden wings
And leave Earth's woe
To slaves and kings.
Oh! I shall know
Of lovely things.

I closed mine eyes
And thro' the blue
Rose tinted skies
Dream-winged I flew
To join the wise
The fair, the true.

TO A LONELY ONE

Why is there sorrow in your soul today?
Why are those tear-drops in your gentle eyes?
The golden corn is gathered, and the way
Is like a road that leads thro' Paradise.

This is the dreamy time when passion fires
Burn softly, like an incense wondrous sweet;
And song-birds strike upon their broken lyres
Their sweetest notes of all, where lovers meet.

Though Nature has donned her shroud of somber brown
Fairer she looks today than when she stood
Wearing upon her brow young Summer's crown;
The winds chant Requiem for her in the woods.

And why's your heart not lightsome, little one?
Are all your great hopes blown to the skies?
That you should stand in tears, the path upon,
A path that seems to wind through Paradise.

TO A CHILD I KNOW

O Beautiful Child, you came to me
In my darkest hour of misery
When I'd almost fallen among the fallen
You whispered into my ear a song
Like the voice of Hope in the desert callin'.
O! And I've faltered long.

O Beautiful Child of the lily hand!
And the purest soul in Patrick land!
You came to me like a dream of bliss
And I going the way that most men go;
O! The magic and wonder of that kiss
No other heart can know.

IN OCTOBER

There is another voice in the glens today
Another form on the hill,
There's a child going down the darksome way
Very pale and ill.
There's a sweet voice hushed that made me glad
There's a faded rose in the gutter pad.

There's a wild wind blowing without tonight
Blowing black sinful rain.
But here by the flickering firelight
I dream old dreams again.
From Memory's garden I cull fair blooms
To deck in splendour my heart's bare rooms.

TILL LOVE CAME

Darkness came down, and then
I doubted all;
And there was no one in the lonely glen
To hear my call.

I doubted God, and I doubted
My secret soul;
The legions of Heaven were routed
And I had no goal.

I doubted Beauty and Love
And wandered forth
A child of despair, to rove
The faithless earth.

And then like an angel she came;
I ceased to rove;
In her heart was a pure white flame
And she was love.

THRALLDOM

O! Must I ever struggle here,
Murmuring faintly to the throngs
Who cannot hear, or will not hear
My sorrow-laden songs?

And shall I ever wander forth
Across the wide unknown expanses
To learn the secrets of the earth
And linger where romance is?

To muse where mighty spirits rose
In Learning's great and radiant morning
And calm the soul that overflows
With philosophic yearnings.

To launch a shop upon the stream
That down the years bore Homer's song;
My ship is but a childish dream
The rocks will pierce ere long.

I might stand on a mountain top
And dream a dream that wouldn't perish,
Or sing of proud undying hope
In all that dreamers cherish

But Fate! Thou has't declared that I
Must grovel here and wear thy chains;
There is no sunshine in my sky
No flowers on my plains.

A PURE WHITE SCROLL

What of the vows we've made and broken
As we kneel at the altar again?
In our soul depths let the word be spoken
We will be better men.

What of the things we did not do—
Sworn to the King of Kings!
O'er the Eastern world the sky breaks blue—
We will do better things.

What of the chasms that opened wide
Huge mouths hell-wide yawning?
The past is dead and we stand beside
The door of a golden dawning.

Faith's lighted her lamp on a mystic height
Bright angels are watching o'er us.
Naught matters now but the words we write
On the pure white scroll before us.

THE TRAMP WOMAN

She was so fair to see
Fragile—and she had been broken.
O the world is a hard place to be!
'Tis truth I have spoken.
HAD BEEN was her name, yet her face
Was lit with the saintliest grace.

The road was a long road—
A road that for her had no ending;
Her shoulders 'neath a wearisome load
Earthwards were bending.
And still for her stoop and her sack
I half-wished to beckon her back!

Night folded wings grey
Above the dark and the fair,
She faded out of my day
I know not where.
But fancy brings back to my mind
A tramp woman rounding the wind.

TO FAME

You did not hear my cries,
You did not mind
Whether I led the crowd and triumphed
Or fell behind—
Among Earth's conquered children—
Clutching the wind

What was the prize to you
Who could not know
When the vessel of dreams is broken
A dreamer's woe.
'Twill all be the same at the closing,
You answered low.

I knocked at your door and craved
One grain of gold,
It would not open to my knocking
The night was cold.
I lay where the vanquished lie
Now as of old.

TO ALL CHILDREN

I tell you little children, not to hurry across the years:
All that age has for you is a field of worry, a sea of tears;
A mountain hard to climb where many fall,
And why should you not wander, pure and small?

Romance around our early morning lingers, but not for long,
And Beauty moves no more her magic fingers o'er cords of song.
Sweetness will pine amid the sunless glades,
And innocence be gathered to the shades.

I tell you, little children, not to squander sunny hours
Too soon will come the storms of life, the thunder and leaden
    showers:
O children, you are growing up too soon,
And you will weep the morning when tis noon.

A MEMORY

An humble song
Sung in the autumn gloom—
'Twas but a childish lay, and yet
I listened, and my eyes were wet.
A winged bird it flew
Across the sky-ie blue,
By laughing plane and hill
I hear that lyric still
Though the lyricist has wandered home.

A dream trudges on
Beneath a darkening dome—
But across Time's hoarsely shouting seas
From that far land of memories
It comes to me again
That tender deep refrain
And sorrow steals away.
I know that singer gay
I singing, now, at home.

TO A DISTANT FRIEND

You spoke that little word of praise;
'Twas nothing much and still
It lighted up my tearful days
Like sunrise on a hill.

Like silver rain on desert sands
It fell upon my heart,
In gratitude I joined my hands
In humble prayerful art.

378

Some day when all the shadows rise
And beauty wanders free,
We too shall rove 'neath laughing skies
But now such cannot be.

O deep within my soul I'll hold
That simple word of praise
And when the world denies me gold
I'll flout it in her gaze.

From THE DUNDALK DEMOCRAT February 2nd 1929

ADDRESS TO AN OLD WOODEN GATE

Battered by time and weather, scarcely fit
For firewood; there's not a single bit
Of paint to hide those wrinkles; and those scringes
Break hoarsely on the silence—rusty hinges.
A barbed wire clasp around one withered arm
Replaces the old latch with evil charm.
That poplar tree you hang upon is rotten
And all its early loveliness forgotten.
This gap ere long must find another sentry
If the cows are not to roam the open country.

They'll laugh at you, Old Wooden Gate, they'll push
Your limbs asunder, soon, into the slush.
Then I will lean upon your top no more
To muse and dream of pebbles on a shore,
Or watch the fairy-columned turf-smoke rise
From white-washed cottage chimneys heavenwise.
Here have I kept fair tryst and kept it true
When we were lovers all and you were new;
And many a time I've seen the laughing-eyed
School-children, on your trusty back astride

But time's long silver hand has touched our brows
And I'm the scorn of women—you of cows.

How can I love the iron gates which guard
The fields of wealthy farmers? They are hard
Unlovely things, a-swing on concrete piers—
Their finger-tips are pointed like old spears.
But you and I are kindred, Ruined Gate,
For both of us have met the self-same fate.

Addenda: Other Poems and Fragments

Page 264. Add the following lines to CYRANO DE
BERGERAC

She told me I was subtle, her
Love distress to note
She was in love and worried
Over someone who was not.

And she always thought when looking at
My loving priestly face
That here was surely some one
Who could give her love advice. . . .

And from the mirror going out
The lecher looked at me
And winked before resuming
His priestly dignity.

ALADDIN

Do not be greedy for these jewels,
Aladdin said to me,
For these that lie at the Cave's mouth
Are touched materially.

Any coward can pick these up
Back to the world run
Bragging of how he robbed the nest
Of the Enchanted One.

But we will go farther and not fear
The monsters Hatred, Hunger,
Meanness, greasy-faced Piety,
Defeat, whose stench grows stronger

As we grope through the Cave of Wonder.
Do not fill so soon
Your pockets out of that pile,
For Time will wear out the tune

That flows in the brilliance of
The Truth you see.
At the foot of a Cross is the Utterness
Of humanity.

Every atom of clay,
Every worn stone,
Becomes your wish for beauty,
The world cannot own

Or steal or buy for boasting . . .
Friendless now, we
Are close to the Secret of Life's Cave
Aladdin said to me.

> Patrick Kavanagh.
> On the forepage of a copy of *The Great Hunger*
> presented to Lord Dunsany 1st November
> 1944.

A PATHETIC BALLAD OF A BIG DINNER
By Eusebius Cassidy

You foolish young fellows that follow the pen
A song I will sing you if you will attend,
It's all about a dinner that I did endure
One Saturday evening all for Thomas Moore.
The truth for to spake it was a fine menu
And the Royal Hibernian Hotel was the venue.

I record that the victuals were found without fault
Likewise the sherry, the port and the malt,
It was, pon me soudy, a terrible great feed
The cabbage well boiled and the praties well peeled.

Well, our troubles began when a piper he came
And played round the flure to the cheers that we gave
But it wasn't enough for to play round the flure,
There was more in the bag that we had to endure.
O let Erin remember the price that we paid,
Sure he gave a recital like great Kreisler from the stage.

The first for to spake was a woeful tall man
Lord Dunsany who owns extensive estates of land
He rose up among us to his splendid height
And talked with deep learning for most of the night.
He read all Moore's poems, likewise Lalla Rookh
And explained for us the fine points of the book.

Then Seamus McCall of great fame and renown
Rose up with his eyes in the folds of a frown.
He was angry with some poets of our modern time
Whose names, sad to state, he did not specify.
Was it Auden or Eliot or young Harry Brown
Or some of the bards of fair Dublin town?
Was it Tommy's American sister, the sweet Marianne
Or Conrad Aiken (Frank's brother) who angered the man?
Was it Spender or Osbert Sitwell or sporting Johnnie B.
Late of Upper Mount Street, or could it be me?

The toast of Our Guests he next did propose
And many warm compliments he paid unto those
Who play on the fiddle or act on the stage
And never like writers in thinking engage
Sure we must have some culture yet safe we must be
So we'll back up the fiddlers and actors, says he
And if the flag of poetry must be unfurled

Father Senan is there to introduce it to the world
And Patrick J. Little from Waterford fair
Sends out gelded culture each night on the air.
And the rich men are backing with money and kind
All culture that hasn't to do with the mind.
So we drank to Our Guests and we emptied our glasses
And praised the safe slopes of our phoney Parnassus.

So the torture went on as I here do relate
Dr. Ryan was there and his wife in great state,
The Earl of Wicklow and Vincent O'Brien
And stout Dr. Mackey at the head of the line.
There were diplomats splendid accredited to this nation
And many others of most exalted station,
There were fiddlers and fluthers and harpers also,
And singers who won gold and silver at the recent Feis Ceoil.
And so ends my song of a feed on a grave,
If I have detained you your pardon I crave.

The Bell July 1947, Vol. 14, No. 4.

THE GHOST LAND

Not a stir, not a stir in the land
The cloudless sky
Of a ghost world
Businessmen hurrying to their offices
Businessmen hurrying to their homes
Businessmen hurrying to their golf clubs
Their souls locked in their cars.

Not a kick, not a kick in the heart
Of the land
But only a slow desperation—
Girls hurrying to their sodality meetings,

Girls hurrying to the theatre,
Girls with girls,
Walking to their chastity graves.

Not a kick, not a stir
In heart or in air.

P. J. McCabe, *Kavanagh's Weekly*, 26th April 1952.

THE GOD OF POETRY

I met a man upon the road
And a solemn man was he
I said to him: You surely are
The god of poetry.

He never answered my remark
But solemnly walked on
Uttering words like "splendour" and
"Picasso fingered dawn".

Then walked on until I met
Another man and he
Danced with delight —this surely is
The god of poetry.

All day I walked, all day I searched
And had no eyes to see
The genuine god who never looks
A bit like poetry.

Ann McKenna, *Kavanagh's Weekly*, 24th May 1952.

DEIRDRE

O the dear impartial tenderness of hands
That love filled, love willed, loose the bands
Of soul's self-bound, ice-chilled, in wound.
Though may the needle of your being set towards a star
To all be ever what within your pure heart you are—
Cool water from a spring
Sun's candid caressing.

To others leave cold flint-edged pride
Fear's lie to love, impulse to deride,
Singing and free, flow as you do flow
A golden ample stream.
You were born to love.
And love's healing.

N. Caffrey, *Kavanagh's Weekly*, 14th June 1952.

ENJOY YOURSELF

The Agha Khan gave the above as his philosophy of life to a
Daily Mail reporter. Patrick's response was as follows,
Kavanagh's Weekly, 28th June 1952.

Enjoy yourself
It's harder than you think
Enjoy yourself
And that means sex and drink.
Enjoy yourself
The sea will let you sink
Enjoy yourself
Says a fat old gink
Get yourself fifty wives

Give them coats of mink.
Enjoy yourself
Let them endure the stink.

> All the above verses by Patrick Kavanagh
> under various pseudonyms.

BIRTH

We will not hold an inquest on the past—
The Word died, the mistake was made, the sin
Was committed as the wheel turned again
And again, exactly as it had turned last.
In the mornings we made promises to ourselves as the fresh
Air of the street gave us that springtime feeling
That is to say, sad hope. Our wills were willing
And plenty of years in the future said, wish your wish.
Yet there was something of the dead past polluting
The New Word we had created out of the water and the spirit
And everything seemed over bar the shouting
When out of the holy mouth came angelic grace
And the will that had fought in vain had found new merit
And all sorts of beautiful things appeared in that place.

> From: *Studies* (Dublin) Spring 1958

UNTITLED

It is when a man is under pressure that art
Comes up and talks to him bravely, heart to heart
And damn the pettifogging
Rascals in pubs and the mean nagging.

> Handwritten on what looks like a cutting from *Quick
> Ques*, London. Has a mention of him on the other
> side by Elizabeth Smart, *circa 1965*.

EX TEMPORE AT POETRY CENTENNIAL '67
London 14th July 1967

But since the arrival of the Beatles and the Stones
Anything goes
And I am glad
That Freedom is mad
Dancing with pot.
Hurray hurray
I say
For this beautiful day.

NOTES TO *COMPLETE POEMS*
Peter Kavanagh

1 The Intangible was the first poem by Patrick ever printed in a literary magazine—*The Irish Statesman* 19 October 1928. Cf. p. 209.

Ploughman: When Patrick received a letter from Æ accepting this poem he was actually ploughing with the primitive "swing" plough.

Lea-green: A field lying fallow in grass for a number of years.

2 Blackbird: A type of thrush with a fair singing voice and common in our area.

Poplars: A common type of tree around wet land. Grows tall and fast. Worthless as lumber unless it be kiln-dried. When I was a boy there were squirrels down Brennan's Lane and elsewhere but not any more.

3 Gold Watch: This watch was given to Patrick in 1928 by relatives visiting from Chicago. After testing, it turned out to be merely gold-plated. I sold it in 1940 to Sam Parr in Inniskeen for £2.50.

4 This copper beech together with a number of sallies was planted by Patrick along the bog-line opposite our house as a shelter against the wicked east wind.

5 Slieve Donard is in Co. Down. In 1936 Patrick visited there in connection with a talk on the county for B.B.C. Northern Ireland.

6 To a Child: "In that little thing I had become airborne and more: I had achieved weightlessness. And then I heard about having one's roots in the soil, of being a peasant. And I raged at Monaghan and the clay and all that. But poetry has to do with the reality of the spirit, of faith and hope and sometimes even charity. It is a point of view. A poet is a theologian." *Self Portrait*.

Mary: A local girl.

7 Coltsfoot: *Tussilago farafara*. A low, wide-leafed plant that blossoms around February. A section of one of our

fields was "infested" with it and since it smothers all other plants we were forced to eradicate it. This was not easy because it has a long soft root. Patrick dug it out with a graip. It took him three weeks or more but observation in 1982 shows he did a good job.

10 Check-reins: In a team of horses, the ropes that tie their heads together. The seed (usually oats) was contained in a sack made from a bed-sheet and tied around the neck. The sower shook the seed, tempering his shake to the force of the wind. The seed settled in the arris between the turned up sods. Pulling a harrow over the ground at the right angle covered the seed. Letting the harrow play on the surface demanded a certain skill—otherwise the seed could easily be smothered.

Celia: Patrick's sister. She entered the Presentation Convent, Matlock, England, in 1933; R.I.P. July '84.

11 M: A local girl.

12 My Room: The upstairs room in our house on the north side. There almost every night Patrick practised writing verse. His description is accurate.

13 Shancoduff: From the Gaelic meaning Black Hollow. The townland in which Patrick's "out-lying farm" was situated. We owned three additional fields near our house but these were in Drumnagrella and Mucker. Patrick wrote: "Shancoduff's watery hills could have done the trick, but I was too thick to take the hint. Curious this, how I had started off with the right simplicity, indifferent to crude reason and then ploughed my way through complexities and anger, hatred and ill-will towards the faults of man and came back to where I started." *Self Portrait.*

18 Inniskeen Road: Patrick loved the sonnet form because, as he explained, it forced the mind to activity without itself being forced.

21 Aldebaran: The eye of the bull in the constellation Taurus. Patrick had read *The Stars in their Courses* by Sir James Jeans which had been given him by Æ. The

390

Bear refers to the constellation of that name.

23 Portobello Bridge, Dublin—favourite haunt of street preachers.

24 Names mentioned here are those of Patrick's neighbours.

25 Sanctity: In the 1960s this verse was taken as a theme song by homosexuals. Patrick was offended by this interpretation, said so, and was offended whenever he saw it quoted.

26 Poplar Memory: These trees were planted along Caffrey's Bog adjoining our "middle field". Several have since fallen blocking the drain. Cf. p. 49.

27 Two Ways: Written after a visit to London.

30 The Girl in the Lending Library: The Dundalk Public Library.

31 The Hired Boy: Forerunner of *The Great Hunger*. Published in the Left-wing magazine *Ireland Today* in 1936. Patrick did not like to be reminded that he had published in this magazine.
Hiring Fair: Twice a year in Carrickmacross and surrounding towns a fair was held where men and girls rented their labour to well-to-do farmers for six months. It was Ireland's version of the slave market.

32 The Mournes: The Mourne mountains in South Armagh.
Forkhill: A small town in south Armagh.

41 The Last Lap: Patrick was a good middle-distance runner. He also engaged in putting the shot, the high jump and the hop-step-and-jump. He had a very powerful physique and he could carry a sixteen-stone bag of wheat at a threshing up a flight of ten or more steps.

49 Poplars: See p. 26.

51 The Rustic: Same local girl already mentioned as M.

52 Yankee tourist: The same as mentioned on p. 3.

54 Anna Quinn: Now Mrs. Carragher of Castleblayney. She met Patrick in 1937 at Rassan Carnival on the Dundalk-Blaney Road, near Flinty McArdles. See also p. 61.

56 Burial Service: I don't know what old mare he is speak-

ing of here. We sold "the kicking mare" to the knackers.

58 In the Same Mood: Longing for companionship, difficult to find in Inniskeen—difficult for Patrick.

61 Anna Quinn: See note p. 54.

64 Ethical: First published in *The Spectator* 15 July 1938. Receiving the letter of acceptance from the editor, Peter Fleming, was one of the greatest thrills of his life. He had broken the barrier into the British literary world.

69 I knew Father only superficially. He died when I was thirteen years old and had been doting for a year or more before that. Patrick and he were good companions.

70 Primrose: The bank along the path to the well in Mecgan's field was packed with primroses in April and May: their aroma could be smelled a hundred yards away.

70 Christmas 1939: A Christmas poem was always a sure-fire seller and worth a pound note—no small amount in those days. As will be seen, he wrote a number of such poems.

71 With the pound received for this Chrismas poem Patrick was able to pay his train-fare from Dublin to Inniskeen. As usual, I met him at the railway station, the train coming in on time at 8.20 p.m. It was a romantic moment on Christmas eve, the lights on the train pulling in, the hissing steam, the storm-lamp being swung by the Guardman. Then the walk home the Inniskeen road under starry skies.

72 To prevent "the blight" potatoes had to be sprayed at least twice—in June and July, using a mixture of copper-sulphate and washing soda melted in a forty-gallon barrel of water. The barrel was placed conveniently on the headland. A two-gallon capacity back-carried sprayer was rented in the Village. Patrick sprayed the potatoes by walking up and down each furrow, the sprayer on his back. Around forty pounds weight or more. You came home tired after that day's work.

Kerr's Pinks and Arran Banners were varieties of potatoes.

This verse was published in *The Irish Times* during the course of a noisy controversy over a book review by Patrick. It was his response to the controversy.

73 Mandril: That part of the plough on which the sock was mounted.

74 Weasel itch: When working in the fields in summer it was customary to leave your coat on the headland or even in the ditch. A weasel (stoat) might come along and leave his stench on the coat. It was said that this stench caused an unpleasant itch. The weasel is of the same family as the skunk.

Coulter: The blade fixed in front of the share in a plough.

74 Kednaminsha: A townland, meaning the field of the kids (goats). The references are to mythologies of the district.

75 Amiens Street: Now Connolly Station.

77 Turn our wheels against the sun: When finished ploughing for the day the plough was always placed facing north.

78 Wangel: A fistful of straw tied at one end. A roof was thatched with wheaten straw made into wangels.

79 The Great Hunger: Written September 1941 while we both lived in a bedsitter at 122 Morehampton Road, Dublin. Written in pen in slightly less than three weeks. No re-writing as far as I can remember. The original is lost but there are several holograph copies. Under the title of "The Old Peasant" the first section of it was published in *Horizon* (Magazine) 1942. *Horizon* was seized by the Irish police, not it is claimed because of The Great Hunger but because of an article in the magazine on contraception, by Frank O'Connor. The complete poem was published by The Cuala Press in 1942. It was never banned.

For Patrick's view of the poem see November Haggard pp. 15-16. It was, he said, too concerned with the woes of the poor to succeed as a great poem. Tragedy is merely undeveloped comedy. Comedy is the ideal which must be sought.

80 Spanging: Long fast steps.

81 Straddle the horse: Place the straddle on the horse.
Coulter: c.f. note p. 74.

84 Headland: The unploughed part of a field where the horses turn when ploughing.

86 The coward's blow: A light blow as a challenge to the other party to start a fight.

96 Matt Talbot: A Dublin ascetic.

97 Tanner: Sixpence.
Double-tree: In a team of horses it is a wooden beam tied in the centre to the plough and at each end attached to a separate horse. Usually about four feet long.

102 Lammas Day: 1st August. Loaf-Mass. Harvest festival in the early church. A common festival in the north of Ireland.

103 Oboe: At this time I was learning to play the oboe.

104 Lough Derg: An island in a small lake in Co. Donegal, popular as a place for penitential pilgrimage. Patrick went there twice: I not at all. Patrick went as poet and pilgrim. Although the pilgrim is supposed to spend three days there fasting I packed sandwiches and a bottle of whiskey for Patrick. You cannot observe or even feel well if you are fasting.

When he returned he wrote the poem "Lough Derg" in a week or more. He gave it to Frank O'Connor for his opinion who suggested that each new theme mentioned should be extended and developed. Patrick made no changes but refused to publish it lest he intrude on sacred ground. I kept the manuscript and published it in 1971 after Patrick's death.

108 Agnus Dei: A cake of wax stamped with the figure of a lamb and blessed by the pope.

111 Tick of chaff: A mattress filled with oaten chaff. A lovely object to sleep on. Unfortunately it had an immense attraction for fleas.

117 A.O.H.: Ancient Order of Hibernians. A fraternal organization, sentimental and absurd.

124 Jack Yeats' novel: *Ah Well*.
Advent: The original title was "Renewal".

127 The harrow was a farm implement in two sections hinged together. Altogether it consisted of eight wooden beams (called bulls) about 4 by 4 inches and about four and a half feet long. They were attached to each other in the form of a gate by steel bars. Each bull had five iron spikes in it, called harrow-pins.
Wyandots: A breed of chicken.

129 Saddle-harrow: A light-weight iron harrow shaped like a saddle and used to remove an inch or two of clay from the top of the potato drill to allow the buds to reach the surface easily.
Leaf-lapped furrow: The leaves of one drill stretch over and join with the leaves of the next drill.
'Shenko, Montgomery, Rommel: Generals in World War II. Timoshenko, the Russian General, Montgomery, British, and Rommel, German.

131 P. Beaslai: A contemporary Gaelic writer. I believe the translation here is by myself and not by Patrick.
Inis Foley: Ireland.

132 A Knight at the Tournament: Sir John Mahaffy, British Representative in Ireland during World War II, challenged Patrick to write a sonnet on this heavyweight bout.

133 Published 4 January 1943 in memory of an Irish ship lost at sea. The Irish Government being neutral and squeezed by the British Government, needed ships badly. They bought some old non-seaworthy hulks and sent them to sea. This one sank with all hands lost.
The President's Birthday: Douglas Hyde.

134 Jack Doyle, a noted Irish boxer and horizontal champion.
Brown Joe: Joe Louis.

136 F. J. McCormick: Abbey Theatre actor.

138 Seed Wheat: Celebrating the 1916 Rising. Recalling with unction this Rising was part of the policy of *The Irish Press* for which Patrick was writing. The seed Patrick sowed by this verse fell on stony soil for his column was soon to be harrassed by the editor and shortly afterwards Patrick was dropped completely. As Patrick later wrote: "You haven't got a chance with fraud/And might as well be true to God."

139 A Toast to G.B.S.: Translation:
O, George Bernard Shaw
I a bottle of Guinness
Or two
To you!
For I be
No teetotaler.

140 Budda: A contemporary Irish verse writer.
Jerome Connor: Sculptor. He did the Lusitania memorial.
Candida: Daughter of Sir John Betjeman.

141 Scraw: Matted grass mixed with mud that forms over a drain or a bog. Occasionally it is strong enough for a man to stand on it. When cleaning a drain it is necessary to cut the scraw into sections and pull it to the bank with a drag.

142 Camogie: A form of Irish hurling or field hockey designed to be played by women. Astoreen = A stóirín = darling.
Mount Street Bridge is in Dublin.

143 White bread. During World War II the bread in Ireland was more black than white.

144 Bellows wheel: A coal fire—unlike a turf fire—has to be kept alive by blowing it with a bellows, usually operated by a wheel.

145 Legend: The boxer mentioned here was Martin Thornton from Spiddal. In a championship boxing match in Dublin with a British champion Thornton was expected to win easily. Instead he himself threw in the towel in the third round. He went home disgraced but loaded with cash since he had bet on himself. He died in 1982 and before dying admitted that he had in fact "thrown" the fight.

146 Curtain: For a short time during the war Patrick attended musical at-homes in the house of a family called Darley. He was trying to fit into society in the hope of getting a job that would make him a living. The pain he suffered on this score was excruciating. At these at-homes he met Joseph Holloway, the fellow who kept an immense diary of his visits to the theatre. I knew Joe Holloway well and for the sake of posterity I must record that a more witless bore I never met before or since. Patrick was very ashamed of having written the above bread-and-butter screed. He would not allow it to be reprinted.

147 Brother Michael: One of the Four Masters, the 17th century annalists. In 1944 a celebration was held in their honour. Patrick was also ashamed of this verse, not because of the sentiment but because of the rhetoric. Anger has no place in poetry.

148 A Tom Moore Society, founded at this time, began the practice of hanging a wreath around the statue of Moore in College Green. We often thought of tearing it off and throwing it in the Liffey.

149 Pegasus: Another verse Patrick came to dislike because he felt there was a whine in it and it was lacking dignity.

151 Bardic Dust: Austin Clarke was a contemporary verse writer. This is Patrick's review in *The Irish Times* of Clarke's verse play, *The Viscount of Blarney.*

153 O'Connor: Frank O'Connor, Irish writer.

154 na gCopaleen: Otherwise Myles na gCopaleen. Pseudonym for Brian O'Nolan, witty Irish writer.

155 Tarry Flynn: When Patrick was struggling withTarry

Flynn I suggested he could solve all his problems by writing it completely in verse. He took me up on the idea but gave up after writing a few pieces. He said verse was not the answer. Boortree: The alder tree.

156   Drilling-bar: A wooden bar similar to the double-tree (see note p. 97) but a foot longer which connects the plough to the team of horses when forming drills for potatoes.
Haws: The fruit of the hawthorn bush.

157   Stooks: Sheaves of corn, usually four, standing against each other to dry.
Rick: A pile of hay or of oats built in the shape of a rectangle and coming to a point as with the roof of a house.
Flaggers: The wild-iris, abundant in bogs around Inniskeen.

158   Roosevelt: When news came of the death of F. D. Roosevelt Patrick was visiting with R. M. Smyllie, editor of *The Irish Times*. With encouragement from Smyllie and to earn a quick pound Patrick rushed home and composed this sonnet. It was published the following day together with Roosevelt's Obituary.

160   Mother's death gave both Patrick and me a bad jolt. Together we wrote her Obituary for *The Dundalk Democrat*. At my suggestion Patrick wrote not one but two verses in her honour. The second one here was printed by me for the first time. It is the better of the two. A contemporary Irish verse-writer and a smart aleck thought he saw a contradiction between the references to sycamores and poplars. I explained that in front of the house we had sycamores and out the back window we saw poplars.

163   Country Shop: A fashionable Dublin Restaurant on St. Stephen's Green.

164   Hilda: A lady with whom Patrick was in love. Eventually she married a minor politician. See, "The Lay of the Crooked Knight" in *Sacred Keeper*, pp. 138 ff.

166 Homeward: It was customary to lead the funeral cortege the long way round to the graveyard.

167 Peadar O'Donnell: A contemporary editor and writer. Why Sorrow? Written and re-written from 1941 onwards but never finished. Parts published separately, *The Listener* 19 December 1941, et al.

172 Seola: A townland of Inniskeen.

174 Hunter-hoe: A horse-drawn implement for cultivating furrows.

187 Raglan Road: A street off Pembroke Road, Dublin. This ballad originally published in *The Irish Press* under the title "Dark Haired Miriam Ran Away". It was written about Patrick's girl-friend Hilda but to avoid embarrassment he used the name of my girl-friend in the title.

188 Jim Larkin: A noted Irish labour leader.

192 Navy-serge: A popular style of suit worn by the poor.

196 R.D.S.: Royal Dublin Society.

198 Gradh: Love.

199 Nemo me impune lacessit: Let no one dare insult me. A Latin tag supplied by me.

203 Ná habair é! Say nothing about it.

206 Pembroke Road: Patrick and I lived at 62 Pembroke Road, Dublin.

207 Joan Russell: An attractive Dublin girl with whom Patrick was in love. She died in her early twenties. I placed a verse from this poem on the cross on Patrick's grave.

209 First printed: Juvenilia in *The Weekly Irish Independent* 1 September 1928.

211 Film critic: Patrick was film critic for *The Standard* 22 February 1946 to 8 July 1949.

212 Patrick's Note on The Paddidad: "This satire is based on the sad notion with which my youth was infected—that Ireland was a spiritual entity. I had a good deal to do with putting an end to this foolishness, for as soon as I found out, I reported the news widely. It is now only propagated

399

by the B.B.C. in England, and in the Bronx, New York, and in the departments of Irish literature at Princeton, Yale, Harvard and New York universities."

There has been speculation on who was the model for the Devil, with M. J. McManus, a popular journalist, as a front runner. My recollection puts Maurice Walsh, a popular novelist of the period, in the main role. The law of libel prevents my identifying all the characters involved.

400

257 Poems from pages 257 to 273 were written in the period following the closing of *Kavanagh's Weekly*.

260 The Rowley Mile: A racetrack at Newmarket one mile straight. A gruelling race. Named after Charles II's favourite horse.

262 *The Collins Pocket Guide to Wild Flowers* by David McClintock and R. S. R. Fitter. 1955.

266 Irish Stew: In 1950 Patrick had an opportunity to visit the U.S. on a literary junket but the visit was vetoed by Frank Aiken, Government Minister. See *Sacred Keeper* p. 203.

274 Prelude. Published in part in *The Irish Times*, 12 February 1955, but written some months earlier. When about to enter hospital for cancer of the lung on March 1st he added two verses dedicated to me. They are included in this edition. See, *Sacred Keeper*, p. 262.

277 Matthew Meers: Based on an old rhyme of the same name.

278 Pembrokeshire. An area of Dublin around Ballsbridge.

279 The Duke of Wellington: A London pub.
George Barker: A contemporary poet.
The Rialto Hospital, Dublin, where Patrick had a lung removed.

280 House Party: The two principal characters are identifiable by me. Compare also, "Pages From a Literary Novel", in *The Bell*, February 1954.

282 In 1956 Patrick was invited to the U.S. by a Mrs. Farrelly. While there he wrote this letter in verse to Paddy Swift, a painter friend of his in London.

283 The lectures referred to here were given at University College, Dublin, in 1956. They were never published except in bits and pieces—in *Collected Pruse* (London 1967) and in a tape recording made in New York by Ann Keeley Kavanagh in 1957. A copy of this tape is in T.C.D. library and in the library of R.T.É. I have The Forgiven Plough ms. His second series of lectures on poetry—ten in number—much better and more compact than the first, were published by me (misdated 1956 series) in

401

November Haggard (New York 1971).

Hanover: The name of a bank.

285   Edward Lear: Writer of nonsense verse.

Plymouth the Hoe: An invented name, it seems.

287   The following fifteen or so pages are sometimes referred to as Canal Bank poems. Patrick wrote them after lying in an ante-natal roll on the bank of the Grand Canal near Baggot Street Bridge, Dublin, following his operation for cancer. He remarked that he was re-born there, born to "not caring". He sent his new poems to me for my opinion. I reported back that they were lush and exotic. At that moment I decided to become a publisher if only for the privilege of publishing these poems. I called the book *Recent Poems* and issued them in 1958 in New York.

289   Requiem for a Mill: One of our local grinding mills, Carolans of Lannett, closed down. It had a romantic association for us. Even the weir, I notice, is gone.

290   Kitty Stobling: An imaginary person, the name intended to have a somewhat outrageous effect.

294   Canal Bank Walk: Near Baggot Street Bridge, Dublin.

295   "O memorial me with no hero-courageous": Originally this read "O commemorate me . . ."

O'Brien: A prominent Limerick and Dublin family.

299   Franz Stampl: Apparently another imaginary name, invented partly for fun and partly as a way of suggesting that one important scholar is no better than the next. It also follows the point of view of "not caring". (A noted soccer coach/manager had a similar name.)

306   The Gambler: Performed as a ballet under the title "Gamble no Gamble" at the Olympia Theatre, Dublin, 30 May to 3 June 1961.

307   Annie Besant (1847-1933): An English theosophist.

311   P. Potts: A contemporary commentator on literature.

312   King Edward Pub, London.

John Heath Stubbs: A contemporary writer.

316   Bachelor's Walk: A Dublin street.
Journal Friends: Readers of *The Irish Farmer's Journal*
for which Patrick had been writing a weekly column.

317   Seán a' Cóta: Pseudonym for Seán Kavanagh—no
relation. Author of a Dictionary of the Gaelic language,
not as yet published. The ms. is reported to be eight feet
high. He had several law suits over it with the Government.

318   Trap: A partly enclosed horse-drawn passenger vehicle. A
cousin to the jaunting car.

319   John Jordan: An Irish writer of verse.

322   Flaggers: The wild iris.

325   Pelman: C. L. Pelman, founder of a method of memory
training.

326   Behaned: Reference to Brendan Behan, an Irish writer of
wild personal behaviour and disregard for integrity. Hence
the phrase means, you are exiled from the truth.

327   My love lies at the gates of foam: The opening line of "The
Churchyard on the Sands" by J. B. L. Warren (Lord de
Tabley) 1835-1895.

329   The Beaver: Lord Beaverbrook, newspaper owner.
On the blower: On the phone.

330   Edith burns her vestments: Edith Sitwell.

331   Beckett's garbage can: Reference to play by Samuel
Beckett.

334   Candlefort Lane: In Inniskeen.
Clegs: Horse-flies.

336   Laws of Oray: Invented term, presumably.

338   Henry Rago: Editor, *Poetry Chicago*, and a friend of
mine.

339   Hidalgoishly: Like Spanish landed gentry.

344   Forte's caffs: Fast-food cafés in London.

345   MacGonagall: A Scottish ballad writer who used excessive
images.

347   C. P. Snow: A British writer.
Golding Lord of the Flies: William Golding author of
Lord of the Flies (1954).

Kinsella: Contemporary Irish writer of verse.

348   In 1938 Patrick was given shelter in London by John Gawsworth, a poetry anthologist, who had the habit of holding on to mss. sent to him. In 1964 Patrick extracted from him a sheaf of his unpublished verse as well as the ms. of *The Green Fool*, both now in the National Library.

352   Church & Binyon: British writers of the 1930s.
      Lowenfels: Walter Lowenfels wrote for *The Irish Statesman* 1929-30.

369   Published in the *Weekly Irish Independent*: 1928: Sept. 1st, 15th, 22nd, 29th, Oct. 6th, 13th, Nov. 10th, Dec. 29th. 1929: Jan. 5th, 19th, Feb. 16th, March 2nd, 23rd, April 6th, June 8th.

INDEX TO FIRST LINES

Excluding Juvenilia

413